The Garde

and Othe

*by the same author*

LIVING IN TRUTH
LETTERS TO OLGA
DISTURBING THE PEACE

*plays*

LARGO DESOLATO
TEMPTATION
REDEVELOPMENT

# The Garden Party and Other Plays

VÁCLAV HAVEL

Grove Press
*New York*

*First published in Great Britain in 1992 as* Selected Plays 1963–83 *by Faber and Faber Limited*
*Published simultaneously in Canada*
*Printed in the United States of America*

Library of Congress Cataloging-in-Publication Data
Havel, Václav.
[Plays. Selections. English]
The garden party and other plays/ Václav Havel.
ISBN-10: 0-8021-3307-X
ISBN-13: 978-0-8021-3307-6
1. Havel, Václav—Translations into English. I. Title.
PG5039.18.A9A2 1993 891.8'625—dc20 93-8656

Grove Press
an imprint of Grove/Atlantic, Inc.
841 Broadway
New York, NY 10003

Distributed by Publishers Group West

www.groveatlantic.com

10 12 11 10 9 8

# CONTENTS

# THE GARDEN PARTY

# CHARACTERS

HUGO PLUDEK
PLUDEK, his father
MRS PLUDEK, his mother
PETER PLUDEK, his brother
AMANDA
MAXY FALK
CLERK at the Liquidation Office
SECRETARY at the Liquidation Office
DIRECTOR of the Inauguration Service

# ACT ONE

## SCENE I

*The flat of the* PLUDEK *family. Present are:* PLUDEK, MRS PLUDEK, PETER *and* HUGO. HUGO *is playing a solitary game of chess. He makes a move, goes around to the other side of the board, deliberates, makes another move, etc.*

PLUDEK: (To HUGO) Dear son! (To MRS PLUDEK) Should I?

MRS PLUDEK: What time is it?

PLUDEK: Twelve.

MRS PLUDEK: Already? You must!

PLUDEK: Dear son!

HUGO: (*Makes his move*) Check! (*Changes sides.*)

PLUDEK: Still at it?

HUGO: Yes, Dad.

PLUDEK: And how goes it?

HUGO: Badly, Dad, badly.

MRS PLUDEK: Peter! What about going to the cellar for a while, do you mind?

(PETER *exits.*)

Kalabis will be here any moment. Heaven forbid that he should meet Peter! Everybody says Peter looks like a bourgeois intellectual. Why should you get into trouble because of him?

PLUDEK: Quite right, Berta. I'm the grandson of a poor farmhand, damn it! One of six children. I've five proletarian great-uncles!

MRS PLUDEK: Peter is the black sheep of the family.

PLUDEK: The blackguard! (*To* HUGO) Dear son! The middle classes are the backbone of the nation. And why? Not even a hag carries hemp seed to the attic alone. Jaros wished to be a goldsmith and he became one. Soon you'll be finishing school. Have you asked yourself?

HUGO: No, Dad.

PLUDEK: Did you hear that, Berta?

MRS PLUDEK: Never mind, Albert. Did somebody ring?

PLUDEK: No.

MRS PLUDEK: Listen, Bertie –

(HUGO *makes his move and changes sides.*)

Well, how goes it?

HUGO: All right, Mum.

PLUDEK: What is it?

MRS PLUDEK: What time is it?

PLUDEK: One.

MRS PLUDEK: He should have been here by now –

PLUDEK: Unless he's been a bit delayed.

MRS PLUDEK: What do you mean, 'delayed'?

PLUDEK: Well, he might have met somebody and forgot to watch the time.

MRS PLUDEK: But whom?

PLUDEK: A chum from the army –

MRS PLUDEK: But you said he's never been in the army.

PLUDEK: There you are! He'll surely come. Should I?

MRS PLUDEK: Let's hope so! You must!

PLUDEK: Dear son! The middle classes are the backbone of the nation. And why? He who fusses about a mosquito net can never hope to dance with a goat. Jaros used to say – life is a blank page. You mean to tell me you don't know what to write on it?

HUGO: I don't, Dad.

PLUDEK: Did you hear that, Berta?

MRS PLUDEK: Never mind, Albert. Did somebody ring?

(PETER *enters.*)

PLUDEK: No. (*To* HUGO) Dear son! (*To* MRS PLUDEK) Should I?

MRS PLUDEK: What time is it?

PLUDEK: Two.

MRS PLUDEK: Already? You must!

PLUDEK: Dear Son!

HUGO: (*Makes his move*) Check! (*Changes sides.*)

PLUDEK: Still at it?

HUGO: Yes, Dad.

PLUDEK: And how goes it?

HUGO: Badly, Dad, badly.

MRS PLUDEK: Peter! What about going to the attic for a while, do you mind?

(PETER *exits.*)

If he was merely an intellectual, well, all right. Intellectuals are sort of tolerated these days. But he keeps insisting on being bourgeois as well!

PLUDEK: Pig-headed, that's all. (*To* HUGO) Dear son! Not even the Hussars of Cologne would go to the woods without a clamp. Jaros thought about his future and so he studied, and studied, and studied. Have you thought about yours?

HUGO: No, Dad.

PLUDEK: How's that?

HUGO: I've studied, Dad.

PLUDEK: Did you hear that, Berta?

MRS PLUDEK: Never mind, Albert. Did somebody ring?

PLUDEK: No.

MRS PLUDEK: Listen, Bertie –

(HUGO *makes his move and changes sides.*)

Well, how goes it?

HUGO: All right, Mum.

MRS PLUDEK: What time is it?

PLUDEK: Three.

MRS PLUDEK: He should have been here by now.

PLUDEK: Unless he's been a bit delayed.

MRS PLUDEK: What do you mean, delayed?

PLUDEK: Well, he might have met somebody and forgot to watch the time.

MRS PLUDEK: But whom?

PLUDEK: A childhood chum.

MRS PLUDEK: You know very well he had no childhood!

PLUDEK: He had no childhood, but he had childhood chums. Am I not his childhood chum?

MRS PLUDEK: But he couldn't have met you!

PLUDEK: There you are! He'll surely come! Should I?

MRS PLUDEK: Let's hope so! You must!

PLUDEK: Dear son! He who knows where the bumblebee hides

his stinger never rolls up his leggings. When one calls Jaros, Jaros calls back, and that's the whole point. The basis of life is the idea you form of life. You think anybody will form it for you?

HUGO: Yes, Dad. Jaros. (*Makes his move.*) Check. (*Changes sides.*)

PLUDEK: Did you hear that, Berta?

MRS PLUDEK: Never mind, Albert. Dear Hugo! Without the warp not even the woof can be buried. That's why your father has invited for today – well, go on, ask Father whom he has invited!

HUGO: Whom have you invited, Daddy?

PLUDEK: My colleague Kalabis. Well, ask Mother who is my colleague Kalabis!

HUGO: Who is Daddy's colleague Kalabis, Mummy?

MRS PLUDEK: Your father's schoolmate. Well, go on, ask Father what did he do with his colleague Kalabis when they were boys!

HUGO: What did you do with your colleague Kalabis when you were boys, Daddy?

PLUDEK: We used to break windows!

MRS PLUDEK: Of rich farmers!

PLUDEK: Yes. And ask Mother what is my colleague Kalabis now!

HUGO: What is Daddy's colleague Kalabis now, Mummy?

MRS PLUDEK: A Deputy Chairman! And your father has invited him –

PLUDEK: For a game of chess with you –

MRS PLUDEK: And at the same time –

PLUDEK: To give you advice –

MRS PLUDEK: Just in the way of information –

PLUDEK: How to go about –

MRS PLUDEK: This or that –

PLUDEK: In life –

MRS PLUDEK: You know what I mean, don't you. Not even a hag would go to the woods without a clamp!

PLUDEK: Well, have you ever seen a Hussar of Cologne carry hemp seed to the attic alone?

HUGO: Never, Daddy.

PLUDEK: There you are! Did somebody ring?

MRS PLUDEK: No.

(HUGO *makes his move and changes sides.*)

Well, how goes it?

HUGO: All right, Mum. (*Makes his move.*) Check! (*Changes sides.*)

PLUDEK: How goes it?

HUGO: Badly, Dad. Very badly, in fact! (*Makes his move and changes sides.*)

MRS PLUDEK: How goes it?

HUGO: Super, Mum! (*Makes his move.*) Checkmate!

PLUDEK: You lost?

HUGO: No, I won.

MRS PLUDEK: You won?

HUGO: No, I lost.

PLUDEK: Come now. Did you win or did you lose?

HUGO: Lost here – and won here.

MRS PLUDEK: When you win here, you lose here?

HUGO: And when I lose here, I win here.

PLUDEK: You see, Berta? Instead of a total victory one time or a total defeat another, he prefers to win a little and lose a little each time.

MRS PLUDEK: Such a player will always stay in the game.

PLUDEK: Quite! You can't fry chickenweed without a straw. And why? Whereas all other classes in history kept exchanging their historical positions, the middle classes have come down through history untouched, because no other class has ever tried to take their position, and so the middle classes never had anything to exchange with anybody and have thus remained the only really permanent force in history. And that's why, dear son, they cement the fragments of history into one unified whole and indeed create history and make it what it is. Hence the most important eras are those that have known how to lean on the middle classes and put all ideals into their care, which they then look after as their own, before passing them on to the next generation. No era can exist without the middle classes, whereas – on the contrary –

the middle classes can exist independently of all eras. And perhaps even without them altogether. I hope you don't think one can shoot kites while keeping a stable in Beroun? There you are! And the only country –

MRS PLUDEK: What time is it?

PLUDEK: And the only country which doesn't need the middle classes is Japan –

MRS PLUDEK: What time is it?

PLUDEK: And the only country which doesn't need the middle classes is Japan, because only in Japan are there enough people –

MRS PLUDEK: What time is it?

PLUDEK: And the only country which doesn't need the middle classes is Japan, because only in Japan are there enough people even without the middle classes. Besides, Japan –

MRS PLUDEK: What time is it?

PLUDEK: Five. Besides, Japan –

MRS PLUDEK: What time was he supposed to come?

PLUDEK: At twelve. Besides Japan – what did I actually want to say about Japan?

HUGO: You probably wanted to say that if we don't realize in time the historical role of the middle classes, the Japs, who don't need the middle classes, will come, remove them from history, and send them to Japan.

MRS PLUDEK: At twelve? And what if he doesn't come?

PLUDEK: Quite right, Hugo. Heaven forbid that you should still be about when that terrible day arrives! (*To* MRS PLUDEK) If he doesn't come, somebody else will!

(*Just then the doorbell rings.*)

MRS PLUDEK: Nobody will come! Nobody will write! Nobody will call! We're alone. Alone in the whole world!

HUGO: And there are more and more Japs every day. Did somebody ring?

(PETER *enters.*)

MRS PLUDEK: Peter! Go and hide in the pantry! Kalabis is here!

(PETER *exits.* AMANDA *enters.*)

PLUDEK: Is something the matter?

AMANDA: There's nothing the matter. Here is a –

ALL: Letter!

AMANDA: No, telegram!

PLUDEK: Well, go on. Read it!

AMANDA: (*Opens it and reads*) DEAR ALBERT, CANNOT COME TODAY, MUST GO TO GARDEN PARTY OF LIQUIDATION OFFICE. Have you got it, Ann dear? Are you all right? Why? Oh, I see. At half past seven. But you'll be there, won't you? May I go on? SORRY. HOPING TO SEE YOU SOME OTHER TIME. Very much! It does something for your figure! Well, why not at the corner where you used to get off! Ah, the voice of nature! Listen, what about a trip to the country this weekend? GREETINGS YOURS. Come on! You're not made of glass, are you? FRANCIS KALABIS.

PLUDEK: He won't come! We're finished! Nobody cares for us, Berta!

MRS PLUDEK: Stop being hysterical, Albert. If he doesn't come to Hugo, Hugo will go to him!

PLUDEK: Where?

MRS PLUDEK: To the garden party.

PLUDEK: To the garden party! Hugo! Where's your tie – and your jacket –

AMANDA: Well, I'd better be going – (*Lingers.*) Well, goodbye –

MRS PLUDEK: Never mind, love. When I was starting out I used to get even smaller parts than this.

AMANDA: But those were different times, madam! (*Exits.*)

PLUDEK: I hope Hugo is being careful when she's about!

MRS PLUDEK: You do realize, Albert, she's the daughter of a caretaker!

PLUDEK: All the more reason for taking care!

MRS PLUDEK: You do realize, Albert, what kind of times we happen to live in!

PLUDEK: Quite! Tomorrow Hugo will take her for a walk!

MRS PLUDEK: That's right. Hugo! Get your tie – and your jacket – and run along to the garden party!

HUGO: I must play the return game.

PLUDEK: Did you hear that, Berta? I've been feeding a chipmunk so long that my pipe fell into the rushes! What if Jaros heard that! To play a return game! When the destiny of man is at stake! The future of a family!

MRS PLUDEK: Father speaks of the family and you don't even bother to stand up?

PLUDEK: Oh no! The times when they used to stand up are gone! Then they were both little, they strolled through the high grass, chased the butterflies, and we were changing their nappies like the apples of our eyes, we were giving them the backs of our shirts –

MRS PLUDEK: Never mind, Albert! Hugo! Life is actually a sort of a big chessboard. Does that mean anything to you?

HUGO: It does, Mum! Without the warp you cannot bury the woof. Where's my tie? And my jacket?

(PLUDEK *and* MRS PLUDEK *are moved and kiss* HUGO.)

MRS PLUDEK: Our darling little dope!

PLUDEK: Dear son! Life is a struggle! And you are a dog! Stone walls do not an iron bar! To be or not, aye there's the rub! Consider the lilies of the valley, they spoil not, neither do they tin. You are my son! He who doesn't know how to wade through the rye must go to Prague for his wits! You're a Pludek! Farewell! Or else –

(PETER *arrives.* HUGO *exits. They are all moved and watch him go.*)

MRS PLUDEK: I'll drink to you only with mine eyes
For parting is such sweet sorrow
I could tomorrow and tomorrow
O Mother, dear Mother
One day he will say
Home, O sweet home
It's here I shall stay –

PLUDEK: (*Sings*) You'll take the low road and I'll take the high road –

MRS PLUDEK: Bertie –

PLUDEK: What?

MRS PLUDEK: Do you remember that lovely summer just before the war? All the wonderful, mad plans we made then! You were going to study – to organize – to direct – Peter! Where are you off to again? Can't you stay for a while within the family circle?

(PETER *exits*.) We must brace ourselves up again, Bertie! You know what I mean! We must soar up from the earth – spread our wings – in short – live! Yes, live, live, live! We shall start a new and a better life!

PLUDEK: Lentils are lentils and oats are oats. New life? Why the hell not?

## SCENE 2

*Entrance to the garden where the party of the Liquidation Office is taking place. A* CLERK *and a* SECRETARY, *employees of the Liquidation Office on duty at this entrance, sit at a desk covered with heaps of papers, various rubber stamps, etc.* HUGO *enters.*

HUGO: Good evening. Lentils are lentils and oats are oats. Is colleague Kalabis in?

CLERK: Kalabis Josef, born January 2nd, 1940, Kalabis Vaclav, born June 18th, 1891, or Kalabis Francis, born August 4th, 1919?

SECRETARY: Kalabis Francis, born August 4th, 1919, has been excused. He's lecturing tonight at a house committee meeting on the future of mankind.

CLERK: Do take off your jacket and tie.

SECRETARY: You are now at the main entrance B13. You can buy here a general ticket which entitles you to move freely throughout the whole area of the garden and to visit almost all the events organized within the framework of the Liquidation Office Garden Party.

CLERK: There is, for example, an informal chat with the Head of the Development Department about new liquidation methods, taking place in the area around the Little Pond –

SECRETARY: An entertaining Quiz Programme on the history of the Liquidation Office, taking place in Summerhouse No. 3 –

CLERK: Or the programme of humorous stories from the liquidation practice of Section 5 which have been written down and will be narrated by the Head of Section 5 –

SECRETARY: And in which you yourself can participate, provided you have sent the exact text of your story together with a health certificate and a permit from the Head of your Section to the Secretariat of Humour and to the Ideological Regulation Commission at the latest two months before the date of this garden party.

CLERK: Provided you can obtain a permit from the Organizing Committee, you may even dance – i.e. in the area of the large Dance Floor A – between 11.30 and 12 p.m. Large Dance Floor A is reserved until 11.30 p.m. for the Liquidation Method Section, and between 12 and 12.45 a.m. for the People's Commission and the Delimitation Subcommission.

SECRETARY: If you are interested in making use of Aids to Amusement, such as paper hats, gay *papier-mâché* noses, etc., you may pick them up via the Head of your Section in the Sectional Warehouse and then you may go and amuse yourself with them within the area of Small Dance Floor C.

CLERK: Of course you'll have to respect the queue which has been forming outside the Small Dance Floor C since early afternoon and which, I'm sorry to say, is inevitable in view of the relatively large interest in Self-Entertainment with Aids to Amusement, and the limited accommodation within the space of Small Dance Floor C.

SECRETARY: The sooner you start queuing, the sooner you get in.

HUGO: Excuse me, but Small Dance Floor C is clearly smaller than the Large Dance Floor A. Why not move Self-Entertainment with Aids to Amusement to large Dance Floor A and the dance of Sections to the Small Dance Floor C? Why stick one's nose into the hedge when even the robin sings alone? Check!

(*The* CLERK *and the* SECRETARY *exchange meaningful glances.*)

SECRETARY: At first glance there's logic in it –

CLERK: Unfortunately, this kind of logic is merely formal –

SECRETARY: Moreover, the actual content of the suggestion testifies to an ignorance of several basis principles.

CLERK: You mean you'd approve if the dignified course of our garden party were disrupted by some sort of dadaistic jokerism which would certainly ensue if such an important and, as it were, junctional area as the Large Dance floor A were to be opened to unbridled intellectualities?

SECRETARY: Moreover, what makes you think that Large Dance Floor A is larger than Small Dance Floor C? Why deceive oneself?

CLERK: Surely our colleagues of the Organizing Committee knew very well why they restricted Self-Entertainment with Aids to Amusement precisely within the confines of Small Dance Floor C.

SECRETARY: You mean you don't trust the resolutions of the Organizing Committee?

CLERK: Composed of the leading officials of the Liquidation Office?

SECRETARY: Old, experienced men who long before you were born were devotedly liquidating?

CLERK: In conditions which your generation cannot even begin to imagine?

FALK: (*Enters*) Well, well, well! How are things at the entrance? Having fun? Conversation flowing? The garden party is for everyone!

CLERK: Thank you. It's flowing –

SECRETARY: It's flowing –

FALK: Well, that's good! It's really sort of pretty good that you're here on duty – go on, sit down – make yourselves comfortable – relax – undress, if you like – take off your shoes – damn it, aren't you just among yourselves? Well, how did you like my inauguration speech? Good, eh? I just gave it a sort of human touch, you know, to liven up things a bit out here. Right down the popular level, wasn't it? Well now, I wasn't putting it on, you know. It comes sort of naturally to me. In fact, I hate phrase-mongering and I resolutely reject all sterile cant. That's the way I am. You see, I'm quite an ordinary chap made of flesh and bones, milk and blood, in short – as they say – I'm one of you! Go on, if you have something to eat, eat! We don't want to bother about formalities, do we? You know, really, nothing foreign is human to me. I mean it! Well, never mind. Main thing, I've managed to establish this friendly, informal atmosphere among you. That's the way I am. Wherever I come there's lots of fun. Never mind. The Liquidation Office is a useful institution with a complicated and a large administrative agenda. But in spite of it, I'm sorry to say, you do sometimes slip into bureaucratic practices. Sections have already noticed it, it was discussed above – and the result is this garden party. But don't worry. Now – in the first stage – it's only a matter of letting your hair down in a human sort of way, establishing among yourselves a nice, warm, human relationship and then frankly stopping to think how to ventilate the whole shop. Good gracious, chums, you really don't live like people, and that's a fact! You know a woman can become pregnant on the Moon? Of course she can. On the honeymoon! Damn it, aren't we all sons of one big mother? Oh well – I must run along now. Have to make sure that conversation in the whole area is flowing. Try and have some sort of fun here while I'm away! (*Exits.*)

(*A long pause.*)

CLERK: Well, how are things at home? What about the children? Quite a handful, eh?

SECRETARY: They aren't really – I haven't any – I haven't –

CLERK: What? What's that? Aren't you married?

SECRETARY: No, I'm not – No – Are you?

CLERK: No – neither am I –

SECRETARY: And what about the children?

CLERK: Well – you know how it is – quite a handful – you know – (*Pause.*)

SECRETARY: Listen – Large Dance Floor. A – when we look at it from the distance of time –

CLERK: Yes?

SECRETARY: Is in a certain sense really –

CLERK: Yes?

SECRETARY: Larger than Small Dance Floor C –

CLERK: In the context of the new historical situation, certainly.

SECRETARY: They concealed it from us, didn't they?

CLERK: But now let's not be afraid to say openly: if we move Self-Entertainment with Aids to Amusement to Large Dance Floor A –

SECRETARY: We shall thus enable a greater number of employees to entertain themselves with Aids to Amusement.

CLERK: Today we no longer have to be afraid of Aids to Amusement!

SECRETARY: Wait – isn't it just another mouse-trap?

CLERK: I beg your pardon!

SECRETARY: I'm sorry. Large Dance Floor A is indeed large! I admire the courage with which it has been revealed to us! Well, how are things at home? What about the children? Quite a handful, eh?

HUGO: Excuse me, but in direct proportion to the amount by which Large Dance Floor A is larger than Small Dance Floor C is the number of employees who can entertain themselves with funny noses at one and the same time. He who fishes near Klatovy doesn't need to jump into the mulberry bush. Check!

CLERK: So what? To say these things today is no sign of courage. Don't you see that if we're going to repeat over and over the truth for which the struggle has long ago been won, namely that the Large Dance Floor A is indeed large, we're only substituting one hackneyed phrase for another. No, no! The point is that today we need action, not words!

SECRETARY: Precisely what I had in mind a moment ago –

FALK: (*Enters*) Well, well, well! How are things at the entrance? Having fun? Conversation flowing? The garden party is for everyone!

SECRETARY: Thank you, it's flowing –

CLERK: It's flowing –

FALK: Well, I'm glad to hear that! I see I've hit the nail on the head with my inaugurating. And why the hell not! I'm no beginner at inaugurating.

SECRETARY: Do you often inaugurate?

FALK: What a question! Good gracious, it's sort of my job! After all, I'm an expert Inaugurator of Parties, Conferences, and Celebrations. I work at the Inauguration Service, Section 02.

CLERK: As soon as you opened your mouth we knew you were a real expert.

FALK: I've had a long inaugurational practice and I specialize in garden parties. But I inaugurate from a sort of burning human need, not just because it's my job.

SECRETARY: Are all inaugurators like you?

FALK: I'm afraid not. There are two camps at the Inauguration Service: old dogmatic phrase-mongers, and we young chaps with a sense of humour. You see, even we have our internal problems. How then could one expect you to be without them! No, not every inaugurator has reached the level where we'd like to see him. Not by a long shot!

CLERK: But you've reached the level where you'd like to see yourself!

FALK: I'm trying to help my weaker colleagues, to show them the way. But actually the main thing is that, in spite of all, the Inauguration Service as a whole stands today in the forefront of the struggle for the new approach to man!

SECRETARY: We'll have to learn a lot from you!

CLERK: A lot!

FALK: A lot! Have you read my booklet *Towards the Popular Character of Garden Parties Organized by our Institutions*?

SECRETARY: I was just about to –

CLERK: So was I –

FALK: Well! No wonder, chums! I mean, really, one must sort of follow what's going on! That's the least one can do, damn it! In my book I've developed the thesis that every garden party ought before anything else to be a platform for a healthy, popular and at the same time well-disciplined entertainment of all employees. As a matter of fact, your garden party has all the earmarks of becoming such a platform.

SECRETARY: Thank you –

CLERK: Thanks –

FALK: I like to work for you, you know. We inaugurators like you liquidation officers sort of off the tops of our heads, as is usual among workers.

SECRETARY: We liquidation officers like you inaugurators as well.

FALK: There you are! At a certain stage it's really important that people frankly say to one another that they're sort of people. However, progress progresses and we mustn't get stuck with mere abstract proclamations. You know, I always say man – man lives! And so, in the same way, you too – now let's not be afraid to open our trap and say it aloud – you too must live! You see, chums, life – life is a bloody marvellous thing. Don't you think?

CLERK: It is –

SECRETARY: Bloody marvellous –

FALK: And even a liquidation officer has a right to his slice of a really full – I mean, you know – er – full life! And each one is bound to have a human defect. They sort of – you know – belong to people. I hope that you – and you too – have some defect or other. If not, we'll never really sort of get along together. That's a fact. I refuse to work with paper abstractions. You may stake your life on that!

SECRETARY: I have a defect –

CLERK: So have I. I'm obscene –

FALK: In what way?

CLERK: I've a filthy picture at home –

FALK: Do you? And what about you?

SECRETARY: So do I.

FALK: That's the spirit! Give it a go, chums, give it a go! Goodness knows, I hate them scrags that sticks their heads in the sand when faced with problematicals such as, let's say, a slice of emotional life! Now, take love, for example. Ain't it a bloody useful thing – so long as one knows how to latch on to it! Damn it, to catch hold of these things is after all a part of working with human material. As they say in my home town: catch a rabbit and you'll have it! Well, what do you say –

SECRETARY: Oh, we agree. Absolutely.

CLERK: Catch a rabbit and you'll have it!

FALK: Oh well – I must run along now. Have to make sure that conversation in the whole area is flowing. Try and have some sort of fun here while I'm away! (*Exits.*)

(*Pause.*)

CLERK: Look –

SECRETARY: Yes?

CLERK: Look – a sparrow! It's flying – moss blossoms – meadows are a-humming – nature!

SECRETARY: What?

CLERK: I say, sparrows are flying – the boss mlossoms – the meadows are a-humming –

SECRETARY: Oh, I see – nature!

CLERK: Yes. Well now. You have hair! It's pretty – gold – like buttercrumbs – I mean buttercups – and your nose is like a rose – I'm sorry – I mean like a forget-me-not – white –

SECRETARY: Look – a sparrow!

CLERK: What?

SECRETARY: It's flying!

CLERK: And you have breasts.

SECRETARY: I know.

CLERK: Two – like two – like two – two little founts – (*Pause.*) I'm sorry – I mean footballs – like two footballs, that's what I meant to say – sorry –

SECRETARY: That's all right – go on –

CLERK: And your eyes are like two – two – like two footballs – I mean buttercups –

SECRETARY: How are things at home?

CLERK: Well, you know – nature – I mean forget-me-nots –

SECRETARY: How about the footballs? Quite a handful, eh?

CLERK: Not really – they blossom – you know –

SECRETARY: I see, you're not married!

CLERK: I mean they're humming – No! Sparrows – moss – boss – like two – two – To hell with it! I'd like to know who thought up this stupid campaign! Catch a rabbit and you'll have it! Bloody fool!

SECRETARY: I beg your pardon!

CLERK: I'm sorry. The Large Dance Floor A is indeed large. I admire the courage with which it has been revealed to us. Look – a sparrow!

HUGO: Excuse me, but if an hour ago the Self-Entertainment with Aids to Amusement had been moved to Large Dance Floor A, the queue could have been shorter by at least a hundred yards. If we're going to repeat over and over the truth for which the struggle has long ago been won, namely that the Large Dance Floor A is indeed large, we're only going to substitute one hackneyed phrase for another. The point is that today we need action, not words! One should never fire a blunderbuss into the nettles. Check!

SECRETARY: I do disagree! Most emphatically! There are truths which can never become trite. And I shall never allow any truth as dear to us as the truth that the Large Dance Floor A is indeed large to be maliciously belittled by any references to its seeming self-evidence. For nothing is self-evident, so long as there still lurks among us even one of those who would prefer to see us removed from every dance floor!

CLERK: Precisely what I had in mind a while ago –

FALK: (*Enters, wearing a gay* papier-mâché *nose*) Well, well, well! How are things at the entrance? Having fun? Conversation flowing? The garden party is for everyone!

CLERK: Thank you, it's flowing –

SECRETARY: It's flowing –

FALK: And what are you talking about, eh?

CLERK: About love –

FALK: Well, that's lovely. Even love sort of belongs to man. And the man of today has rich feelings, much, much richer than any preceding man! But that's exactly why we must make damned sure that our love doesn't go and spill over a certain optimum level of manageability. Otherwise our love might go and awake in people some temporary sadnesses as well.

SECRETARY: And these must be fundamentally eradicated!

CLERK: As long as they don't belong among constructive sadnesses – for we know those, too. We mustn't proceed mechanically, so we don't pour out the bath with the baby.

SECRETARY: As long as the bath of constructive sadnesses doesn't conceal destructive ones as well, of course –

CLERK: Regarding the question of sadness, I'm an optimist.

SECRETARY: I, on the contrary, am an enemy of cheap optimism!

FALK: I'm so glad you're discussing! Today we must discuss! And while we're doing it we mustn't be afraid of contrary opinions. Everybody who's honestly interested in our common cause ought to have from one to three contrary opinions – as was so nicely put in the resolution of the 23rd Inaugurational Conference. You know that a woman can get pregnant on the Moon?

SECRETARY: Yes, on the honeymoon.

FALK: (*Irritated*) Jokes – jokes – nothing but jokes! Why don't you talk about art, for example? There you've jolly rich material for discussion, all nice and ready. Good gracious, you mean we haven't still got a whole damned heap of burning problems in matters of art?

SECRETARY: I was just going to mention art –

FALK: Art – that's what I call a fighting word! I myself – sort of personally – fancy art. I think of it as the spice of life. I think our time directly calls for great dramaticals full of full-blooded heroes – for courageous, audacious painting of landscapes – the contemporary spectator needs more and more contemporary plays – the more contemporary, the better! Art ought to become an organic part of the life of each one of us –

SECRETARY: Absolutely! At the very next meeting of the Delimitation Subcommission I suppose to recite a few lyrico-epical verses!

HUGO: (*To himself*) 'Lyrico-epical verses' –

FALK: Mind you, it's good that you're inflamed by the question of art, but at the same time you mustn't sort of one-sidedly overrate art and so sink into unhealthy aestheticism profoundly hostile to the spirit of our garden parties. As if we didn't have in technology a whole damned heap of burning problems.

CLERK: I was just going to change the subject and mention technology.

FALK: Technology – that's what I call a fighting word! You know, I maintain that we're living in the century of technology – the magnet – the telephone – the magnet – not even Gill Vernon could imagine anything like this!

CLERK: I've just read *Twenty Thousand Leagues under the Sea*.

FALK: Soon we'll be able to read at even greater depths!

CLERK: About the discoveries of Captain Nemo. He hasn't got –

FALK: Of course he hasn't! He hasn't got a clue – this Vernon – about the discoveries of our captains of science. Technology ought to become an organic part of the life of each one of us –

CLERK: Absolutely! At the very next meeting of the Liquidation Methodology Section I'll suggest that we reconsider the possibilities of the chemification of liquidation practice.

HUGO: *(To himself)* 'The chemification of liquidation practice' –

FALK: Mind you, it's good that you're inflamed by the question of technology, but at the same time you mustn't sort of one-sidedly overrate technology and so sink into perilous technicism which changes man into a mechanical cog in the dehumanized world of a spiritless civilization. As if we didn't have a whole damned heap of burning problems in matters of art!

SECRETARY: I was just going to change the subject and mention art –

FALK: Art – that's what I call a fighting word! The colleagues in the Department of Culture surely know very well why they're planning to publish a decree about artistic courage! It'll take effect already in the second quarter.

SECRETARY: Quite right! Art must provoke through audacious experimantation in form – Impressionism – that sort of thing –

HUGO: *(To himself)* Impressionism –

FALK: It's good that you're inflamed by the question of art. But you shouldn't underrate technology –

CLERK: I was just going to change the subject and mention technology –

FALK: Technology – that's what I call a fighting word! The colleagues of industry surely know very well why they're planning the introduction of machines already in the next quarter.

CLERK: Quite right! Technology must make use of the latest discoveries – the periodic table of the elements, for example –

HUGO: (*To himself*) 'The periodic table of the elements' –

FALK: It's good that you're inflamed by the question of technology. But you shouldn't underrate art.

SECRETARY: Art – that's what I call a fighting word!

FALK: It's good that you're inflamed by the question of art –

CLERK: But you shouldn't underrate technology!

SECRETARY: Technology – that's what I call a fighting word!

CLERK: It's good that you're inflamed by the question of technology!

SECRETARY: But you shouldn't underrate art!

CLERK: Art – that's what I call a fighting word!

SECRETARY: It's good that you're inflamed by the question of art –

FALK: Stop it, for God's sake! This way we'll never get along together! If you mean to torpedo the friendly atmosphere I've managed to create among you under the guise of an open discussion, and furthermore, to undermine the success of our garden party – then there's no place for you in the close-knit ranks of our collective! I won't stand for any rowdyism here! If anybody starts a rumpus in this place I'll catch hold of him with these two grabbers and send him out of here spinning like a top! Don't you dare come near me until you've made it up with one another in a human sort of way! Hooligans!

(*The* CLERK *and the* SECRETARY *back out in terror.* HUGO *softly mumbles to himself.*)

HUGO: Lyrico-epical verses – chemification of liquidation practice – Impressionism – the periodic table of the elements – lyrico-epical verses – chemification –

FALK: Hey, you! What do you think about all this?

HUGO: Me? Well, at the beginning the argument was quite interesting, but then it got a bit out of hand, didn't it?

(*Pause*) I mean from the beginning a wrong personal tone was maintained, although throughout an interesting topical problem was under discussion, wasn't it? (*Pause.*) Of course one may look at it from different angles, sides and positions, but at the same time one must never forget to consider all the pros and cons, must one? (*Pause.*) In fact, they were both sort of right and sort of wrong – or rather, on the contrary – both were wrong and both were right, weren't they? I mean they were, were they not? (*Pause.*) Yes, I agree, they were not, though I don't think they were. In fact, they both seemed to have forgotten that in the future art and technology will sort of harmoniously supplement each other – the lyrico-epical verses will help in the chemification of liquidation practice – the periodic table of the elements will help in the development of Impressionism – every technological product will be specially wired for the reception of aesthetic brain waves – the chimneys of the atomic power stations will be decorated by our best landscape painters – there will be public reading rooms twenty thousand leagues under the sea – differential equations will be written in verse – on the flat roofs of cyclotrons there will be small experimental theatres where differential equations will be recited in a human sort of way. Right?

(FALK *stares at* HUGO *who fearfully takes out his identification card and shows it to him.* FALK, *mistaking his action, shows his card to* HUGO. *Then they both calm down.*)

FALK: I like the way you speak. In a human sort of way. And you're with it! I like you, you know! You're a born inaugurator! Come on, tell me – when did you leave the team?

HUGO: I've always fancied inaugurating –

FALK: Goodness gracious, how did you get stuck in the Liquidation Office? Some injustice from the past?

HUGO: Well, you know how it is, one gets blown this way and that –

FALK: Or an assignment, perhaps?

HUGO: We all have our assignments –

FALK: Special field assignment, eh? That's it, isn't it? Pity, I wasn't really in good form today!

HUGO: You weren't too bad –

FALK: You're all right, you know. Now you mustn't think I'm trying to butter you up – that's not my way – but I must say I've grown a soft spot in my heart for you – I mean it!

HUGO: Same here.

FALK: My name's Maxy Falk. Why don't you call me Maxy!

HUGO: Why not, you old Falk, you!

FALK: Listen, chum, what about a nice little chat straight from the heart?

HUGO: Sort of man to man, Maxy?

FALK: That's it! What about it?

HUGO: Why not! As a matter of fact, all this time I've been thinking how nice it'd be if we two could have a sort of real man-to-man chat! (*He puts on* FALK*'s gay nose.*) Well, how's the boss? Quite a handful, eh?

FALK: The skipper? Has his faults, you know, but does his share. You'll find him at his desk even at this hour.

HUGO: At night?

FALK: What are you liquidating, in fact?

HUGO: So I could go and see him right now?

FALK: Are you going to?

HUGO: You mean I couldn't?

FALK: Why not? By the way – what for?

HUGO: Just like that – have a little chat – that's all.

FALK: I see. I don't want to pry –

HUGO: Pry away –

FALK: May I?

HUGO: Sure.

FALK: Well – er – what for?

HUGO: Just like that – have a little chat – that's all.

FALK: I see. I don't want to pry –

HUGO: Pry away –

FALK: May I?

HUGO: Sure.

FALK: Well – er – what for?

HUGO: Just like that – have a little chat – that's all.

FALK: Well, the Inauguration Service isn't perfect, we all know that. There were mistakes. Main thing, the whole affair will now be in the hands of a pro.

HUGO: Listen, he won't give me a hard time, will he?

FALK: Dictate of history is the dictate of history – he'll see that. Much greater men have had to see it.

HUGO: I'm really quite an ordinary chap, you know, made of flesh and bones, milk and blood – and also to me nothing foreign is human.

FALK: At least you'll proceed with feeling – you do understand people – and that's damned good.

HUGO: But of course I hate phrase-mongering and I resolutely reject all cant!

FALK: I mean it, chum! You know me, don't you?

HUGO: And I haven't even mentioned them scrags that sticks their heads in the sand when faced with burning problematicals!

FALK: I've never been afraid of the truth! When the cause is at stake, all personal interests must go overboard!

HUGO: I'm sure he'll meet me halfway. Damn it, aren't we all sons of one big mother?

FALK: You bet! But you mustn't put us all, as they say, in one basket! Even in liquidating one must sort of appreciate the differences! Take a chap like me, for example –

HUGO: Never mind. Main thing, I've managed to create here a sort of friendly, informal atmosphere – but now I must really run along! Don't worry, we're not seeing each other for the last time. Who knows, tomorrow I might be quite at home among you!

FALK: You'll be through with us in no time!

HUGO: Well, that's that. Now try and have some sort of fun here while I'm away!

FALK: I see what you mean. These are tempestuous times – everything's on the move –

HUGO: Do have a rest –

FALK: Everything's evolving at breakneck speed –

HUGO: Calm down –

FALK: What's new today will be old tomorrow –

HUGO: Relax –

FALK: We're searching for new paths –

HUGO: Make yourself comfortable –

FALK: Opening windows –

HUGO: Undress, if you like –

FALK: The ice is breaking – the thaw –

HUGO: Take off your shoes –

FALK: Yesterday the Inauguration Service was in the forefront, tomorrow it'll bring up the bloody rear –

HUGO: Have a nap, if you like! Even inaugurators are sort of men, damn it! As they say in my home town – catch a rabbit and you'll have it. Check!

(HUGO *quickly leaves.* FALK *sits down in despair. The* CLERK *and the* SECRETARY *gingerly approach. Pause. Then the* CLERK *slowly begins to deliver his 'message'.* FALK *sits motionlessly, stares ahead and ignores them.*)

CLERK: We've made up with one another now – we exchanged various facts from our private lives – we threw pine cones at each other – we tickled each other – nudged each other – tried to throw each other off balance – I pulled my colleague the Liquidation Secretary by the hair – my colleague the Liquidation Secretary bit me – but all just in fun, you know! Then we showed each other various peculiarities of our persons – we both found it very interesting – and we also touched each other – and, finally, we even called each other by our first names a few times!

FALK: Shut up! Well, why are you staring at me? You think I care about you! Not at all! Not in the least! You're nothing but air for me! You don't exist! I don't even see you! Well – go on! the Inauguration Service is being liquidated, so you'd better be there! You'd better not miss it! Hurry up!

(FALK *angrily stalks out. The* CLERK *stares blankly after him for a while. Then the penny drops and he begins to pace joyfully up and down the stage.*)

CLERK: They're clever! They are clever! (*Halts.*) Now, let's see. Will the Inauguration Service be liquidated under letter A, or under letter B? (*Again paces.*) Christ, they're clever!

SECRETARY: (*Sadly*) Joe! Is that all you can say to me now?

CLERK: Oh, come on! Be glad it's all over! We must hurry and liquidate – Miss! We mustn't be late!

(*The* SECRETARY *begins to sob. Quickly she starts towards the exit. The clerk, smiling happily, is about to follow. But before they have time to leave, Falk, furious, runs on the stage, faces them and shouts.*)

FALK: You know what? By the time you start liquidating, I'll be in bed! That's where I'll be! In bed! (*Puts his tongue out at them.*)

## ACT TWO

### SCENE 3

*Head Office of the Liquidation Service. The* DIRECTOR *sits at his desk, covered with masses of papers, next to the* SECRETARY, *who is carrying out the liquidation. She is taking papers and files from the* DIRECTOR *and stamping them with various rubber stamps. Having classified each object, she puts it into a huge basket, placed nearby. The following dialogue does not in any way interfere with the process of liquidation.*

DIRECTOR: Miss –

SECRETARY: Yes?

DIRECTOR: May I ask you something?

SECRETARY: Go on.

DIRECTOR: Will this liquidation take a long time?

SECRETARY: Why do you ask?

DIRECTOR: You don't want to go to bed?

SECRETARY: What do you mean by that?

DIRECTOR: Nothing wrong –

SECRETARY: It shouldn't take long. The organizational structure of the Inauguration Service allows us to proceed in a new way – under letter C – which is a combination of letters A and B. I'm working from the bottom under letter A – which is the preliminary registrationally formal liquidation – and my colleague works from the top under letter B – which is the proper, normal delimitational liquidation. We simply proceed from opposite directions towards each other.

DIRECTOR: I see. So you're going to meet somewhere in the middle –

SECRETARY: Well, not exactly. According to the liquidation harmonogram, we should meet on the third floor. But it's quite possible that my colleague will be there before me. He works very hard.

DIRECTOR: Some fool, eh?

SECRETARY: Please don't speak of him like this! At least not in my presence –

DIRECTOR: Sorry. I didn't realize –

(*Short pause. Then the* SECRETARY *flares up.*)

SECRETARY: Good gracious! You think I'm not a woman?

DIRECTOR: I didn't mean to –

SECRETARY: I beg your pardon.

DIRECTOR: In other words, your colleague might appear here any minute.

SECRETARY: Yes. We must hurry.

(*Meanwhile the* SECRETARY *has classified and put into the basket all the papers. During the following dialogue she takes the* DIRECTOR*'s tie, stamps it and throws it into the basket. The same happens with his jacket, shirt and trousers. From then on until the end of the scene the* DIRECTOR *will stay in his underwear.*)

Have you the list of the liquidation forms?

DIRECTOR: Yes.

SECRETARY: And the list of the delimitation norms?

DIRECTOR: No, not that one.

SECRETARY: Size (*referring to the tie*)?

DIRECTOR: No size. Regular, I suppose.

SECRETARY: But the list of the liquidation forms is invalid without the list of the delimitation norms!

DIRECTOR: Wouldn't a list of liquidation norms supported by a list of delimitation forms be enough?

SECRETARY: That, I'm afraid, would make the whole liquidation invalid.

DIRECTOR: Goodness, isn't this norm a bit formal?

SECRETARY: On the contrary, it's a perfectly normal form.

(*Holding up the jacket.*) Size?

DIRECTOR: Forty.

SECRETARY: Lining a bit torn –

DIRECTOR: I'd hate to argue, but where –

SECRETARY: By the left sleeve.

DIRECTOR: I'd hate to argue, but where –

SECRETARY: It was stipulated in the *Volume of Collected Liquidation Decrees*.

DIRECTOR: I'd hate to argue, but where were the decrees enacted?

SECRETARY: At this year's Liquidation Action Committee Meeting.

DIRECTOR: And where were they unanimously voted on?

SECRETARY: At last year's Liquidation Conference.

DIRECTOR: And finally validated?

SECRETARY: At the Liquidation Sitting of the year before last which you yourself inaugurated, quite nicely, as a matter of fact. You quoted Shakespeare, remember? 'Shall I compare thee to a summer's day' –

DIRECTOR: 'Thou art more lovely and more temperate' –

SECRETARY: And then, 'When daffodils begin to peer' –

DIRECTOR: 'With heigh! the doxy of the dale' –

SECRETARY: And then from Sramek, 'Farewell clover, 'tis the end' –

DIRECTOR: 'I may no longer call him friend' –

SECRETARY: Oh God! (*Bursts into tears.*)

DIRECTOR: There, there, miss! There's lots of good fish in the sea! Chin up, old girl – you're a woman –

SECRETARY: (*Recovers and at once resumes her official tone*) So you don't know the stipulation regarding the list of delimitation norms?

DIRECTOR: 'A thousand violins and flutes I heard' – and so I missed the stipulation.

SECRETARY: There you are! If this was another sort of liquidation I could perhaps turn a blind eye –

DIRECTOR: What sort of liquidation is this?

SECRETARY: This is liquidation through delimitation.

DIRECTOR: Does it mean we'll be reassigned?

SECRETARY: To the tinkers, probably.

DIRECTOR: Blimy, 'ow are we to be organized?

SECRETARY: In so-called 'col-tinks', I suppose, which are sort of complex collectives made up of one tinker and eight inaugurators each.

DIRECTOR: Are the col-tinks going to inaugurate, or to tink?

SECRETARY: Tink of course. Collar?

DIRECTOR: Sixteen.

SECRETARY: Well – that sort of winds up letter A. (*Folds her papers and closes the basket.*) Now I'm going up to the next floor. I'll collect the basket on the way back. My colleague will be here any minute to do letter B – Oh God! I'm not a woman, I'm a tree!

(*She walks out sobbing. The* DIRECTOR *goes to the basket, opens it, and for a while stares sadly inside. Then he sighs.*)

DIRECTOR: Difficult times –

(*After a while he collects himself, sits down at this desk. His eyelids begin to close. He struggles against his sleepiness, partially recovers.*)

Must try and hold out! (*Falls asleep.*)

HUGO: (*Enters, still wearing the* papier-mâché *nose*) Hello there, skipper!

DIRECTOR: (*Jumps up at once*)What? – Ah yes! Yes – that's me – I mean – sort of –

HUGO: Gave you quite a turn, eh?

DIRECTOR: On the contrary! Thank you!

HUGO: Do sit down! We're human, aren't we? Well, how are the kidneys?

DIRECTOR: Thanks. Liver.

HUGO: Same thing. Aren't we sort of among ourselves? Eh?

DIRECTOR: Yes – of course –

(*Pause.*)

HUGO: Well, how are things, chum? How are we?

DIRECTOR: Well, we know – we live – we inaugurate – chum –

HUGO: Good that we live! Let's live!

(*Pause.*)

DIRECTOR: Well now – how do we – so to say – begin –

HUGO: That – so to say – depends on us, doesn't it?

DIRECTOR: No doubt – it does, doesn't it?

(*Pause.*)

HUGO: So we're the boss here, are we?

DIRECTOR: We are.

HUGO: Honest?

DIRECTOR: If it's all right with us – yes – honest!

HUGO: Well, that's quite stimulating! We respect us! We think it's a sort of pretty honourable and responsible position we hold! Do we smoke?

DIRECTOR: No, thanks – We've been expecting us, we know?

We've been looking forward – shall we sit down? Do we smoke?

HUGO: No, thanks. We know – we sort of appreciate the inspiring significance of the Inauguration Service within the framework of our society – and the inspiring significance of the skipper within the framework of the Inauguration Service – do we smoke?

DIRECTOR: No, thanks. We know, not that we wouldn't like to tink, we'd love to tink, but – how should we put it – do we smoke?

HUGO: No, thanks. Soon this'll be sort of our second home, we believe. Am we right?

DIRECTOR: We am. Do we smoke?

HUGO: No, we don't.

DIRECTOR: Oh!

(*Pause.*)

HUGO: If we may, we'd like to start sort of from Eve. Already as a little child we inaugurated all our little childish games –

DIRECTOR: Charming!

HUGO: When we grew up a bit –

DIRECTOR: As a generation?

HUGO: As an individual. I've never set up any artificial barriers between the generations.

DIRECTOR: Neither have I.

HUGO: All people are really one generation, aren't they?

DIRECTOR: Absolutely.

HUGO: Well then, when I grew up a bit I inaugurated all school celebrations and parties.

DIRECTOR: Nice!

HUGO: And until now I've never let an opportunity for inaugurating slip by –

DIRECTOR: Impressive!

HUGO: Thanks.

DIRECTOR: I'm glad it's precisely you who've come to us.

HUGO: Thank you.

DIRECTOR: Clearly, you'll appreciate our particular situation.

HUGO: I'll do my best.

DIRECTOR: So the work will just hum along.

HUGO: Right!

DIRECTOR: Promise?

HUGO: Yes. You see, I've a number of qualities and potentialities particularly suited to inaugurating and I understand, I think, sort of its meaning and its mission.

DIRECTOR: Inaugurating, to my mind, is sort of a specific form of education, isn't it?

HUGO: Yes. But it's also its specific method.

DIRECTOR: Well – form or method?

HUGO: Both. It's precisely this peculiar unity which guarantees its specificity.

DIRECTOR: Stimulating!

HUGO: Isn't it?

DIRECTOR: All right, but what is specific for the content of inauguration?

HUGO: Its specific form.

DIRECTOR: Stimulating!

HUGO: Isn't it?

DIRECTOR: All right, but what is specific for the form of inauguration?

HUGO: Its specific method.

DIRECTOR: Stimulating!

HUGO: Isn't it?

DIRECTOR: All right, but what is specific for the method of inauguration?

HUGO: Its specific content.

DIRECTOR: Thrice stimulating!

HUGO: Isn't it, isn't it, isn't it?

DIRECTOR: It is.

HUGO: Yes. And this specific interrelation might be called the basic inauguration triangle.

DIRECTOR: Oh?

HUGO: Yes. While the specific character of this triangle is precisely its triangularity.

DIRECTOR: Oh?

HUGO: Yes.

DIRECTOR: This is indeed a stimulating contribution to the burning problems of inauguration theory.

HUGO: Isn't it? I'm glad we understand each other.

DIRECTOR: So am I. Very glad.

HUGO: I'm always glad when I meet somebody who's sort of close to me. I mean in the way of opinions and emotions. Go on, call me Hugo! Do you smoke?

DIRECTOR: No thanks, Hugo. And you? Do call me Ernie!

HUGO: Thanks, Ernie, neither do I. And you?

DIRECTOR: No thanks, Hugo. And you?

HUGO: Not at all. Listen, Ernie, why don't you think of me as sort of your father!

DIRECTOR: And you of me as your mother!

HUGO: Mummy –

(MRS PLUDEK *looks out from the wings.*)

MRS PLUDEK: Did you want anything, love?

HUGO: From you – nothing.

(MRS PLUDEK *disappears.*)

Well now, as a matter of fact, I came –

DIRECTOR: I know why you came, Hugo. But don't worry, I'll meet you halfway. I agree with you entirely. About time this happened! You'll be pleased with me, you'll see!

HUGO: You know, I mean it, Ernie, really, you see – I think I belong here among you – sort of – am I right?

DIRECTOR: Right!

HUGO: It's clear we'll get along fabulously!

DIRECTOR: We're lucky, that's all. Do you smoke?

HUGO: No. And you?

DIRECTOR: No.

HUGO: Listen, Ernie, cross your heart, aren't you a sort of non-smoker?

DIRECTOR: Goodness no! Not I!

HUGO: I see.

DIRECTOR: Oh well – what about getting down to business?

HUGO: That's up to you, isn't it? It's you who's at home here. I'm the intruder.

DIRECTOR: On the contrary. I'm the one who's delaying you,

Hugo. Well, why don't you sort of inaugurate it?

HUGO: You want to try me out first, eh?! And what am I supposed to inaugurate?

DIRECTOR: What? Well, you know what!

HUGO: No. What?

DIRECTOR: The liquidation!

HUGO: The liquidation? Of what?

DIRECTOR: Of the Inauguration Service of course!

HUGO: Christ! A bloody genius thought up that one! Obviously it's loaded with booby-traps. But I won't be booby-trapped, you know!

DIRECTOR: Oh?

HUGO: I won't!

DIRECTOR: Well, who's going to inaugurate it?

HUGO: Who? Well – surely – the responsible inaugurator!

DIRECTOR: The responsible inaugurator? But the inaugurators cannot inaugurate when they are being liquidated, can they?

HUGO: Right. That's why it ought to be inaugurated by the responsible liquidation officer!

DIRECTOR: The responsible liquidation officer? But the job of a liquidation officer is to liquidate, not to inaugurate!

HUGO: Right. That's why it'll be necessary to organize special inaugurational training of liquidation officers.

DIRECTOR: Oh?

HUGO: Or rather, a liquidational training of inaugurators?

DIRECTOR: Well, you ought to know that!

HUGO: Best if both trainings were organized at the same time. Inaugurators will be training liquidation officers, while liquidation officers will be training inaugurators.

DIRECTOR: And will it then be inaugurated by a liquidation officer trained by an inaugurator, or by an inaugurator trained by a liquidation officer?

HUGO: Another training will have to be organized. Inaugurationally trained liquidation officers training liquidationally trained inaugurators, and liquidationally trained inaugurators training inaugurationally trained liquidation officers.

DIRECTOR: And will it then be inaugurated by a liquidationally trained inaugurator trained by an inaugurationally trained liquidation officer, or by an inaugurationally trained liquidation officer trained by a liquidationally trained inaugurator?

HUGO: By the latter of course!

DIRECTOR: I see you've thought the matter through to the end. In theory. But in practice we're faced with the necessity to act. I want to get to bed as soon as possible. Besides, the liquidation of the Inauguration Service will be no problem. I mean it! My papers are all in order and letter A is already finished.

HUGO: Is the Inauguration Service being liquidated?

DIRECTOR: Unfortunately.

HUGO: (*Takes off his* papier-mâché *nose and puts it on the desk*) What do you mean 'unfortunately'? You mean fortunately, don't you?

DIRECTOR: Well, yes, I mean fortunately. I did say fortunately.

HUGO: Did you really say fortunately?

DIRECTOR: Of course. I wouldn't have said unfortunately, would I?

HUGO: All right, I'm going to believe you did say fortunately. We must have sort of faith in man, mustn't we? Unfortunately.

DIRECTOR: You mean fortunately, don't you?

HUGO: Of course I mean fortunately. You mean it's unfortunate?

DIRECTOR: I mean nothing of the sort. Now look here. We all know very well that the Inauguration Service is an outworn vestige of the past. And while it cannot be denied that in the era of the struggle against certain manifestations of bureaucratism in the activity of the Liquidation Office the Inauguration Service has played – thanks to certain inaugurators who by means of a healthy, unconventional, fresh, dynamic approach to man managed to hew their way even through this unploughed field to many valuable ideas – no doubt –

HUGO: A positive role, nevertheless there exists a danger of sinking –

DIRECTOR: Into liberal extremism – which would happen to any who failed to see these positive short-term characteristics from the perspective of the later development of the Inauguration Service –

HUGO: And who failed to see behind their possibly positive intent – from the subjective point of view –

DIRECTOR: Their clearly negative impact – from the objective point of view –

BOTH: (*Together*) Caused by the fact that as a result of an unhealthy isolation of the whole office certain positive elements in the work of the Inauguration Service were uncritically overrated, and at the same time certain negative elements in the work of the Liquidation Office were one-sidedly magnified, which finally resulted in the fact that the era – (*The* DIRECTOR *cannot keep pace with* HUGO *any more.*)

HUGO: When the new activization of all the positive forces inside the Liquidation Office placed the Liquidation Office once more in the forefront of our work as a firm and mighty stronghold of our unity, it was unfortunately precisely the Inauguration Service which succumbed –

DIRECTOR: To the hysterical atmosphere of certain imprudent excesses –

HUGO: Insinuating themselves by means of effective arguments taken from the arsenal of abstract humanistic cant – which however in reality did not span the confines of the generally conventionalized types of work – and these clichés are reflected in their typical form, for example, in –

DIRECTOR: The hackneyed machinery –

HUGO: Of the pseudo-familiar inaugurational phraseology hiding behind the routine of professional humanism a profound dilution of opinions which finally and necessarily led the Inauguration Service into the position of one who undermines the positive endeavour of the Liquidation Office towards consolidation, and the absolute historical necessity of all this is expressed in the wise act of its liquidation.

DIRECTOR: I couldn't agree more.

HUGO: You keep agreeing, but you do nothing about it! This way we'll never finish the liquidation. Time is money. Bring me a cup of coffee!

DIRECTOR: Excuse me, but –

HUGO: After all this, I can't imagine what the hell you mean by 'but'!

DIRECTOR: I don't mean 'but', but I want to say – but –

HUGO: So, on top of everything, you want to say 'but'!

DIRECTOR: I don't want to say 'but', but –

HUGO: Perhaps you don't want to say 'but but', but you do want to say 'but', and that's quite enough! You can't but me up with your 'buts', you know!

DIRECTOR: Excuse me, but – how much sugar do you take?

HUGO: Twenty-four lumps. And do stop messing about! This is no time for tongue-twisters!

(*The* DIRECTOR *backs out in terror.* HUGO *becomes the master of the situation. He paces importantly up and down the stage, examines everything with an official air, finally opens the basket and begins to throw out of it with disgust the* DIRECTOR*'s clothes. The* CLERK *enters, papers in hand, to continue his work of liquidating.*)

CLERK: Good evening. Well, let's get down to business, shall we?

HUGO: Let's! Where's the safe?

CLERK: You ought to know that!

HUGO: You don't work here? Good evening.

CLERK: I came here to work.

HUGO: Well, where do you work?

CLERK: At the Liquidation Office. (*Offers his hand to* HUGO.) How do you do. I'm Josef Dolezal.

HUGO: You want to work here?

CLERK: I've got to work here.

HUGO: Is the Liquidation Office being liquidated?

CLERK: Is the Liquidation Office supposed to be liquidated?

HUGO: (*Shakes hands with the* CLERK) How do you do. I'm Hugo Pludek. You mean it ought not to be liquidated?

CLERK: I mean nothing of the sort. We all know very well that the Liquidation Office is an outworn vestige of the past. And even though it cannot be denied that in the era of the struggle against certain imprudent excesses in the activity of the Inauguration Service the Liquidation Office has played – thanks to certain wise liquidational interventions – an undoubtedly positive role, nevertheless nothing but sinking into a sentimental hankering after the past –

HUGO: And into bureaucratic conservatism –

CLERK: Awaits him who fails to see the work of the Liquidation Office from the perspective of its later development when thanks to many imprudent liquidational interventions against many positive elements in the work of the Inauguration Service –

HUGO: The Liquidation Office undoubtedly played a negative role which was the result of the activities of some liquidation officers –

CLERK: Who progressively superimposed –

BOTH: (*Together*) The administrative part of liquidation practice over its social content, with the result that the activity of the Liquidation Office assumed an unhealthy, sterile character, since it was thus wrenched from life –

(CLERK *cannot keep pace with* HUGO *any more.*)

HUGO: And drawn into the muddy waters of fossilized bureaucratism which necessarily opened the door to the irresponsible activity of a small gang of liquidational adventurers who abused –

CLERK: The wise endeavour –

HUGO: Towards the suppression of certain one-sided excesses in the activity of the Inauguration Service so as demagogically to attack all its positive forces which successfully came through the era of its temporary crisis, and by their new far-reaching activization managed to place the Inauguration Service again in the forefront of our endeavour towards a revaluation of faulty methods and thus imposed on the Liquidation Office the role of an actual brake on our development and thus literally forced our era to perform the bold act of its liquidation. Signed, Hugo Pludek.

CLERK: I couldn't agree more. Signed, Josef Dolezal.

HUGO: You'd better agree! (*Points at the clothes which he had been throwing about a while ago.*) See this mess? It's their work! The Liquidation Office is being liquidated and they just keep liquidating here as if nothing was the matter.

CLERK: Is the Liquidation Office indeed being liquidated?

HUGO: Just imagine! Even now when they've been earmarked for extinction they're acting as if the place belonged to them. It makes me sick! I'm going to go there. Now!

(HUGO *briskly walks out. The* DIRECTOR *arrives with a cup of coffee. When he sees the* CLERK *he halts.*)

DIRECTOR: Good evening.

CLERK: Good evening.

DIRECTOR: Assistant?

CLERK: Whose?

DIRECTOR: Of the chap who's liquidating here.

CLERK: I beg your pardon! I wouldn't assist those who act as if the place belonged to them even now when they've long been earmarked for extinction!

(*The* DIRECTOR *drops the cup. Freezes, amazed.*)

Clearly, it'd be rather foolish to liquidate at the very time the Liquidation Office is being liquidated. The absurdity of such behaviour was pointed out to me by Hugo Pludek himself.

DIRECTOR: Who's he?

CLERK: I'm sorry, I don't know precisely, but he seems to be very closely involved with the liquidation of the Liquidation Office. Who knows, perhaps he's actually in charge of it. (*Pause. The* DIRECTOR *picks up the cup.*) Oh well, I'd better be going.

DIRECTOR: (*Suddenly slaps him on the back*) Don't go away! Do sit down! Let's have a little chat, shall we? Now, tell me, why did you come here? What for?

CLERK: Well, you know – just like that – to have a look around – have a little chat – oh well, I'd better be going –

DIRECTOR: (*Again slaps him on the back*) Don't go away! Do sit down! Let's have a little chat, shall we? Now, tell me, why did you come here? What for?

CLERK: Well, you know – just like that – to have a look around – have a little chat – oh well, I'd better be going –

DIRECTOR: (*Again slaps him on the back*) Don't go away! Do sit down! Let's have a little chat, shall we? Now, tell me, why did you come here? What for?

CLERK: Well, you know – just like that – to have a look around – have a little chat – (*suddenly explodes*.) Good gracious! Why all this fuss! I simply didn't know about it, that's all!

DIRECTOR: (*Calming him down*) Gracious, why all this fuss? You simply didn't know about it, that's all!

CLERK: (*Calming down*) I simply didn't know about it, that's all.

DIRECTOR: You simply didn't know about it, that's all.

CLERK: (*Calmed down*) Gracious, why all this fuss?

DIRECTOR: Gracious, aren't we friends?

CLERK: What?

DIRECTOR: We're friends, aren't we?

CLERK: What did you say?

DIRECTOR: I said we're friends.

CLERK: What do you mean by that?

DIRECTOR: Good gracious, don't you know? Aren't we all sons of one big mother, damn it!?

CLERK: That's not the point. The point is, I'd better go and liquidate the Liquidation Office. Bye – see you later – cheerio!

(*The* CLERK *walks out. The* DIRECTOR *looks about conspiratorially a few times, then very carefully drags out from his desk a stuffed sack and puts it on top.* HUGO *enters. The* DIRECTOR, *alarmed, hides the sack again inside his desk.*)

HUGO: What the hell are you doing?

DIRECTOR: What? Nothing. I'm liquidating –

HUGO: Come, come, old boy! You don't really mean it, do you? You wouldn't want to be liquidating at the very time the Liquidation Officer is being liquidated! Goodness, you're a grown-up man, you wouldn't want to act like a child now, would you? Or are you perhaps trying to make me report on you above? If you insist on digging your own grave in the name of sham heroism – by all means! But in that case I can't be expected to master myself!

DIRECTOR: It's the liquidation I'm liquidating – the liquidation!

HUGO: Let's hope so! Has Dolezal left?

DIRECTOR: I'm terribly sorry, he's left. But I may be able to catch him on the stairs. Shall I run and see if I can catch him?

HUGO: I was on my way to give the chaps a hand with liquidating the Liquidation Office and I clean forgot to ask who's actually in charge. You see, I'd like to go straight to the horse's mouth.

DIRECTOR: Pludek.

HUGO: Which? Hugo?

DIRECTOR: That's the one.

HUGO: Good. I'll go and see him right now. I hope you won't start any rumpus in this place. I quite like you, you know, and I'd hate to be forced to send you spinning out of here like a top! Well – be good! Bye!

(HUGO *briskly walks out, then he returns for his* papier-mâché *nose, puts it on and leaves. The* DIRECTOR *stares after him for a while, then he puts his tongue out after* HUGO, *again carefully drags out his sack, puts it gently on the desk and suddenly starts to hit it furiously. The* SECRETARY *enters.*)

SECRETARY: Hitting the sack? Again?

DIRECTOR: Sorry – I'm sorry –

(*He tries to hide the sack quickly, but* SECRETARY *energetically wrenches it from him and throws it in the basket.*)

SECRETARY: Aren't you ashamed? You think we aren't tired? But we all must carry on! Was Josef here?

DIRECTOR: Dolezal?

SECRETARY: Yes.

DIRECTOR: He left some time ago.

SECRETARY: Be glad you're not a woman! (*Bursts into tears.*)

DIRECTOR: Wouldn't you like to stay a moment? Sort of unofficially? You do need some distraction, you know. After all, you too are only human!

SECRETARY: You should be ashamed of yourself! (*Marches resolutely out.*)

DIRECTOR: One goes around so long lugging a liquidation basket, that one day it gets left behind. Oh well – at least I've place to take a nap.

(*The* DIRECTOR *climbs into the basket. The* SECRETARY *enters.*)

SECRETARY: 'When daffodils begin to peer – '

DIRECTOR: 'With heigh! the doxy of the dale – '

(*The* SECRETARY *steps into the basket as though it were a river. The lid slowly closes.*)

## SCENE 4

*Again the flat of the Pludek family. Present are:* PLUDEK *and* MRS PLUDEK , *both in night-clothes.*

PLUDEK: Besides, as far as Japan is concerned – what time is it, actually?

MRS PLUDEK: Almost six. Did you hear that?

PLUDEK: He should have been here by now. Hear what?

MRS PLUDEK: Unless he was a bit delayed. Isn't it footsteps?

PLUDEK: What do you mean, 'delayed'? It's the wind. Besides, as far as Japan is concerned –

MRS PLUDEK: He might have got drunk at the garden party. You're right, it's only the wind.

PLUDEK: He drinks nothing but milk, and I bet there was no milk on tap there. Isn't it footsteps, after all? Besides, as far as Japan is concerned –

MRS PLUDEK: Why shouldn't there be milk on tap? If there are milk bars, why not milk garden parties? Is it really footsteps?

PLUDEK: I haven't thought of that. No question, he got stoned on milk and delayed. Who'd be walking in the pantry at this hour? It's the wind.

MRS PLUDEK: Was it in the pantry? But I closed the window there last night.

PLUDEK: Footsteps? After all? I'm going to go there and see! What did I actually want to say about Japan? (*Walks offstage and bangs on a door.*) I repeat: Who's there? Who's there? I repeat: Open up at once! Open up at once!

(*He backs onstage in terror, followed guiltily by* AMANDA *and*

PETER, *each wearing only a hastily arranged overcoat.*)

MRS PLUDEK: Goodness gracious me! Is something the matter?

AMANDA: There's nothing the matter. Here is a letter. I mean a telegram.

PLUDEK: Read it!

AMANDA: (*Reading*) DEAR ALBERT, I HEAR THAT YOUR SON HUGO HAS BEEN PUT IN CHARGE OF LIQUIDATING THE LIQUIDATION OFFICE. Have you got it, Ann darling? We'll push off at twelve. Don't bother, love, I'll take the ham in its own juice. I SHOULD LIKE TO TAKE THIS OPPORTUNITY TO CONGRATULATE HIM ON HIS SIGNAL SUCCESS. You mean you've never been in Nespeky? Carbons? In Hirsch's desk. Just wait till you see the woods! Please carry on. WE OUGHT TO MEET ONE DAY . Don't forget to take – YOURS FRANK KALABIS – your swimsuit.

MRS PLUDEK: Did you hear that, Albert? The liquidation of the Liquidation Office!

PLUDEK: I heard it, Berta. Jaros wished to be a goldsmith and he became one. Hugo asked himself – and there you are – a signal success. Besides, as far as Japan is concerned –

MRS PLUDEK: (*To* AMANDA) What exactly were you doing in the pantry the whole night?

AMANDA: Sorting the post. Goodbye.

(AMANDA *and* PETER *leave in opposite directions.*)

MRS PLUDEK: Listen, Bertie –

PLUDEK: What is it?

MRS PLUDEK: Hugo is nicely taken care of. Shouldn't we now look out for something for Peter? After all, he too is our child.

PLUDEK: Oh, we'll find something for him. He might go to work for some paper.

MRS PLUDEK: Wouldn't they mind him looking like a bourgeois intellectual? If only he'd stop wearing those glasses!

PLUDEK: They haven't got a single intellectual among them, so they're bound to think better a bourgeois one than none at all. At least he knows which way is up. Did somebody ring?

MRS PLUDEK: No.

(*The doorbell rings.*)

PLUDEK: It's Hugo!

MRS PLUDEK: At last!

(HUGO *enters, still wearing his gay* papier-mâché *nose.*)

I was sure our darling little Hugo would get ahead!

PLUDEK: Well done, you rascal! What about giving him something good to eat?

MRS PLUDEK: Now what would he like? A nice little glass of milk perhaps?

PLUDEK: A nice little cup of coffee, I'd say. The poor bugger's been up the whole night.

MRS PLUDEK: He may have got no sleep, but he got ahead! Who knows, he might not feel like talking to us now that he has this important position, Albert!

HUGO: He has a friendly word for everyone, even for the simplest folk. As a matter of fact, I'm counting on it myself. I've come here to have a little chat with him and see if perhaps I might not give him a hand with this or the other. What about that nice cup of coffee?

MRS PLUDEK: Yes, of course, as soon as our darling little Hugo arrives.

HUGO: He's not home yet?

PLUDEK: He was probably delayed by that liquidation.

MRS PLUDEK: Liquidating a Liquidation Office is no easy matter, you know!

HUGO: Your Hugo is liquidating at the very time the Liquidation Office is being liquidated?

PLUDEK: That's not what my wife meant. She just meant to say that Hugo shouldn't be doing this liquidation.

HUGO: And who'd liquidate the Liquidation Office?

PLUDEK: Our Hugo.

HUGO: You mean your Hugo would be liquidating at the very time the Liquidation Office is being liquidated?

MRS PLUDEK: That's not what my husband meant. He just meant to say that Hugo shouldn't be doing the liquidation.

HUGO: And who'd liquidate the Liquidation Office?

MRS PLUDEK: Our Hugo.

PLUDEK: Precisely.

MRS PLUDEK: Why should our Hugo be liquidating at the very time the Liquidation Office was being liquidated?

PLUDEK: And who'd liquidate the Liquidation Office?

MRS PLUDEK: Our Hugo.

PLUDEK: Why should our Hugo be liquidating at the very time the Liquidation Office is being liquidated?

MRS PLUDEK: And who'd liquidate the Liquidation Office?

PLUDEK: Our Hugo.

MRS PLUDEK: Why not?

PLUDEK: Provided nobody hears about it.

MRS PLUDEK: These things can't be kept quiet.

PLUDEK: Hugo shouldn't have accepted that liquidation.

MRS PLUDEK: If he hadn't accepted it, the Liquidation Office wouldn't have been liquidated and liquidation would go on. And why then should Hugo be the only one who isn't liquidating? It's good he didn't turn it down!

PLUDEK: Because he didn't, the Liquidation Office will be liquidated, liquidation will stop, and it'll be only Hugo who'll keep on liquidating. It's bound to get him into trouble, sooner or later –

MRS PLUDEK: He should have turned it down –

PLUDEK: On the contrary, he should have not accepted it –

MRS PLUDEK: On the contrary, he should have not turned it down –

PLUDEK: Shouldn't he have at the same time accepted it and not turned it down?

MRS PLUDEK: Rather, turned it down and not accepted it!

PLUDEK: In that case, rather not accepted it, not turned it down, accepted it and turned it down!

MRS PLUDEK: And what if he'd at the same time turned it down, not accepted it, not turned it down and accepted it?

PLUDEK: Hard to say. What do you think?

HUGO: Me? Well, I'd say he should have not accepted it, not turned it down, accepted it and turned it down, and at the same time turned it down, not accepted it, not turned it down and accepted it. Or the other way around. Did somebody ring?

PLUDEK: No.

(*Just then the doorbell rings.*) It's Hugo!

MRS PLUDEK: At last!

(AMANDA *and* PETER *enter from opposite directions.*)

AMANDA: (*Reading*) DEAR ALBERT, I HAVE JUST HEARD THAT THE INAUGURATION SERVICE IS BEING LIQUIDATED AND THAT THE RESPONSIBLE TASK OF CONDUCTING THIS IMPORTANT LIQUIDATION HAS ALSO BEEN ENTRUSTED TO YOUR HUGO . Have you got it, Ann? What? Good God, a bit of rain on the way back! No, much later. CONVEY TO HIM PLEASE MY SINCEREST CONGRATULATIONS UPON HIS GREAT SUCCESS . That's why, dear, that's precisely why! And what about me? She won't give me a divorce! WE MUST MEET SOON ALBERT AND HAVE A GOOD CHAT . Try and understand – I've got children! DO YOU REMEMBER WHAT WE DID WHEN WE WERE BOYS ? Careful, Hirsch is coming! YOURS FRANCIS.

MRS PLUDEK: Did you hear that, Albert? The liquidation of the Inauguration Service!

PLUDEK: I heard it, Berta. What was it Jaros used to say? Life is a blank page. Hugo knew what to write on it – and there you are – a great success! Besides, as far as Japan is concerned –

MRS PLUDEK: (*To* AMANDA) Have you been sorting post the whole night? In the dark?

AMANDA: The bulb broke.

MRS PLUDEK: The bulb! If you don't marry Peter now –

AMANDA: But we want to get married –

MRS PLUDEK: My poor girl, Peter is a bourgeois intellectual!

AMANDA: Peter is going to study microbiology! Goodbye!

(AMANDA *and* PETER *leave in opposite directions.*)

MRS PLUDEK: Listen, Bertie –

PLUDEK: What is it?

MRS PLUDEK: Did you hear that?

HUGO: So your Hugo is liquidating not only the Liquidation Office, but the Inauguration Service as well?

PLUDEK: And he's right! Both institutions ought to be liquidated as soon as possible, because both are outworn vestiges of the past. You do agree, don't you?

HUGO: Well, we all –

MRS PLUDEK: Please try and understand, my husband didn't mean to say that – on the contrary – they shouldn't both be preserved, if this turned out to be a matter of good tactics –

HUGO: Well, we all –

PLUDEK: Please try and understand, my wife didn't mean to say that the Inauguration Service shouldn't be liquidated and the Liquidation Office preserved, or the Liquidation Office liquidated and the Inauguration Service preserved, if this turned out to be a matter of good strategy –

HUGO: Well, we all –

MRS PLUDEK: Please try and understand, my husband didn't mean to say that both institutions shouldn't be in good measure preserved –

PLUDEK: And at the same time both in good measure liquidated –

MRS PLUDEK: Or the other way round –

PLUDEK: If this turned out to be –

MRS PLUDEK: Good strategical –

PLUDEK: Tactics –

HUGO: Well, we all –

MRS PLUDEK: Well – what?

HUGO: Well, please try and understand – we all are only sort of searching in these tempestuous times for our particular standpoint – did somebody ring?

PLUDEK: No.

(*Just then the doorbell rings.*)

It's Hugo!

MRS PLUDEK: At last!

(AMANDA *and* PETER *enter from opposite directions.*)

AMANDA: (*Reading*) MY VERY DEAREST ALBERT, YOU CANNOT IMAGINE HOW VERY PLEASANTLY I WAS SURPRISED BY THE NEWS THAT YOUR HUGO – Only yesterday he had a full drawer of carbons! I didn't eat them! What? You'd be wanting a mink coat next! Carry on, will you! – WAS ASSIGNED THE EXTREMELY HONOURABLE AND IMPORTANT TASK OF CONSTRUCTING ON THE RUINS OF THE FORMER LIQUIDATION OFFICE AND THE FORMER

INAUGURATION SERVICE A GREAT NEW INSTITUTION, A CENTRAL COMMISSION FOR INAUGURATION AND LIQUIDATION. I can't stand a woman crying! All right, all right! GIVE HIM PLEASE MY FERVENT BROTHERLY GREETINGS ON THE OCCASION OF HIS OUTSTANDING SUCCESS . Oh, come off it! I don't believe it. And if you are – you must get rid of it, that's all! I AM MISSING YOU MOST TERRIBLY AND I CANNOT WAIT TO SEE YOU AGAIN . I won't be blackmailed by you, you know! YOUR OLD – Liar! – FAITHFUL – Whore! – FRANK – Silly goose!

MRS PLUDEK: Did you hear that, Albert? The construction of a Central Commission for Inauguration and Liquidation!

PLUDEK: I heard it, Berta. Jaros always thought of his future, he studied and studied and studied. Hugo thought of his – and there you are – an outstanding success! Besides, as far as Japan is concerned –

MRS PLUDEK: (*To* AMANDA) Peter and microbiology! Nonsense! A member of the middle classes won't waste his time on such piddling matters!

AMANDA: Peter and I are in love with each other. He's moving out of here and coming to live with me! Goodbye!

PETER: Goodbye!

(AMANDA *and* PETER *leave together, theatrically holding hands.*)

MRS PLUDEK: Listen, Bertie –

PLUDEK: What is it?

MRS PLUDEK: Did you hear the way he shouted at us?

PLUDEK: Berta, I can't help feeling that we've just lost a son. But I can't help adding that it's no great loss, since our future daughter-in-law is the child of a caretaker!

MRS PLUDEK: But a caretaker is really the working class, isn't he?

PLUDEK: Not all that much. But let's face it, he knows a lot about the working class –

MRS PLUDEK: Amanda and microbiology were stronger than us, so now Hugo remains the only real hope of the family. What did you actually want to say about Japan?

PLUDEK: (*To* HUGO) Listen, who are you, in fact?

HUGO: Me! You mean who I am? Now look here, I don't like this one-sided way of putting questions, I really don't! You think one can ask in this simplified way? No matter how one answers this sort of question, one can never encompass the whole truth, but only one of its many limited parts. What a rich thing is man, how complicated, changeable, and multiform – there's no word, no sentence, no book, nothing that could describe and contain him in his whole extent. In man there's nothing permanent, eternal, absolute; man is a continuous change – a change with a proud ring to it, of course! Today the time of static and unchangeable categories is past, the time when A was only A, and B always only B is gone; today we all know very well that A may be often B as well as A; that B may just as well be A; that B may be B, but equally it may be A and C; just as C may be not only C, but also A, B, and D; and in certain circumstances even F may become Q, Y, and perhaps also H. I'm sure you yourselves must feel that what you feel today you've not felt yesterday, and what you felt yesterday you don't feel today, but might perhaps again feel tomorrow; while what you might feel the day after tomorrow you may never have felt before. Do you feel that? And it's not hard to see that those who today understand only today are merely another version of those who yesterday understand only yesterday; while, as we all know, it's necessary today somehow to try and understand also that which was yesterday, because – who knows – it may come back again tomorrow! Truth is just as complicated and multiform as everything else in the world – the magnet, the telephone, Impressionism, the magnet – and we all are a little bit what we were yesterday and a little bit what we are today; and also a little bit we're not these things. Anyway, we all are a little bit all the time and all the time we are not a little bit; some of us are more and some of us are more not; some only are, some are only, and some only are not; so that none of us entirely is and at the same time each one of us is not entirely; and the point is just when it is better to be more, and to not be less, and when – on the contrary – it is better less to be and more to not be; besides, he who is too much may soon not be at all, and he who – in a certain situation – is able to a certain extent to not be, may in another situation be all the better for that. I don't know whether you want more to be or not to be, and when you want to be or not to be; but I know I want to be all the time and that's why all the time I must a little bit not be. You see, man when he is from time to time a little bit not is not diminished thereby! And if at the moment I am – relatively speaking – rather not, I assure you that soon I might be much more than I've ever been – and then we can have another chat about all these things, but on an entirely different platform. Checkmate! (*Walks out.*)

MRS PLUDEK: Listen, Bertie –

PLUDEK: What is it?

MRS PLUDEK: Not bad what he said, was it?

PLUDEK: It was excellent! And you know why?

MRS PLUDEK: Why?

PLUDEK: Because clearly he has in his veins the healthy philosophy of the middle classes! You know, without gumboots not even Kubes can get to Kravovec!

(*Sings*) Rule Bohemia!
Bohemia rules the waves
Bohemians
Never, never, never –

MRS PLUDEK: So long as the Japs don't overrun us! When they come, all the hounds of hell will bark!

(*Just then a hell-hound barks inside the cupboard.*)

PLUDEK: Berta, they're here!

(FALK *steps out of the cupboard and comes right down to the footlights.*)

FALK: (*Addressing the audience*) And now, without sort of much ado – go home!

# THE MEMORANDUM

# CHARACTERS*

JOSEF GROSS, *Managing Director*
JAN BALLAS, *Deputy Director*
OTTO STROLL, *Head of the Translation Centre*
ALEX SAVANT, *Ptydepist*
HELENA, *Chairman*
MARIA, *Secretary at the Translation Centre*
HANA, *Secretary to the Managing Director*
MARK LEAR, *Teacher of Ptydepe*
FERDINAND PILLAR
GEORGE, *Staff Watcher*
PETER THUMB, *A clerk*
MR COLUMN
THREE CLERKS

The action takes place in three office rooms within one large organization. Each office differs frcm the other in its particulars (placement of furniture, office equipment, etc.), but they all exude the same atmosphere and thus resemble each other. In each, there are two exits: a back door and a side door.

*TRANSLATOR'S NOTE: Some names of the *dramatis personae* in this translation differ from those of the original. This is the reason: The original text of the play was dedicated by Václav Havel to the theatre ensemble of the first Prague production and he used the first names of his cast for those of his characters. I was delighted to find that their last names happened to be translatable, and so–with the agreement of the author–I used the translated names of the Czech cast, rather than those given in the original text (though the part acted by Mr. Lir was merely adapted to read 'Lear', and his first, unpronounceable name was changed). For clarity's sake, however, the names of the two main characters, Gross and Ballas, were preserved. In other words, this discrepancy between the translation and the original is the result of a little inside joke between me, Havel and the cast.

V.B.

# ACT ONE

## SCENE I

*The Director's office. Large office desk, small typist's desk, a fire extinguisher on the wall, a coat rack in the background. The stage is empty. Then* GROSS *enters by the back door, takes off his coat, hangs it on the rack, sits at his desk and begins to go through his morning mail. He skims each letter, then puts it either into the waste-paper basket or into the out tray. One letter suddenly arrests his attention. He glares at it and then starts to read it aloud.*

GROSS: (*Reads*) Ra ko hutu d dekotu ely trebomu emusohe, vdegar yd, stro reny er gryk kendy, alyv zvyde dezu, kvyndal fer tekynu sely. Degto yl tre entvester kyleg gh: orka epyl y bodur depty-depe emete. Grojto af xedob yd, kyzem ner osonfterte ylem kho dent de det detrym gynfer bro enomuz fechtal agni laj kys defyj rokuroch bazuk suhelen. Gakvom ch ch lopve rekto elkvestrete. Dyhap zuj bak dygalex ibem nyderix tovah gyp. Ykte juh geboj. Fyx dep butrop gh–
(GROSS *does not notice that meanwhile* BALLAS *and* PILLAR *have quietly entered by the side door.* BALLAS *coughs discreetly.*)
Are you here?

BALLAS: Yes, we are.

GROSS: I didn't hear you come.

BALLAS: We entered quietly.

GROSS: Have you been here long?

BALLAS: Not long.

GROSS: What is it?

BALLAS: We've come to ask your advice, Mr Gross.

GROSS: Go on.

BALLAS: Where should Mr Pillar record the incoming mail?

GROSS: Couldn't be more obvious, Mr Ballas. In the incoming-mail book.

BALLAS: It's full, isn't it, Mr P?
(PILLAR *nods.*)

GROSS: So soon?

BALLAS: I'm afraid so.

GROSS: Good gracious! Well, he'll have to get a new one.

BALLAS: We've no funds to get a new one, have we, Mr P?

(PILLAR *shakes his head.*)

GROSS: What do you mean no funds? As far as I recall a purchase of two incoming-mail books was budgeted for this quarter.

BALLAS: It was. But in accordance with the new economy drive all budgeted expenditures were cut by half, with the result that we were able to purchase only one incoming-mail book which is, as I've just mentioned, full. Isn't it, Mr P?

(PILLAR *nods.*)

GROSS: (*Hands* PILLAR *some money.*) Here. Buy yourself a new one.

(PILLAR *pockets the money. Both bow respectfully.*)

BALLAS: We thank you, Mr Gross. Thank you very much.

(*They leave by the side door.* GROSS *picks up his letter and examines it with curiosity.* HANA *enters by the back door, wearing a coat and carrying a vast shopping bag.*)

HANA: Good morning.

GROSS: (*Without looking up*) Good morning.

(HANA *hangs her coat on coat rack, sits down at the typist's desk, takes a mirror and a comb out of her bag, props the mirror against the typewriter and begins to comb her hair. Combing her hair will be her main occupation throughout the play. She will interrupt it only when absolutely necessary.* GROSS *watches her stealthily for a moment, then turns to her.*)

Hana–

HANA: Yes, Mr Gross?

GROSS: (*Shows her the letter*) Any idea what this is?

HANA: (*Skims the letter*) This is a very important office memorandum, Mr Gross.

GROSS: It looks like a hodgepodge of entirely haphazard groups of letters.

HANA: Perhaps, at first glance. But in fact there's method in it. It's written in Ptydepe, you see.

GROSS: In what?

HANA: In Ptydepe.

GROSS: In Ptydepe? What is it?

HANA: A new office language which is being introduced into our organization. May I go and get the milk?

GROSS: There's a new language being introduced into our organization? I don't remember having been informed.

HANA: They must have forgotten to tell you. May I go and get the milk?

GROSS: Who thought it up?

HANA: It seems to be a full-scale campaign. Elsie said it's being introduced into their department, too.

GROSS: Does my deputy realize what's going on?

HANA: Mr Ballas? Of course he does. May I go and get the milk?

GROSS: Run along.

(HANA *takes an empty bottle from her shopping bag and hurries out by the back door.* GROSS *paces thoughtfully up and down. Again does not notice when* BALLAS *and* PILLAR *enter by the side door.* BALLAS *coughs.*)

Are you here again?

BALLAS: We've come to tell you that we've just purchased a brand new incoming-mail book. It's lying on Mr Pillar's desk. Isn't it, Mr P?

(PILLAR *nods.*)

GROSS: Good.

BALLAS: But the Department of Authentication refuses to authenticate it.

GROSS: Why?

BALLAS: The new book hasn't been registered by the Purchasing Department on account of its not having been purchased with the department's funds. So, legally, it doesn't exist, does it, Mr P?

(PILLAR *shakes his head.*)

GROSS: Say I ask them to authenticate it on my personal responsibility. My position's solid now, I think I can go so far.

BALLAS: Excellent! Would you mind giving it to us in writing? It'll simplify things a great deal.

GROSS: I would. I don't mind taking risks, but I'm not a gambler. A verbal order will have to do.

BALLAS: Well, then we must try to talk them into accepting it. Mr P, let's go.

(*They turn to leave.* GROSS *stops them.*)

GROSS: Just a moment, Mr Ballas.

BALLAS: Yes, Mr Gross?

GROSS: Do you know anything about a new language?

BALLAS: I think I've heard about it. I seem to recall Mr Pillar told me about it some time ago, didn't you, Mr P?

(PILLAR *nods.*)

GROSS: Do you also recall who ordered its introduction into our organization?

BALLAS: Who was it, Mr P, do you know?

(PILLAR *shrugs.*)

GROSS: Mr Ballas. You are my deputy, aren't you?

BALLAS: Yes.

GROSS: Well then. I didn't order it. So it could only have been you.

BALLAS: One gives so many orders every day, one can't be expected to remember them all.

GROSS: Don't you think you ought to consult me on such matters?

BALLAS: We didn't want to bother you with trifles.

GROSS: Actually, why is it being introduced?

BALLAS: As a sort of experiment. It's supposed to make office communications more accurate and introduce precision and order into their terminology. Am I putting it correctly, Mr P?

(PILLAR *nods.*)

GROSS: Was it ordered from above?

BALLAS: Not directly–

GROSS: To tell you the truth, I'm far from happy about it. You'll have to find a way to stop the whole thing at once. We don't want to be somebody's guinea-pig, do we?

(HANA *re-enters by the back door with a bottle of milk.*)

HANA: (*To* BALLAS) Good morning.

(*She puts the bottle on her desk, opens it, drinks, then continues combing her hair.*)

BALLAS: All right, I'll cancel my directive, and try to retrieve all the Ptydepe texts sent out so far, and have them translated back into natural language. (*To* HANA) Good morning.

GROSS: Kindly do that.

BALLAS: We don't want to be somebody's guinea-pig, do we?

GROSS: Exactly.

BALLAS: Mr P, let's go.

(*They leave by the side door.* GROSS *crosses to* HANA'*s desk, reaches for her milk bottle.*)

GROSS: May I?

HANA: Yes, of course, Mr Gross.

(GROSS *drinks, returns to his desk, sits down. Pause.*)

GROSS: Strange relationship between those two.

HANA: I know a great many particulars about it.

GROSS: I don't want to hear them! They're both exceptionally good workers. The rest is not my business. (*Pause. Again stares at his letter. Then turns to* HANA.) Thank God, I've nipped it in the bud. Did they seriously think anybody would want to learn this gibberish?

HANA: Special Ptydepe classes have been set up for all departments.

GROSS: Indeed! Anybody joined them?

HANA: Everybody except you, Mr Gross.

GROSS: Really?

HANA: It was an order.

GROSS: Whose order?

HANA: Mr Ballas's.

GROSS: What! He didn't tell me anything about that! (*Pause.*) Anyway, I fail to see how our staff could be expected to use this Ptydepe when most of them couldn't possibly have learned it yet.

HANA: That's why a Ptydepe Translation Centre has been set up. But it's supposed to be only temporary, until everybody has learned Ptydepe. Then it'll become the Ptydepe Reference Centre. May I go and get the rolls?

GROSS: Well, well! A Translation Centre! Where on earth did they find room for it all?

HANA: The Translation Centre is on the first floor, room 6.

GROSS: But that's the Accounts Department!

HANA: The Accounts Department has been moved to the cellar. May I go and get the rolls?

GROSS: Also on his order?

HANA: Yes.

GROSS: That's the limit!

HANA: May I go and get the rolls?

GROSS: Run along.

(HANA *pulls a string bag from her shopping bag and leaves by the back door.* GROSS *again does not notice when* BALLAS *and* PILLAR *enter by the side door.* BALLAS *coughs.*)

Now what?

BALLAS: Mr Gross, I'm afraid you'll have to give us the order in writing, after all.

GROSS: I'll do nothing of the sort.

BALLAS: It'd be in your own interest.

GROSS: What do you mean–in my own interest?

BALLAS: If you'll give it to us in writing, you'll greatly simplify the work of our clerical staff. They won't have to fill out a special voucher to go with each incoming letter, you see. And in view of the rumours which have lately been circulating among them, it would certainly be a good tactical move on your part. Am I not right, Mr P?

(PILLAR *nods.*)

GROSS: What rumours?

BALLAS: Oh, about that unfortunate rubber stamp.

GROSS: Rubber stamp? What rubber stamp?

BALLAS: Apparently during the last audit it transpired that you're in the habit of taking the bank endorsement stamp home for your children to play with.

GROSS: That's ridiculous. Of course I have taken that particular rubber stamp home a few times. But not as a plaything. There are nights when I have to take my work home to get it all done.

BALLAS: You don't have to explain it to us, Mr Gross. But you know how people are!

GROSS: And you think this bit of paper you want would smooth things over?

BALLAS: I'll guarantee you that.

GROSS: All right then. As far as I'm concerned, have it typed, and I'll sign it.

(BALLAS *at once produces a typed sheet of paper, unfolds it, and places it on* GROSS*'s desk.*)

BALLAS: Here you are, Mr Gross.

(GROSS *signs.*)

(BALLAS *snatches the document and quickly folds it.*) Thank you, Mr Gross. We thank you very much in the name of the entire organization.

(BALLAS *and* PILLAR *are about to leave.*)

GROSS: Mr Ballas.

BALLAS: Yes, Mr Gross?

GROSS: Have you cancelled the introduction of Ptydepe?

BALLAS: Not yet.

GROSS: Why not?

BALLAS: Well, you see, we've been waiting for the right moment. There doesn't seem to be the right sort of atmosphere among the authorities for this move just now. We wouldn't like it to be used against us in any way, would we, Mr P?

(PILLAR *shakes his head.*)

GROSS: That's just an excuse.

BALLAS: Mr Gross, you don't believe us and we're hurt.

GROSS: You've bypassed me. You've moved the Accounts Department to the cellar.

BALLAS: That's only half the truth!

GROSS: What's the other half?

BALLAS: That I've ordered a ventilator to be installed in the cellar next year. Mr P, speak up, didn't I give such an order?

(PILLAR *nods.*)

GROSS: What about the light?

BALLAS: The Temporary Accountant has brought a candle from her home.

GROSS: Let's hope so!

BALLAS: Mr P, speak up! She did bring a candle, didn't she?

(PILLAR *shrugs.*)

Mr P doesn't seem to know about it. But she did! You can go and see for yourself.

GROSS: Be that as it may, you bypassed me. You organized Ptydepe classes, you set up a Ptydepe Translation Centre, and you made the study of Ptydepe obligatory for all staff members.

BALLAS: Outside their working hours!

GROSS: That's beside the point.

BALLAS: Mr Gross, I fully agree that I may not bypass you in things concerning the activity of our staff during their working hours. But as for anything outside those hours, I believe I can do as I please.

GROSS: I don't quite know what answer to give you at this moment, but I'm sure there is a fitting one somewhere.

BALLAS: Perhaps there is, perhaps there isn't. In any case, at this point we're not concerned with anything but the good of our organization. Are we, Mr P?

(PILLAR *nods.*)

Naturally, we hold the same critical attitude towards Ptydepe that you do, Mr Gross. Only we think that if, before the inevitable collapse of the whole campaign, we can manifest certain limited initiative, it'll be of great help to our whole organization. Who knows, this very initiative may become the basis on which we might be granted that snack bar which we have been trying to get for so long. Imagine that our staff would no longer have to travel all that way on their coffee break.

GROSS: All right. It's quite possible that in this way we might indeed get the snack bar. This, however, in no way changes the fact that you've bypassed me a number of times and that, lately, you've been taking far too many decisions on your own authority.

BALLAS: I? I beg your pardon! Haven't we just been consulting you about such a trifle as a new incoming-mail book? You're not being fair to us, Mr Gross. You're not at all fair.

GROSS: Mr Ballas, let me make a suggestion.

BALLAS: Yes?

GROSS: Let's be quite blunt with each other for a while shall we? It'll simplify the situation a great deal and speed up the clarification of our points of view.

BALLAS: Shall we accept, Mr P?

(PILLAR *nods.*)

I accept.

GROSS: Why did you say that you hold a critical attitude towards Ptydepe and that you're only interested in the snack bar, when in fact you believe in Ptydepe and do everything you can to get it quickly introduced?

BALLAS: Matter of tactics.

GROSS: A little short-sighted.

BALLAS: I wouldn't say so.

GROSS: It never occurred to you that sooner or later I'd see through your tactics?

BALLAS: We knew you'd create obstacles and therefore we arranged it so you wouldn't see what we were after until we were strong enough to surmount your obstacles. There's nothing you can do to stop us now. The overwhelming majority of our staff stands resolutely behind us, because they know that only Ptydepe can place their work on a truly scientific basis. Isn't that so, Mr P?

(PILLAR *nods.*)

GROSS: You seem to forget that it is I who bear the full responsibility for our organization, I in whom the trust has been placed. Thus, it is up to me to judge what is good for our organization, and what is not. So far it is I who am the Managing Director here.

BALLAS: We cannot ignore the stand of the masses. The whole organization is seething and waiting for your word.

GROSS: I won't be dictated to by a mob.

BALLAS: You call it a mob, we call it the masses.

GROSS: You call it masses, but it is a mob. I'm a humanist and my concept of directing this organization derives from the idea that every single member of the staff is human and must become more and more human. If we take from him his human language, created by the centuries-old tradition of national culture, we shall have prevented him from becoming fully human and plunge him straight into the jaws of self-alienation. I'm not against precision in official communications, but I'm for it only in so far as it humanizes Man. In accordance with this my innermost conviction I can never agree to the introduction of Ptydepe into our organization.

BALLAS: Are you prepared to risk an open conflict?

GROSS: I place the struggle for the victory of reason and of moral values above a peace bought by their loss.

BALLAS: What do you say to this, Mr P?

(PILLAR *shrugs in embarrassment.*)

GROSS: I suggest to you that we all forget what has just happened between us and that we part in peace before I'm forced to take the whole matter seriously.

(*A short pause.* HANA *enters by the back door, carrying a string bag full of rolls, puts it into her shopping bag, sits down and begins to comb her hair.*)

BALLAS: (*Turns to* PILLAR) It seems he's not yet ripe for realistic discussion. We've overrated him. Never mind. Let's give him–(*looks at his watch*)–what do you say, an hour?

(PILLAR *nods.*)

Time is on our side. An hour from now we'll no longer be handling him with kid gloves. The patience of the masses is great, but it is not infinite. He'll be sorry. Let's go.

(*They leave by the side door.*)

GROSS: Unheard of! (*Sits down, notices his memorandum, stares at it, turns to* HANA.) Hana!

HANA: Yes, Mr Gross?

GROSS: Do you know Ptydepe?

HANA: No.

GROSS: Then how did you know this was an official memorandum?

HANA: They say that in the first stage Ptydepe was used only for important official memoranda and that these are now being received by some of the staff.

GROSS: What are these memos about?

HANA: They are supposed to inform the recipients about decisions based on the findings of the last audit in their departments.

GROSS: Indeed? What sort of decisions?

HANA: All sorts, it seems. Very positive and very negative ones.

GROSS: Damn that rubber stamp! Where on earth did you learn all this?

HANA: Oh, in the dairy shop this morning.

GROSS: Where did you say the Translation Centre is?

HANA: First floor, room 6. To get to it one must go through the Ptydepe classroom.

GROSS: Ah yes! Former Accounts Department. Well, I'm off to lunch.

(*He takes his memorandum from his desk and hurries out through the back door.*)

HANA: (*Calls after him*) You'll like it, Mr Gross. They have goose in the canteen today!

## SCENE 2

*The Ptydepe classroom. Teacher's desk in the background; in the foreground five chairs.* LEAR *is standing behind his desk, lecturing to four clerks who are seated with their backs to the audience. Among them is* THUMB.

LEAR: Ptydepe, as you know, is a synthetic language, built on a strictly scientific basis. Its grammar is constructed with maximum rationality, its vocabulary is unusually broad. It is a thoroughly exact language, capable of expressing with far greater precision than any current natural tongue all the minutest nuances in the formulation of important office documents. The result of this precision is of course the exceptional complexity and difficulty of Ptydepe. There are many months of intensive study ahead of you, which can be crowned by success only if it is accompanied by diligence, perseverance, discipline, talent and a good memory. And of course, by faith. Without a steadfast faith in Ptydepe, nobody yet has ever been able to learn Ptydepe. And now, let us turn briefly to some of the basic principles of Ptydepe. The natural languages originated, as we know, spontaneously, uncontrollably in other words, unscientifically, and their structure is thus, in a certain sense, dilettantish. As far as official communications are concerned, the most serious deficiency of the natural languages is their utter unreliability, which results from the fact that their basic structural units–words–are highly equivocal and interchangeable. You all know that in a natural language it is often enough to exchange one letter for another (goat–boat, love–dove), or simply remove one letter (fox–ox), and the whole meaning of the word is thus changed. And then there are all the homonyms! Consider what terrible mischief can be caused in inter-office communications when two words with entirely different meanings are spelled exactly the same way. P-o-s-s-u-m. Possum–possum. The first, designating an American small arboreal or aquatic nocturnal marsupial mammal with thumbed hind foot–(THUMB *giggles.*)

The second, the Latin equivalent of 'I am able'. Such a thing is quite unthinkable in Ptydepe. The significant aim of Ptydepe is to guarantee to every statement, by purposefully limiting all similarities between individual words, a degree of precision, reliability and lack of equivocation quite unattainable in any natural language. To achieve this, Ptydepe makes use of the following postulation: if similarities between any two words are to be minimized, the words must be formed by the least probable combination of letters. This means that the creation of words must be based on such principles as would lead to the greatest possible redundancy of language. You see, a redundancy–in other words, the difference between the maximum and the real entropy, related to the maximum entropy and expressed percentually–concerns precisely that superfluity by which the expression of a particular piece of information in a given language is longer, and thus less probable (i.e., less likely to appear in this particular form), than would be the same expression in a language with maximum entropy; that is to say, one in which all letters have the same probability of occurrence. Briefly: the greater the redundancy of a language, the more reliable it is, because the smaller is the possibility that by an exchange of a letter, by an oversight or a typing error, the meaning of the text could be altered.

(GROSS *enters by the back door, his memorandum in his hand, crosses the room and leaves by the side door*)

How does, in fact, Ptydepe achieve its high redundancy? By a consistent use of the so-called principle of a 60 per cent dissimilarity; which means that any Ptydepe word must differ by at least 60 per cent of its letters from any other Ptydepe word of the same length (and, incidentally, any part of such a word must differ in the same way from any Ptydepe word of this length, that is from any word shorter than is the one of which it is a part). Thus, for example, out of all the possible five-letter combinations of the 26 letters of our alphabet–and there are 11,881,376–only 432 combinations can be found which differ from each other by three letters, i.e., by 60 per cent of the total. From these 432 combinations only 17 fulfil the other requirements as well and thus have become Ptydepe words. Hence it is clear that in Ptydepe there often occur words which are very long indeed.

THUMB: (*Raising his hand*) Sir–

LEAR: Yes?

THUMB: (*Gets up*) Would you please tell us which is the longest word in Ptydepe? (*Sits down.*)

LEAR: Certainly. It is the word meaning 'a wombat', which has 319 letters. But let us proceed. Naturally, this raises the question of how Ptydepe solves the problem of manageability and pronounceability of such long words. Quite simply: inside these words the letters are interspersed with occasional gaps, so that a word may consist of a greater or smaller number of so-called 'sub-words'. But at the same time the length of a word – as indeed everything in Ptydepe – is not left to chance. You see, the vocabulary of Ptydepe is built according to an entirely logical principle: the more common the meaning, the shorter the word. Thus, for example, the most commonly used term so far known – that is the term 'whatever' – is rendered in Ptydepe by the word 'gh'. As you can see, it is a word consisting of only two letters. There exists, however, an even shorter word – that is 'f' – but this word does not yet carry any meaning. I wonder if any of you can tell me why. Well? (*Only* THUMB *raises his hand.*)

LEAR: Well, Mr Thumb?

THUMB: (*Gets up.*) It's being held in reserve in case science should discover a term even more commonly used than the term 'whatever'.

LEAR: Correct, Mr Thumb. You get an A.

## SCENE 3

*The Secretariat of the Translation Centre. It is something between an office and a waiting room. A large desk, a typist's desk, a few straight chairs or armchairs, a small conference table.* STROLL *is seated on it, a paper bag full of peaches in his lap. He is consuming them with gusto.* GROSS *enters by the back door, his memorandum in hand.*

GROSS: Good morning.

STROLL: (*With his mouth full*) Morning.

GROSS: I've dropped in to get acquainted with the activities of the Translation Centre. I'm the Managing Director.

STROLL: (*With his mouth full*) So you're the Managing Director?

GROSS: Yes. Josef Gross.

(STROLL *slowly lets himself down from the table, finishes his peach, wipes his hands on his handkerchief and walks over to* GROSS.)

STROLL: Very glad to meet you. Sorry I didn't recognize you. I've been here only a very short time and so I still haven't met everybody. My name's Stroll. Head of the Translation Centre. Do sit down. (STROLL *folds his handkerchief and shakes hands with* GROSS. *Both sit down.* STROLL *lights a cigarette.* GROSS *tries all his pockets, but cannot find his.*)

Everything here is still so to speak at the nappy stage.

GROSS: I understand.

STROLL: We're still grappling with a great many teething troubles.

GROSS: That's clear enough–

STROLL: It's no easy matter, you know.

GROSS: No, quite.

STROLL: Tell me, exactly what would you like to find out?

GROSS: I'd like to see how you've organized the process of making translations. Do you do them while one waits?

STROLL: We'll make a translation from Ptydepe while you wait for any member of our organization who is a citizen of our country and has an authorization to have a Ptydepe text translated.

GROSS: Does one need a special authorization?

(SAVANT *enters by the side door.*)

SAVANT: Morning, Otto. Have you heard that there's goose for lunch today?

STROLL: (*Jumps up*) What! Did you say goose?

SAVANT: That's what the chaps in the Secretariat said. Pick you up on the way to the canteen, right?

STROLL: Right! The sooner the better!

(SAVANT *leaves by the side door.*)

I love goose, you know! Now, what were we talking about?

GROSS: You were saying that one needs an authorization to get a translation made.

STROLL: Right. Well now, look here. We, the staff, do use Ptydepe, but we're no experts. Let's face it, we're no linguists, are we? So, naturally, the exploitation and development of Ptydepe cannot be left in our hands alone. If it were, it might lead to unwelcome spontaneity and Ptydepe might quite easily change under our very noses into a normal natural language and thus lose its whole purpose.

(*Suddenly he halts, becomes preoccupied, then quickly gets up.*)

Excuse me.

(*He hurries out by the side door.*)

(GROSS *stares after him in surprise, then begins another search through his pockets, but finds no cigarettes. Pause.* HELENA *enters by the side door.*)

HELENA: Was Alex here?

GROSS: I don't know who that is.

HELENA: You're not part of this shop, sweetie?

GROSS: On the contrary. I'm the Managing Director.

HELENA: Are you, sweetie? Well, you must do something about this snack bar, I mean it! It's a damned shame to see our girls traipse miles for a cup of tea, it really is. Does anybody think about people in this shop?

GROSS: And who, may I ask, are you?

HELENA: I'm the Chairman. But you can call me Nellie.

GROSS: The chairman of what, if you'll forgive my asking?

HELENA: Of what? Don't know of what just yet. As a matter of fact we're having a meeting about that very thing this afternoon. But I'm already so damned busy I don't know which way to turn. They don't give you time to have a proper look around and they expect you straight away to start cleaning up their smelly little messes. See you later, sweetie.

(*She leaves by the side door.*)

(*Pause.* GROSS *again tries his pockets. Then looks at his watch. Waits. Pause.* STROLL *at last returns by the side door. Walks slowly. Buttons up his trousers while walking.*)

STROLL: You don't like goose?

GROSS: I do. You were saying that Ptydepe cannot be left in your hands alone.

STROLL: Right. That's why every department which starts to introduce Ptydepe is assigned a special methodician, a so-called Ptydepist, who, being a specialist, is supposed to ensure that Ptydepe gets used correctly.

(MARIA *enters by the back door, carrying a string bag full of onions.*)

MARIA: (*Walking towards the side door.*) Good morning.

GROSS: Good morning.

(MARIA *leaves by the side door.*)

STROLL: Our Ptydepist fulfils this task by issuing a special authorization for every translation–

MARIA: (*Offstage*) Here are the onions, Miss Helena.

STROLL: Which enables him to record all outgoing translations from Ptydepe.

HELENA: (*Offstage*) Would you mind putting them over by the filing cabinet, that's a good girl.

STROLL: Thus he obtains all the necessary material for various statistics, on the basis of which he then directs the use of Ptydepe.

(MARIA *returns by the side door, carrying an empty string bag, puts it in the drawer, sits at typist's desk and begins to work.*)

GROSS: So, if I've understood you correctly, you'll give a translation only to those staff members who can produce an authorization from your Ptydepist.

STROLL: Right.

(SAVANT *enters by the side door, knife and fork in hand.*)

SAVANT: Are you ready?

STROLL: (*To* MARIA) Where's my cutlery?

(MARIA *takes a knife and fork from a drawer and hands them to him.*)

GROSS: Who is your Ptydepist?

STROLL: Has it been washed?

MARIA: Of course.

STROLL: (*To* GROSS) What did you say?

GROSS: Who is your Ptydepist?

STROLL: Dr Savant here.

GROSS: (*Shakes hands with* SAVANT.) How do you do. I'm Josef Gross, the Managing Director.

SAVANT: How do you do. I'm Alex Savant, the graduate Ptydepist. My degree is like a doctorate, you know.

GROSS: I'd like a word with you, Dr Savant.

STROLL: Are you going to ask for breast?

SAVANT: Sorry, Mr Gross, but we really must go and have our lunch now. Shouldn't want to miss it. (*To* STROLL) I prefer a leg.

(SAVANT *and* STROLL *leave by the back door.* GROSS *stands for a while in surprise, then slowly sits down. Pause. He looks at his watch. Waits. Again looks at his watch, puts it to his ear. Then tries all his pockets.*)

GROSS: Have you a cigarette, by any chance?

MARIA: I'm sorry, I don't smoke.

(*Pause.* GROSS *again looks at his watch. Then he notices a box on the desk.*)

GROSS: What's that?

MARIA: Cigars.

GROSS: May I take one?

MARIA: Oh no! They belong to Mr Stroll. He's counted them. He'd be very angry if you did.

(*Long pause.* GROSS *stretches, looks at his watch, finally gets up, slowly approaches* MARIA *and peers over her shoulder to see what she is doing.*)

Reports–

GROSS: Mmnn–

(GROSS *slowly walks around the office, examining everything, then again sits down.* HELENA *quietly enters by the side door.* GROSS *sits with his back towards her.* HELENA *gestures to* MARIA *to keep quiet. Tiptoeing, she creeps up to* GROSS *and from behind puts her hands over his eyes.* GROSS *starts.*)

HELENA: (*Changing her voice to make it sound like a man's*) Peep-bo!

GROSS: I beg your pardon!

HELENA: Guess who!

GROSS: Take your hands off at once!

HELENA: First you must guess!

GROSS: (*Hesitates a moment*) The District Inspector.

HELENA: No.

GROSS: The Regional Inspector.

HELENA: No.

GROSS: The Inspector General.

HELENA: No.

GROSS: Ilon.

HELENA: No.

GROSS: Then it's Karel.

HELENA: No, no, no.

GROSS: Do stop it, Ilon! You're being very silly!

HELENA: Shall I tell you?

GROSS: Would you, please!

(HELENA *takes her hands away.* GROSS *turns.*)

HELENA: You're not Alex? Sorry, sweetie. I thought it was Alex Savant. Hasn't he showed up yet?

GROSS: Charming manners!

MARIA: He's gone to lunch.

HELENA: (*To* GROSS) Starchy, aren't you? What the hell! It was just a bit of fun, that's all. See you later, sweetie.

(*She leaves by the side door. Pause.* GROSS *once more tries his pockets.*)

GROSS: Have you a cigarette, by any chance?

MARIA: You've already asked, Mr Gross.

GROSS: I'm sorry, I must have forgotten.

(GROSS *looks at his watch, puts it to his ear, begins to be impatient. Again the same search, then gets up and wanders about the office. Stops behind* MARIA *and peers over her shoulder to see what she is doing.*)

MARIA: Reports–

GROSS: Mmnn–

(*Pause.* GROSS *again notices Stroll's box, slowly approaches, looks at it for a while, opens it quietly, takes a cigar, smells it.* MARIA *watches him.* GROSS *realizes he is being watched, replaces the cigar and returns to his seat. Pause.*)

(*Loudly*) Good God! It wouldn't hurt him, would it?

(STROLL *and* SAVANT *are returning by the back door in lively conversation. They hand their knives and forks to* MARIA, *then sit down.*)

STROLL: That was simply delicious. The way it was cooked! Straight through! And yet so crispy!

SAVANT: I think it was better last time.

STROLL: Not juicy enough. The very best was the time before last.

GROSS: Dr Savant–

STROLL: (*To* MARIA) Would you go and see if Mr Langer is having his lunch today? If not, ask whether he'd mind sending me his voucher.

GROSS: Dr Savant–

(MARIA *quickly walks out by the back door.* SAVANT *watches her with greedy appreciation.*)

SAVANT: (*Turning to* GROSS) Not bad, eh?

GROSS: Rather pleasant.

SAVANT: Sexy little thing, isn't she?

GROSS: Dr Savant–

STROLL: Her? Sexy? Come off it!

SAVANT: (*To* GROSS) Yes?

GROSS: I understand you can authorize the making of a translation from Ptydepe.

SAVANT: Yes, for those who bring me their documents.

GROSS: What sort of documents?

SAVANT: Personal registration.

(STROLL *offers a cigarette to* SAVANT.)

(*Taking it*) Ta.

(STROLL *and* SAVANT *light their cigarettes.* GROSS *again tries his pockets, hesitates, then speaks up.*)

GROSS: I'm sorry–er–could you sell me a cigarette?

STROLL: I wish I could, but I've only three left.

GROSS: Oh, I see. I'm sorry. (*To* SAVANT) Why do you actually need the personal registration documents?

SAVANT: (*To* STROLL) She is sexy, you know. Just wait till someone catches her in the dark! (*To* GROSS) What did you say?

GROSS: Why do you actually need the personal registration documents?

SAVANT: Well, it's like this, you see. Although I've been employed by this organization, I'm no common or garden staff member. I am, as you well know, a scholar. A scholar of a new sort, of course, as everything about Ptydepe is new. And as such I naturally take certain–shall we say–exceptions to some of the rather bureaucratic procedures of my staff colleagues. As a matter of fact, it's not really exceptions I take–it's more like objections. No, objections isn't the right word either. How shall I put it? I'm sorry, Mr Gross. You see, I'm used to speaking in Ptydepe and so it's rather difficult for me to find the right words in a natural language.

GROSS: Please go on.

SAVANT: In Ptydepe one would say axajores. My colleagues sometimes ylud kaboz pady el too much, and at the same time they keep forgetting that etrokaj zenig ajte ge gyboz.

STROLL: Abdy hez fajut gabob nyp orka?

SAVANT: Kavej hafiz okuby ryzal.

STROLL: Ryzal! Ryzal! Ryzal! Varuk bado di ryzal? Kabyzach? Mahog? Hajbam?

SAVANT: Ogny fyk hajbam? Parde gul axajores va dyt rahago kabrazol! Fabotybe! They think they can simply send me a chap, I'll give him an OK, and that'll be the end of it. Byzugat rop ju ge tyrak! Don't they realize that if our statistics are to make any sense at all we must have concrete foundations to build on. We must have detailed information about everybody who comes in contact with Ptydepe, in order to get the greatest possible variety of sociological and psychological data. Otherwise we just couldn't carry on.

GROSS: Wouldn't it be enough if a chap just told you himself everything you want to know about him?

SAVANT: That wouldn't guarantee that everything was hutput.

GROSS: I beg your pardon?

SAVANT: Hutput. Quite exact.

(MARIA *returns by the back door.*)

MARIA: I'm sorry, but it appears that Mr Langer will definitely be eating his lunch today.

STROLL: Pity.

(MARIA *sits at her desk and continues working.*)

GROSS: Excuse me, you were speaking about the uncertainties of verbal statements.

SAVANT: Ah, yes! Well now, all the particulars concerning each employee have long been recorded with the utmost precision and without the risk of any possible subjective zexdohyt–I'm sorry–point of view–

GROSS: I understand–(*Jokingly*) I've a completely hutput zexdohyt of it.

SAVANT: Zexdohyttet! You've forgotten that every noun preceded by the adjective hutput takes on the suffix 'tet'–

STROLL: Or 'tete'.

SAVANT: Or 'tete'. Quite. Many people make this mistake. Even Mr Wassermann in one of his letters–

GROSS: Excuse me, you were speaking about the advantages of the personal registration documents.

SAVANT: Ah, yes! Well now, the personal registration documents often record things which even the particular employee doesn't know about himself. (*To* STROLL) Nuzapom?

STROLL: Zapom. Yd nik fe rybol zezuhof.

SAVANT: Yd nik–yd nek.

GROSS: To sum up. You'll authorize a translation only for those members of the staff who can produce their documents. All right, where does one get them?

(HELENA *enters by the side door.*)

HELENA: Hallo, everybody!

SAVANT: (*Sings*) Hallo, everybody, hallo–

HELENA: You know whose birthday it is today? Eddi Kliment's!

SAVANT: Eddi's? Is it?

HELENA: There's a party going on for him next door. So drop

everything and come along. (*To* MARIA) Seems the grocer's got limes. Would you mind running over and getting me eight?

(MARIA *hurries out by the back door.*)

SAVANT: What are they drinking?

HELENA: Vodka.

SAVANT: Did you hear that, Otto?

(SAVANT *and* STROLL *hasten towards the side door.*)

GROSS: You haven't told me yet where one gets those documents.

SAVANT: Why, right here from our Chairman. From Nellie, of course.

(SAVANT *and* STROLL *quickly walk out by the side door.* HELENA *is about to follow them.*)

GROSS: Miss Helena–

HELENA: (*Halts by the door.*) What?

GROSS: I'd like a word with you.

HELENA: Later, love. You'll have to wait.

GROSS: Here?

HELENA: Where else?

GROSS: You mean you don't mind leaving me here alone? With all this classified material?

HELENA: You won't be alone. There's a chink in the wall, sweetie. You're being watched by our Staff Watcher.

GROSS: Good gracious! A chink?

HELENA: Wouldn't be much good if he was actually in here. That way he'd be able to watch only one office, wouldn't he? This way he can watch five of them at once. You see, his cubicle is surrounded by offices and each is furnished with an observation chink. So all he has to do is to walk–at random, natch–from one to the other and peer.

GROSS: Interesting idea.

HELENA: Isn't it! And it's my idea, too! My point was to stop visitors from having to hang about in the hall when the office is empty. Damned nuisance for them. Even in these piddling details one must be thinking of the good of the people! See you later, sweetie.

(*She runs out through the side door.* GROSS *wanders about investigating the walls.*)

GEORGE: (*After a while, offstage*) Don't bother. The chink is well disguised.

GROSS: I should say it is! One might make use of this idea in other departments as well.

GEORGE: (*Offstage*) Not so easy. This kind of thing has to be planned for by the architect from the very start.

GROSS: I see what you mean. On the other hand, he couldn't very well have planned for it here.

GEORGE: (*Offstage*) He didn't. He made a mistake in his calculations. And when this building was erected it was found that there was this space left over between the offices. So it was used in this way.

GROSS: A really stimulating idea!

(*Pause.* GROSS *sits down, looks impatiently at his watch, gets up, sits down, again looks at his watch, gets up, searches his pockets, again sits down.* MARIA *runs in by the back door.*)

What's the matter?

MARIA: Forgot my purse.

(*She opens the drawer of the typing desk and rummages in it hastily.*)

GROSS: Miss–

MARIA: Yes?

GROSS: Do you know Ptydepe?

MARIA: A bit.

GROSS: Can you translate it?

MARIA: I'm strictly forbidden to make any translations before I've passed my exams.

GROSS: But on my authority you might try to make a translation, mightn't you? It doesn't have to be perfect, you know.

(MARIA *smiles.*)

What's so funny about it?

MARIA: You wouldn't understand. It's impossible, that's all.

GROSS: What's your name?

MARIA: Maria.

GROSS: Maria! A pretty name.

MARIA: Do you like it?

GROSS: Very much. Maria–just for once! Nobody'll know about it.

MARIA: Mr Gross! Somebody might walk in any minute. Please be reasonable!

GROSS: (*Urgently*) Go on, my dear!

MARIA: And what about the Staff Watcher?

GROSS: (*Whispers*) You could whisper the translation to me.

MARIA: The limes will soon be sold out and Miss Helena will be angry. Bye.

(*Having found her purse, she runs out by the back door. Pause.* GROSS, *tired, sinks into his chair. He stares ahead, mechanically begins to try his pockets again. Then gets up and walks straight to the cigar box. When he is about to open it, he quickly takes his hand away and looks around cautiously.*)

GROSS: Mr Watcher–(*Pause.*) Mr Watcher–(*Pause.*) Listen, Mr Watcher, can you hear me? Have you got a cigarette? (*Pause.*) He must have fallen asleep. (*Carefully opens the box.*)

GEORGE: (*Offstage*) What do you mean–fallen asleep!

GROSS: (*Jerks away from the box.*) Well, why didn't you answer me?

GEORGE: (*Offstage*) I wanted to test you out.

GROSS: I beg your pardon! Do you realize who I am? The Managing Director!

GEORGE: (*Offstage*) Habuk bulugan.

GROSS: I beg your pardon?

GEORGE: (*Offstage*) Habuk bulugan, avrator.

GROSS: What did you mean by that?

GEORGE: (*Offstage*) Nutuput.

GROSS: (*Looks at his watch, then walks quickly to the back door, turns by the door.*) I won't put up with any abuse from you! I expect you to come to me and apologize. (*Exits by the back door.*)

GEORGE: (*Offstage*) Gotroch!

## SCENE 4

*The Director's office.* BALLAS *and* PILLAR *are silently waiting for* GROSS. PILLAR *has a notebook in his hand.* HANA *is combing her hair. Then* GROSS *hurries in by the back door, crosses to his desk, sits down with studied casualness. For a while there is menacing silence.*

BALLAS: Well?

GROSS: Well?

BALLAS: The hour has passed. Ready to be more sensible now?

GROSS: Certainly not.

BALLAS: As you may have noticed, the introduction of Ptydepe into our organization successfully proceeds. What are you going to do about it?

GROSS: Put a stop to it.

HANA: Mr Gross, may I go and get the chocolates?

BALLAS: How?

GROSS: By issuing an order that the introduction of Ptydepe be stopped and its use cancelled.

BALLAS: You cannot.

GROSS: Why not?

BALLAS: You never issued any order for its introduction and use, so you're in no position to stop and cancel anything at all.

GROSS: Then you'll do it.

BALLAS: I haven't issued any such order either. Have I, Mr P? (PILLAR *shakes his head.*)

HANA: Mr Gross, may I go and get the chocolates?

GROSS: What do you mean?

BALLAS: It was just a verbal directive, based on an assurance that you'd validate it by a supplementary order.

GROSS: Then I'll simply not give any supplementary order.

HANA: Mr Gross, may I go and get the chocolates?

BALLAS: The introduction of Ptydepe is in full swing and it will naturally go on even without it. (*To* HANA) Run along. (HANA *immediately stops combing her hair and is off by the back door.*)

GROSS: In that case I'll have to report the whole matter to the authorities.

BALLAS: (*Laughs.*) Did you hear that, Mr P? He doesn't know that the authorities have taken a great fancy to Ptydepe.

GROSS: If that's the case, why haven't they made its use obligatory in all organizations?

BALLAS: Playing it safe. If Ptydepe succeeds, they'll have plenty of time to take the credit for it; if it fails, they'll be able to dissociate themselves from it and blame the departments.

GROSS: I hope you don't expect me to be a traitor to my beliefs.

BALLAS: I do.

GROSS: How do you propose to make me?

BALLAS: (*Points at* PILLAR*'s book.*) Do you see this book? Not long ago it was improperly authenticated by your order, although it had not been registered by the Purchasing Department and thus was your own property. Do you know what that constitutes? Abuse of authority.

GROSS: Good God! Don't you make yourself sick?

BALLAS: Do we make ourselves sick, Mr P?

(PILLAR *shakes his head.*)

Of course we don't. When the good of Man is at stake, nothing will make us sick.

GROSS: But you yourself got me to sign it!

BALLAS: I did? I don't seem to remember–

GROSS: By your hints about the rumours concerning that damned rubber stamp!

BALLAS: I wouldn't bring that up, if I were you.

GROSS: Why not?

BALLAS: Because it's no extenuating circumstance at all. Just the reverse, in fact.

GROSS: I don't know what you're talking about.

BALLAS: Don't you? Well, look here. If it weren't for the rubber stamp affair, you might have claimed that you signed the authentication of this book moved by a sincere desire to help our clerical staff, which of course wouldn't have excused your conduct, but would at least have explained it somewhat on humanitarian grounds; while if you do bring up this motive now, you'll be admitting thereby that you signed it moved merely by petty cowardice, so as to silence legitimate inquiries into the circumstances of the rubber stamp affair. Do you follow me? If, on the other hand, you hadn't signed it, you might have pretended that you were indeed taking the rubber stamp home for reasons of work, but your signature proves that you were clearly aware of your guilt. As you see, both your errors are intertwined in such an original way that the one greatly multiplies the other. By publicizing the circumstances which you consider extenuating you would leave nobody in any doubt whatever about the real motives of your conduct. Well then, shall we come to an agreement?

GROSS: All right, I'll resign.

BALLAS: But we don't want you to.

GROSS: Well, what do you want me to do?

BALLAS: Sign the supplementary order for the introduction and the use of Ptydepe in our organization.

GROSS: But you said, didn't you, that Ptydepe will be used even without a supplementary order? Then why do you insist on it now?

BALLAS: That's our business.

(*A long pause.*)

GROSS: (*Quietly*) Are you sure that Ptydepe will really make office communications more precise?

BALLAS: I'm glad our discussion is at last reaching a realistic level. Mr Pillar, would you offer Mr Gross some milk?

(PILLAR *hands* GROSS HANA*'s bottle of milk.* GROSS *drinks mechanically.*)

Look here. You yourself know best how many misunderstandings, suspected innuendos, injustices and injuries can be contained in one single sentence of a natural language. In fact, a natural language endows many more-or-less precise terms, such as for example the term 'coloured', with so many wrong, let's say emotional, overtones, that they can entirely distort the innocent and eminently human content of these terms. Now tell me sincerely, has the word 'mutarex' any such overtones for you? It hasn't, has it? You see! It is a paradox, but it is precisely the surface inhumanity of an artificial language which guarantees its truly human function! After Ptydepe comes into use, no one will ever again have the impression that he's being injured when in fact he's being helped, and thus everybody will be much happier.

(HANA *returns by the back door, carrying a box of chocolates, puts it in her shopping bag, sits down and once more begins to comb her hair. Pause.*)

GROSS: You have convinced me. Have the supplementary order for the introduction of Ptydepe in our organization typed and bring it to me for signature.

BALLAS: Mr Gross, we're overjoyed that you've grasped the demands of the times. We look forward to our further work in this organization under your expert and enlightened leadership.

(*He takes out a sheet of paper and puts it on the desk in front of* GROSS.)

Here is the typed order you request.

(GROSS *signs. When he finishes,* BALLAS *and* PILLAR *begin to applaud.* GROSS *also claps uncertainly a few times. They all shake hands and congratulate each other. Finally,* BALLAS *takes the signed document.*)

Well, that's that. Aren't you hungry, Mr P?

(PILLAR *shakes his head. Pause.*)

I believe that from now on we'll be working very closely together.

GROSS: We'll have to. Without your help it'd probably be rather hard for me to find my bearings in the new situation. Perhaps at the beginning we shan't be able to avoid directing the organization, so to speak, hand in hand.

BALLAS: I have a better idea. What about me being the director and you my deputy. Won't that make things much easier?

GROSS: (*Confused*) But you said, didn't you, that you were looking forward to working under my expert and enlightened leadership?

BALLAS: You will be able to use your expertise and enlightenment just as well as a deputy. I'll go and get my things, while you, Mr Gross, will kindly move out of my desk!

GROSS: As you wish, Mr Ballas.

BALLAS: Mr P, let's go.

(BALLAS *and* PILLAR *leave by the side door.* GROSS *collects his papers from his desk and stuffs them in his pockets, then carefully takes down the fire extinguisher hanging on the wall.*)

GROSS: Things do seem to be moving rather fast.

HANA: Mr Gross–

GROSS: There was nothing else I could do. An open conflict would have meant that I'd be finished. This way–as Deputy Director–I can at least salvage this and that.

HANA: Mr Gross–

GROSS: Anyway, who knows, maybe this–Ptydepe–will turn out to be a good thing after all. If we grasp the reins firmly and with intelligence–

HANA: Mr Gross–

GROSS: What is it?

HANA: May I go and get my lunch?

GROSS: Run along!

(HANA *hastily takes her knife and fork, and hurries out by the back door.* BALLAS *and* PILLAR *enter by the side door.* BALLAS *is carrying a fire extinguisher, identical with the one* GROSS *just took off the wall.* GROSS *halts in the centre and stares sadly ahead.*)

(*To himself*) Why can't I be a little boy again? I'd do everything differently from the beginning. (GROSS *lingers dejectedly for a second longer, then turns and slowly walks out by the back door, the fire extinguisher clasped in his arms. Meanwhile* BALLAS *has placed his own extinguisher in the emptied space,* PILLAR *has taken various papers from his pockets and spread them on the desk. Then they both sit down at the desk, make themselves comfortable, grow still, look at each other and smile happily.*)

## SCENE 5

*The Ptydepe classroom. Again* LEAR *lecturing to four clerks.*

LEAR: Historically, the natural languages originated in all probability through the development of the inarticulate shrieks by which a primitive creature expressed his basic reactions to the surrounding world. The very oldest group of words is thus the interjections. At the same time, the interjections form an unusually easy part of Ptydepe, which is quite obvious, as their frequency in inter-office communications is rather limited. This is why the interjections will form the first few lessons of your curriculum. Well then, let us proceed to the interjections. As you know, every word of a natural language–including the interjections–has several Ptydepe equivalents, which differentiate its several shades of meaning. To start with, for each interjection we shall learn only one, the most common, expression in Ptydepe. Nevertheless, as an example, I'd like to demonstrate to you through the Ptydepe renderings of the interjection 'boo', how rich and precise is Ptydepe, even in this marginal sphere. (GROSS *enters by the back door, fire extinguisher in his arms, walks towards the side door, hesitates, halts, thinks for a moment, then turns to* LEAR.)

GROSS: Sir–

LEAR: What is it?

GROSS: I do hate to interrupt you, but I happen to have with me a little Ptydepe text, and I was wondering if–just as an example, you know–it might not be a good thing to acquaint our colleagues here with the actual shape of Ptydepe. Perhaps if you read it aloud and then possibly translated it, it might be of interest to the class.

LEAR: As regards a sample of an actual Ptydepe text, I've prepared my own, authorized, specimen. However, for the sake of variety, I'm quite prepared to read your text as well, that is, provided you can show that your interest in

Ptydepe is vital and you're not just trying to interfere with the class. You may sit down.

(GROSS, *surprised, mechanically sits in an empty chair, puts the extinguisher in his lap.*)

Generally speaking, the interjection 'boo' is used in the daily routine of an office, a company, a large organization when one employee wants to sham-ambush another. In those cases where the endangerment of an employee who is in full view and quite unprepared for the impending peril is being shammed by an employee who is himself hidden, 'boo' is rendered by 'gedynrelom'. The word 'osonfterte' is used in substantially the same situation when, however, the imperilled employee is aware of the danger. 'Eg gynd y trojadus' is used when an employee who has not taken the precaution, or the time, or the trouble to hide wants to sham-ambush another employee who is also in full view, in case it is meant as a joke. 'Eg jeht kuz' is used in substantially the same situation when, however, it is meant in earnest. 'Ysiste etordyf' is used by a superior wishing to test out the vigilance of a subordinate. 'Yxap tseror najx' is used, on the contrary, by the subordinate towards a superior, but only on the days specially appointed for this purpose. And now let me see if you've been paying attention. Who can tell us how one says 'boo' in Ptydepe when a hidden employee wants to sham-ambush another employee who is in full view and quite unprepared for the danger? Mr Thumb!

THUMB: (*Gets up.*) Gedynrelom. (*Sits down.*)

LEAR: Correct. And when the imperilled employee is aware of the danger? (*Points at* GROSS.)

GROSS: (*Gets up.*) Danger menacing an employee who is in full view?

LEAR: Yes.

GROSS: Who is aware of the danger?

LEAR: Yes.

GROSS: And the perpetrator is hidden?

LEAR: Yes.

GROSS: Aha–yes–I see. Well–in that case one says–damn it, it was on the tip of my tongue.

LEAR: Mr Thumb, do you know?

THUMB: *(Gets up):* Osonfterte. *(Sits down.)*

LEAR: There. You see how easy it is! Well, let's take another case, shall we? For example, how would a superior say 'boo' when he wishes to test out the vigilance of a subordinate?

GROSS: A superior?

LEAR: Yes.

GROSS: The vigilance of a subordinate?

LEAR: Yes.

GROSS: I say, I think I know this one!

LEAR: Well, then tell us.

GROSS: We're translating the interjection 'boo', aren't we?

LEAR: Yes.

GROSS: I'm sure I know it–only–it has sort of slipped my mind.

LEAR: Well, Mr Thumb?

THUMB: *(Gets up)* Ysiste etordyf. *(Sits down.)*

LEAR: Correct, Mr Thumb. Well, shall we try once more? Third time never fails, eh? Let's see if you can tell us, for example, how does an employee who has not taken the precaution, or the time, or the trouble to hide say 'boo' if he wants to sham-ambush another employee who is also in full view, when it is meant in earnest?

GROSS: I'm afraid I don't know.

LEAR: Let me help you. Eg–

GROSS: Eg–eg–eg–

LEAR: Jeht–

GROSS: Yes, I do remember now. Eg jeht.

LEAR: Wrong. Mr Thumb, would you mind telling him?

THUMB: *(Gets up.)* Eg jeht kuz. *(Sits down.)*

LEAR: Correct. Eg jeht doesn't mean anything at all. Those are only two sub-words of the word eg jeht kuz.

GROSS: The third sub-word escaped me.

LEAR: Unfortunately, also the first two sub-words escaped you, just as all the other Ptydepe words which I was trying to teach you only a moment ago. When one considers that the interjections are the easiest part of Ptydepe and that my requirements have indeed been minimal, one cannot avoid concluding that yours is not merely a case of average inattentiveness or negligence, but of that particular inability to learn any Ptydepe whatsoever which stems from a profound and well-disguised doubt in its very sense. Under these circumstances I can hardly be expected to oblige you by reading aloud and, what's more, translating an unauthorized text. Chozup puzuk bojt!

GROSS: Goodness! So much fuss about three little words! (*Claps fire extinguisher in his arms and leaves by the side door.*)

LEAR: Now then, let us proceed. Mr Thumb, can you tell us how a subordinate says 'boo' to a superior in Ptydepe on the days specially appointed for this purpose?

THUMB: (*Gets up.*) Yxap tseror najx. (*Sits down.*)

LEAR: Correct, Mr Thumb. You get an A.

## SCENE 6

*The Secretariat of the Translation Centre. The office is empty, only the noise of a party going on offstage can be heard: gay voices, laughter, clinking of glasses, singing of 'Happy birthday to you', drinking songs, etc. During the first part of the following scene the noise occasionally becomes very loud, then quiets down a little.* GROSS *hurries in by the back door with the fire extinguisher still in his arms, halts in the centre, looks around, listens, then puts the extinguisher on the floor and tentatively sits down.* MARIA *enters by the back door, carrying a paper bag full of limes and walks towards the side door.* GROSS *gets up at once.*

GROSS: Good afternoon.

MARIA: Good afternoon. (*Leaves by the side door, offstage*) Here are the limes. Miss Helena.

HELENA: (*Offstage*) Would you mind putting them down by the coat rack? That's a good girl.

(MARIA *re-enters by side door, sits at her desk and begins to work.*)

GROSS: (*Also sits down.*) Miss Helena is next door?

MARIA: Yes. They're celebrating Mr Kliment's birthday.

GROSS: Do you think she'd mind coming here for a moment?

MARIA: I'll ask–(*Exits by the side door. Returns after a short while.*) Mr Gross–

GROSS: Yes?

MARIA: You're no longer the Managing Director?

GROSS: I'm his deputy now.

MARIA: Oh! Forgive me for asking–but what happened?

GROSS: Oh, well, we just–we exchanged jobs, Mr Ballas and I.

MARIA: Well, Deputy Director is also a very responsible position.

GROSS: It is, isn't it? As a matter of fact, to some extent it's even more responsible than the director's! I can remember, for instance, that when I was the director, my deputy often solved some of the most important problems for me. Will Miss Helena come?

MARIA: You'll have to wait a little, I'm afraid.

(HELENA *looks in at the side door.* GROSS *quickly gets up.*)

HELENA: (*To* MARIA) Come here a moment, will you?

(MARIA *leaves with* HELENA *by the side door.* GROSS *slowly sits down again. Long pause. Loud voices and noise from next door. After a while all quiets down.*)

GROSS: Mr Watcher–

GEORGE: (*Offstage*) What is it?

GROSS: We're friends again, aren't we?

GEORGE: (*Offstage*) Oh, well–why not?

(*Pause. Noise of the party.*)

GROSS: Mr Watcher–

GEORGE: (*Offstage*) What now?

GROSS: Aren't you celebrating?

GEORGE: I'm following the party through the chink.

GROSS: Does it look like a long one?

GEORGE: (*Offstage*) They've finished the vodka.

GROSS: Have they?

(*Pause. Singing offstage, changing into cheers.*)

VOICES: (*Offstage*) For he's a jolly good fellow
For he's a jolly good fellow
For he's a jolly good fellow
Which nobody can deny.
Hip–hip–hurrah!

(*Cheers and shouts culminate in laughter which, however, soon dies down; voices are beginning to recede, a few farewells, then all is quiet. The party is over.* STROLL *and* SAVANT *enter by the side door, absorbed in animated conversation.*)

STROLL: I bet she was shy!

SAVANT: To start with. But then–

STROLL: Then what?

SAVANT: You know what.

STROLL: Come off it! I bet you've made up that part about xachaj ybul!

SAVANT: Absolutely not! Literal truth! Down to the last letter.

STROLL: Come off it.

SAVANT: Mind you, if it hadn't been for kojufer bzal gaftre, we'd have certainly luhofr dyboroch!

STROLL: Does she actually–

SAVANT: I'm telling you. She's a wild 'un! (*Sings*) 'Cigarettes and whisky and wild wild women–'

STROLL: How old is she?

SAVANT: Sixteen.

STROLL: I prefer them a teensy weensy bit younger.

HELENA: (*Enters by the side door.*) Come on, everybody! Let's have some coffee!

STROLL: That's a thought! Where's Maria?

SAVANT: Our sexy little thing? Mr Gross might know.

GROSS: I?

SAVANT: Don't try to deny it! You lust after her!

GROSS: I beg your pardon!

SAVANT: You called her my dear. The Staff Watcher heard you.

GEORGE: (*Offstage*) You talk too much, Alex.

SAVANT: Listen, why don't you shut up and do your watching!

STROLL: Now, now, friends! (*Calls*) Maria!

SAVANT: (*Sings*) 'Maria–Maria–Maria!'

HELENA: Leave her alone, sweetie. She's ironing my slip. I'll make the coffee. (*Calls towards the side door*) Where do you keep the percolator?

(MARIA *runs in by the side door, iron in one hand; with the other she takes the percolator from the drawer, and runs out again.*)

STROLL: You won't mind, Mr Gross, will you, if we don't offer you any coffee? We've very little left, you see. It'll just about make three cups.

GROSS: Never mind. I don't really care for any.

STROLL: Nellie, Mr Gross doesn't care for any coffee. Make it three cups, but make mine double. (*To* SAVANT) I say, what about a cigar with the coffee?

SAVANT: That's a thought!

GROSS: Miss Helena–

HELENA: (*Calling towards the side door*) Where do you keep the coffee?

(MARIA *runs in by the side door with the iron, takes a jar of coffee from another drawer, runs out again. Meanwhile* STROLL *has taken the cigar box off his desk. Offers one to* SAVANT.)

GROSS: Miss Helena–

STROLL: That's what I call a cigar!

SAVANT: (*Takes one.*) Ta.

(STROLL *also takes one. Both light them expertly.* GROSS *watches them. As usual, he first tries all his pockets, then takes out some money and offers it to* STROLL.)

GROSS: Excuse me–may I–if you'd–

STROLL: Sorry, Mr Gross, I wouldn't advise it. I really wouldn't. They're awfully heavy, you're not used to them, they're sure to make you cough.

GROSS: Just one–

STROLL: I mean it. You'd be making a mistake. (GROSS, *disappointed, puts his money back.* STROLL *and* SAVANT *smoke with gusto.*)

GROSS: Miss Helena–

HELENA: Why don't you call me Nellie, sweetie? What is it?

GROSS: Miss Nellie, do you issue the documents one needs to get a translation authorized?

STROLL: Goose, vodka, and a cigar, that's what I call living.

SAVANT: And what a cigar!

GROSS: I said, do you issue the documents one needs to get a translation authorized?

HELENA: (*Calling towards the side door*) Where do you get water?

MARIA: (*Offstage*) I'll get it.

(*She runs in by the side door, iron in hand, grabs the kettle, and runs out through the back door.*)

HELENA: (*To* GROSS) What?

GROSS: Do you issue the documents one needs to get a translation authorized?

HELENA: Yes. To anybody who hasn't received a memo written in Ptydepe.

GROSS: Why?

SAVANT: Downright heady!

STROLL: I should say!

GROSS: I said, why?

HELENA: (*Calling towards the side door*) Where do you keep the cups?

MARIA: (*Offstage*) Coming!

(*She runs in by the back door, carrying the iron and the kettle full of water. Pours water into the percolator, takes out cups and a spoon, hands them to* HELENA *and runs out by the side door.*)

HELENA: (*Spoons out coffee into the percolator.*) Why what?

GROSS: Why this condition?

HELENA: Because I cannot be expected to give the personal registration documents to every Tom, Dick and Harry without making damned sure they don't conflict with the findings of the last audit in his blessed memo!

GROSS: Why can't you look at his memo and see what it says?

STROLL: Poor Zoro Bridel used to smoke only these. And he was a real gourmet!

SAVANT: Pity he passed away!

GROSS: I said, why?

HELENA: (*Calling towards the side door*) Sugar!

(MARIA *runs in, carrying the iron, hands* HELENA *a paper bag of sugar and again runs out.*)

(*To* GROSS) Why what?

GROSS: Why can't you look at his memo and see what it says?

HELENA: I'm forbidden to translate any Ptydepe texts. (*Towards the side door*) It's almost empty.

MARIA: (*Offstage*) There's another bag in the drawer.

GROSS: Good gracious! What can a staff member do in such a case?

SAVANT: Mr Bridel loved goose, didn't he?

STROLL: Zoro? Simply mad about it!

HELENA: (*Calling towards the side door*) Water's boiling.

(MARIA *runs in by the side door, puts the iron on the floor, unplugs the percolator, pours coffee into cups.*)

(*To* GROSS) What?

GROSS: What can a staff member do in such a case?

HELENA: He can have his memo translated. Listen everybody! Today your coffee's hyp nagyp!

(MARIA *passes cups to* STROLL, SAVANT *and* HELENA, *then takes the iron and runs out through the side door.*)

SAVANT: Nagyp avalyx?

HELENA: Nagyp hayfazut!

(STROLL, SAVANT *and* HELENA *pass the spoon around, offer sugar to each other, sip their coffee with gusto, absorbed in their Ptydepe conversation.* GROSS, *growing more and more desperate, turns from one to the other.*)

GROSS: Mr Stroll–

STROLL: Hayfazut gyp andaxe. (*To* GROSS) Yes?

SAVANT: Andaxe bel jok andaxu zep?

GROSS: In order to make a translation from Ptydepe, you require an authorization from Dr Savant–

HELENA: Andaxu zep.

STROLL: Ejch tut zep. Notut?

GROSS: Dr Savant–

SAVANT: Tut. Gavych ejch lagorax. (*To* GROSS) Yes?

HELENA: Lagorax hagyp.

GROSS: In order to grant the authorization, you require the documents from Miss Helena–

STROLL: Lagorys nabarof dy Zoro Bridel caf o abagan.

SAVANT: Mavolde gyzot abagan?

GROSS: Miss Helena–

HELENA: Abagan fajfor! (*To* GROSS) Yes?

STROLL: Fajfor? Nu rachaj?

GROSS: In order to issue the documents, you require that a staff member have his memorandum translated–

SAVANT: Rachaj gun.

HELENA: Gun znojvep?

STROLL: Znojvep yj.

SAVANT: Yj rachaj?

HELENA: Rachaj gun!

STROLL: Gun znojvep?

SAVANT: Znojvep yj.

HELENA: Yj rachaj?

STROLL: Rachaj gun!

SAVANT: Gun znojvep?

GROSS: (*Shouts*) Quiet!

(*At once all three become silent and quickly get up. Not on account of* GROSS, *of course, but because* BALLAS *and* PILLAR *have just quietly entered by the back door.* GROSS*'s back is turned towards* BALLAS *and* PILLAR, *thus he does not see them.*)

I'm the Deputy Director and I insist that you show me some respect! You may sit down.

(*Naturally, they remain standing. Pause.* MARIA, *unaware of what has been happening, enters by the side door carrying the ironed slip over her arm. Seeing the situation, she crumples the slip behind her back and stands like the others.*)

As I've just discovered, any staff member who has recently received a memorandum in Ptydepe can be granted a translation of a Ptydepe text only after his memorandum has been translated. But what happens if the Ptydepe text which he wishes translated is precisely that memorandum? It can't be done, because it hasn't yet been translated officially. In other words, the only way to learn what is in one's memo is to know it already. An extraordinary paradox, when you come to think of it. Ladies and gentlemen, do you come to think of it? I ask you, what must an employee of our organization–whoever he may be–do in order to escape this vicious, vicious circle?

*(For a second there is dead silence.)*

BALLAS: He must learn Ptydepe, Mr Gross. *(To the others)* You may sit down.

*(They all sit down at once.* MARIA, *still hiding the slip behind her, runs fearfully to her desk.)*

GROSS: *(Faintly)* Are you here?

BALLAS: Yes, we are.

GROSS: Have you been here long?

BALLAS: Not long.

GROSS: I didn't hear you come in.

BALLAS: We entered quietly.

GROSS: Excuse me, I–

BALLAS: There are things, Mr Gross, that cannot be excused. And when, at the very time in which the whole organization is conducting a courageous struggle for the introduction and establishment of Ptydepe, an official, referring to the activities of our employees, speaks with such malicious innuendo and mean irony about–I quote–'a vicious, vicious circle', then it cannot be excused at all.

GROSS: I'm sorry, Mr Ballas, but the circumstance I've allowed myself to point out is simply a fact.

BALLAS: We refuse to be bullied by facts!

*(Long pause.)*

GROSS: *(In a quiet, broken voice)* I plead guilty. I acknowledge the entire extent of my guilt, while fully realizing the consequences resulting from it. Furthermore, I wish to enlarge my confession by the following self-indictment. I issued an illegal order which led to the fraudulent authentication of my own, personal notebook. By this action I abused my authority. I did this in order to avert attention from the fact that I'd appropriated a bank endorsement stamp improperly for my private use. I request for myself the most severe punishment.

BALLAS: I think that under these circumstances it is no longer possible for him to remain in our organization. What do you say, Mr P?

(PILLAR *shakes his head.*)

BALLAS: Certainly not. Come to my office tomorrow morning. We'll settle the formalities connected with your dismissal. (*Calls*) George, come out of there! You'll be my deputy. (*To the others*) You may leave now. Mr P, let's go.

(BALLAS *and* PILLAR *leave by the back door,* STROLL, SAVANT *and* HELENA *by the side door,* GROSS *remains standing in the centre. Motionless, he stares ahead.* MARIA *watches him in silence. It seems she would like to help him in some way. Then she takes the cigar box and shyly offers one to* GROSS. GROSS *does not see her.* HELENA *looks in at the side door.*)

HELENA: (*To* MARIA) Seems the grocer's got fresh canteloupes. Would you mind running over and getting me ten? If you're quick about it, I'll give you a taste!

(HELENA *disappears.* MARIA *hastily replaces the cigar box, snatches her string bag and runs out through the back door.* GROSS *hangs his head, takes the fire extinguisher, and slowly, sadly leaves by the back door. Just then a small secret door opens in one of the side walls and* GEORGE *backs out of it on all fours. When he is quite out, he straightens, stretches, arranges his clothes with a dash of vanity, takes a cigar from the box and haughtily struts out by the back door.*)

# ACT TWO

## SCENE 7

*The Director's office.* BALLAS *and* PILLAR *enter by the back door, take off their coats, sit at the desk.* BALLAS *begins to go through the morning mail, like* GROSS *at the beginning of the play. One letter suddenly arrests his attention; he glares at it, then starts to read it aloud.*

BALLAS: (*Reads*) Ak ok utuh d utoked yle umobert ehusome, ragedv dy, orts uner re kyrg ydnek, vylaz edyvz uzed, ladnyvk ref unyked yles–(*Puts down the letter, hesitates, turns to* PILLAR.) You don't know Ptydepe, do you?

(PILLAR *shakes his head.*)

You might have learned it by now!

STROLL: (*Looks in at the side door.*) I hope I'm not interrupting. (*To* PILLAR) Ferry, would you come here a moment?

(PILLAR *gets up once and leaves with* STROLL *by the side door.* BALLAS *looks after them in surprise. Meanwhile* GROSS *quietly enters by the back door, the fire extinguisher clasped in his arms.*)

BALLAS: (*To himself*) 'Ferry'?

(BALLAS, *puzzled, shakes his head, then again stares at his letter.* GROSS *after a while speaks up timidly.*)

GROSS: Good morning.

BALLAS: You're here?

GROSS: I haven't been here long.

BALLAS: What do you want?

GROSS: I was supposed to come to your office today concerning my dismissal from our organization, Mr Ballas.

BALLAS: I'm busy now. Come back in a while–

GROSS: Sorry. Thank you. I'll come later.

(GROSS *quickly backs out by the back door.* PILLAR *returns by the side door and sits at his place.*)

BALLAS: What did he want?

(PILLAR *gestures that it was nothing important.* BALLAS *shakes his head doubtingly, and again stares at his letter.* HANA *enters by the back door, wearing a coat and carrying a vast shopping bag.*)

HANA: Good morning.

BALLAS: (*Without looking up*) Morning.

(HANA *hangs the coat on the coat rack, sits at her desk and begins to comb her hair. After a moment,* BALLAS *turns to her.*)

Hana–

HANA: Yes, Mr Ballas?

BALLAS: You know Ptydepe, don't you?

HANA: I'm sorry, I don't.

BALLAS: Why not? I thought you'd been going to the Ptydepe classes.

HANA: I used to, but I had to give them up. May I go and get the milk?

BALLAS: Why?

HANA: It was too hard for me. May I go and get the milk?

BALLAS: Aren't you ashamed? The secretary to the Managing Director and Ptydepe's too hard for her!

HANA: May I go and get the milk?

BALLAS: Run along.

(HANA *takes the milk bottle and hurries out by the back door.*)

I hope you won't end up like her!

(PILLAR *makes an embarrassed face.*)

SAVANT: (*Looks in at the side door.*) Morning, Jan! Can you spare Ferry a minute?

BALLAS: Be my guest–

SAVANT: Ta. Cheerio!

(SAVANT *gestures to* PILLAR. PILLAR *gets up at once and both leave by the side door.* BALLAS *looks angrily after them. Meanwhile* GROSS *quietly enters by the back door, the extinguisher in his arms.*)

BALLAS: (*To himself*) Ferry! Ferry! Ferry! (*Again stares at his letter.*)

GROSS: Good morning.

BALLAS: You're here again?

GROSS: You said, Mr Ballas, that I should come back in a while.

BALLAS: By that I didn't mean such a short while!

GROSS: Sorry. I'll come later. Sorry–

(*He is backing towards the back door.*)

BALLAS: Listen–

GROSS: Yes, Mr Ballas?

BALLAS: Nothing.

GROSS: Did you want something?

BALLAS: No, no. You may go.

(GROSS *backs out by the back door.* PILLAR *returns by the side door and sits down at his place.*)

What did he want?

(PILLAR *puts on a vague expression.*)

I don't like the way they keep addressing you. Much too familiar.

(PILLAR *shrugs, embarrassed.* HANA *returns by the back door, drinks, then continues combing her hair. Pause.*)

(*To* HANA) Is Ptydepe so difficult to learn?

HANA: It makes great demands on one's memory, Mr Ballas.

BALLAS: Others can learn it–

HANA: Very few can, Mr Ballas. Most of the staff have had to give it up.

BALLAS: Even when all give up, you should persevere!

HANA: But you also dropped out, Mr Ballas, after the first lesson.

BALLAS: That's different. I had to interrupt my studies for reasons of work. You think it's child's play to be at the helm of this colossus? And, what's more, in these times? Come and try it and you'd see.

HANA: But Ptydepe really makes great demands on people. Besides, they say it's based on doubtful principles. May I go and get the rolls?

BALLAS: Who says that?

HANA: Mr Pillar here.

BALLAS: Surely not Mr Pillar! And if, by any chance, he did say such a thing, it was just in fun. Who on the staff actually knows Ptydepe?

HANA: Only the teacher and the personnel of the Translation Centre. May I go and get the rolls?

BALLAS: Run along.

(HANA *takes string bag and leaves by the back door. As soon as she is out,* BALLAS *turns furiously to* PILLAR.)

You talk too much! Far too much!

HELENA: (*Looks in by the side door.*) Morning, all! Ferry, love–would you mind?

(PILLAR *gets up at once.*)

See you later, sweetie.

(HELENA *and* PILLAR *leave by the side door.* BALLAS *jumps up furiously. He does not notice that* GROSS *has again entered with his fire extinguisher by the back door.*)

BALLAS: (*To himself*) I'll teach you a lesson! Ferry! (BALLAS *sits down. Again stares at his letter. Pause. Then* GROSS *speaks up.*)

GROSS: Good morning.

BALLAS: You're here again?

GROSS: You said, Mr Ballas, that I should come back in a while.

BALLAS: By that I didn't mean such a short while!

GROSS: Sorry. I'll come later. Sorry–

(*He is backing towards the back door.*)

BALLAS: Listen–

GROSS: Yes, Mr Ballas?

BALLAS: Nothing.

GROSS: Did you want something?

BALLAS: I just wanted to say that I seem to have overdone it a bit yesterday. You know, there were so many people about, I wasn't sure who might be among them–my nerves were a bit ruffled after what happened–

GROSS: Thank you. You're very kind. Thank you. But the dismissal stands, doesn't it?

BALLAS: Dismissal? Well, for the moment, perhaps we needn't take such drastic measures. You can't be my deputy, of course–

GROSS: Of course–

BALLAS: But there is an opening.

GROSS: Is there? To do what?

BALLAS: The position of Staff Watcher has become free.

GROSS: Do you think I could handle it?

BALLAS: Well, why don't you give it a try for a while? We'll see how it works out.

GROSS: Very kind of you, Mr Ballas. When may I start?

BALLAS: At once, if you like.

GROSS: Thank you, Mr Ballas. Thank you very much.

(GROSS *backs out by the back door.* PILLAR *returns by the side door and sits down at his place.*)

BALLAS: What did she want?

(PILLAR *puts on a vague expression.*)

Don't you play games with me!

(HANA *returns by the back door, her string bag full of rolls. She puts them in her shopping bag, sits down and combs her hair.*)

(*To* HANA) Who else says that Ptydepe is based on doubtful principles?

HANA: All except you, Mr Ballas.

BALLAS: Nonsense!

HANA: Really.

BALLAS: What else do they say?

HANA: That it's only a matter of time before you find it out too.

BALLAS: Indeed! This is the reward one gets for all one has done for them! (*Hands his letter to* HANA.) Couldn't you at least make out what this is about?

HANA: (*Skims the letter.*) It could be either a memorandum concerning the last audit–

BALLAS: Hardly–

HANA: Or a protest.

BALLAS: What sort of protest?

HANA: I don't know.

BALLAS: Why should it be a protest, of all things?

HANA: It's being rumoured that protests written in Ptydepe get preferential treatment.

BALLAS: Where did you hear all this?

HANA: Oh, in the dairy shop this morning

BALLAS: If anybody thinks he can come and protest here, I'll–I'm off to lunch.

(*He grabs his letter and leaves by the back door.*)

HANA: (*Calls after him*) You'll like it, Mr Ballas. They have goulash in the canteen today!

## SCENE 8

*The Ptydepe classroom. All is as before, with the exception that* LEAR *is lecturing to only one clerk,* THUMB. *All other chairs are empty.*

LEAR: And now I shall name, just for the sake of preliminary orientation, some of the most common Ptydepe interjections. Well then, our 'ah!' becomes 'zukybaj', our 'ouch!' becomes 'bykur', our 'oh!' becomes 'hayf dy doretob', English 'pish!' becomes 'bolypak juz', the interjection of surprise 'well!' becomes 'zyk'; however, our 'well, well!' is not 'zykzyk', as some students erroneously say, but 'zykzym'–

(GROSS *with his fire extinguisher enters by the back door, crosses the room and leaves by the side door.*)

'Aow!' becomes 'varylaguf yb de solas', or sometimes, though much more rarely, 'borybaf'; 'bang!' as the symbol of a shot or explosion becomes 'hetegyx ujhoby'; 'bang' as a colloquial expression for sudden surprise is 'maluz rog'. Our 'eek!' becomes 'hatum'–

THUMB: (*Raises his hand.*) Sir–

LEAR: What is it?

THUMB: (*Gets up.*) Would you mind telling us how one says 'oops' in Ptydepe?

LEAR: 'Mykl'.

THUMB: Thank you. (*Sits down.*)

LEAR: 'Psst!' becomes 'cetudap'; 'mmnn' becomes 'vamyl', the poetic 'oh!' is rendered in Ptydepe by 'hrulugyp'. The 'hoooo' of a ghost is translated mostly as 'lymr', although I'd prefer the expansion 'mryb uputr'. Our very important 'hurrah!' becomes in Ptydepe 'frnygko jefr dabux altep dy savarub goz texeres'. And now a little test of your memory. Aow?

(THUMB *raises his hand.*)

Mr Thumb!

THUMB: (*Gets up.*) Varylaguf yb de solas. (*Sits down.*)

LEAR: Eek?

(THUMB *raises his hand.*)

Mr Thumb!

THUMB: (*Gets up.*) Hatum. (*Sits down.*)

LEAR: Psst?

(THUMB *raises his hand.*)

Mr Thumb!

THUMB: (*Gets up.*) Cetudap. (*Sits down.*)

LEAR: Bang?

THUMB: As the symbol of a shot?

LEAR: No, as the colloquial expression for sudden surprise.

(THUMB *raises his hand.*)

Mr Thumb!

THUMB: (*Gets up.*) Maluz rog.

LEAR: (*Correcting his pronunciation*) Maluz–

THUMB: Maluz–

LEAR: M-a-l-u-z–

THUMB: M-a-l-u-z–

LEAR: Listen carefully: m-a-l-u-z–

THUMB: M-a-l-u-z–

LEAR: Your pronunciation isn't too good. How do you say 'well'?

THUMB: Zyk.

LEAR: And 'well, well'?

THUMB: Zykzyk.

LEAR: Zykzym!!

THUMB: I'm sorry, I forgot.

LEAR: Mr Thumb! Mr Thumb! Yippee!

THUMB: We haven't learned yippee yet, sir.

LEAR: Don't try to excuse yourself. You simply don't know it. Hurrah!

THUMB: Frnygko jefr dabux altep dy savarub gop texeres.

LEAR: Goz texeres!!

THUMB: I mean, goz texeres.

LEAR: Such an important word! No, no, Mr Thumb! It won't work this way. I've placed so many hopes in you, and you have what? Well? You have disappointed me! Yes, disappointed! No, no, this way we can't do what? Well? Carry on. Certainly not. This way our class would soon turn into what? Well? Go on, answer me!

THUMB: I don't know.

LEAR: Then try.

THUMB: A kindergarten?

LEAR: No.

THUMB: A borstal?

LEAR: No.

THUMB: Bedlam?

LEAR: Quite correct! Bedlam! No, no! Under these circumstances I can't let you carry on with your studies. You'd only slow down the class and hold up the other students. Please leave the classroom! (THUMB *takes his briefcase and sadly leaves by the back door.)*

*(Addressing the empty classroom)* Let us proceed. 'Hallo!' becomes 'trevunt'; 'gosh!' is translated as 'kavlyz ubahaj kupit'; the American 'gee!' becomes 'hofro gaborte'; 'pooh!' is translated as–

## SCENE 9

*The Secretariat of the Translation Centre. The room is empty, then* MARIA *enters by the back door, carrying a string bag full of onions, crosses the room and leaves by the side door.*

MARIA: *(Offstage)* Here are the onions, Miss Helena.

HELENA: *(Offstage)* Would you mind putting them by the filing cabinet? That's a good girl.

(MARIA *returns by the side door, carrying an empty string bag, sits at the typist's desk and works for a while, then looks about her a few times, takes a mirror from drawer, props it up in front of her, carefully takes out a new hat and tries it on in front of the mirror.)*

GROSS: (*Offstage*) It suits you.

(MARIA *starts, tears the hat off her head, shoves it hastily into the drawer, hides the mirror and fearfully looks about.*)

(*Offstage*) Don't worry. It's only me, Gross.

MARIA: (*Heaves a sigh of relief.*) Oh! But where are you?

GROSS: (*Offstage*) I'm the Staff Watcher now.

MARIA: You? Oh, no!

GROSS: (*Offstage*) Yes, Mr Ballas dropped my dismissal and he's letting me work here for a trial period.

MARIA: You? Staff Watcher?

GROSS: (*Offstage*) Very much so. And in the given circumstances it really seems the best solution for me. I only wish I could get used to the lack of space.

MARIA: Goodness! And I've found a job for you.

GROSS: (*Offstage*) Have you? What sort of job?

MARIA: With a theatre group.

GROSS: (*Offstage*) But I can't act.

MARIA: You could always manage a bit part. There's always bit parts cropping up, you know, a butler, a messenger, a workman, that sort of thing. Well, anyway, if worst came to the worst you could prompt the actors.

GROSS: (*Offstage*) Yes, perhaps. Are you somehow connected with the theatre?

MARIA: My brother works with this group.

GROSS: (*Offstage*) You're kind. (*Pause.*) Maria–

MARIA: Yes?

GROSS: (*Offstage*) Isn't it odd? I have to look at you all the time.

MARIA: Oh, Mr Gross!

HELENA: (*Looks in at the side door.*) Seems the grocer's got limes. Would you mind running over and getting me eight? (*Disappears.*)

(MARIA *takes the string bag from a drawer and runs out by the back door. Short pause, then* BALLAS *stalks in energetically by the back door, his letter in his hand. Looks about, tries his pockets, but finds no cigarettes. Turns towards the secret door.*)

BALLAS: Are you there?

GROSS: (*Offstage*) But of course, Mr Ballas.

BALLAS: Well, how goes it?

GROSS: (*Offstage*) Very well, thank you.

BALLAS: Many strangers?

GROSS: (*Offstage*) Only three visitors in number five.

BALLAS: Alone in the office?

GROSS: (*Offstage*) One, for a moment.

BALLAS: Behaved?

GROSS: (*Offstage*) Correctly.

BALLAS: Good. I think you'll manage. Anything else?

GROSS: (*Offstage*) Sorry, but what else, precisely?

BALLAS: Well, for example, what sort of things are being said about Ptydepe among the staff?

(*Pause.*)

GROSS: (*Offstage*) I'm sorry, Mr Ballas, but I–how should I put it?–I–I'm not an–you know what I mean.

BALLAS: I know. You still haven't shaken off the shackles of outdated prejudice. But you must understand that it's in a good cause. Besides, in a way, it's your moral duty.

(STROLL *enters by the side door and swiftly walks towards the back door.*)

(*To* STROLL) Just a moment!

(STROLL *halts.*)

(*Towards the secret door*) Is that quite clear?

GROSS: (*Offstage*) Quite clear, Mr Ballas.

BALLAS: (*To* STROLL) I say, old boy! How goes the translating?

STROLL: Very well, thank you.

BALLAS: Tell me, how many texts have you translated so far?

STROLL: Into Ptydepe or from Ptydepe?

BALLAS: Well, let's say into Ptydepe.

STROLL: One. I'm just working on the second one now.

BALLAS: So few?

STROLL: That's not so few.

(SAVANT *enters by the side door and quickly walks towards the back door.*)

BALLAS: (*To* SAVANT) Just a moment!

(SAVANT *halts.*)

(*To* STROLL) Slow work, isn't it?

STROLL: Indeed it is. Every expression has several variants in Ptydepe and so one must consult the author of the submitted text regarding each separate word, in order to find out precisely how it was meant and which of the Ptydepe variants to use. Am I not right, Alex?

SAVANT: Quite right. Often the authors themselves aren't sure. They simply don't know such precision from their mother tongue.

STROLL: The shades of meaning of individual words in Ptydepe are so subtle that most of the staff can't grasp them at all.

BALLAS: Why don't you get some help?

STROLL: Help? But you know how things are! Am I not right, Alex?

SAVANT: So far, nobody has really managed to learn Ptydepe. Only Pekarek, and then he left for steam navigation.

BALLAS: Well, you'll have to speed up your translating. The world won't come to an end if an occasional little word isn't exactly right.

(PILLAR *looks in at the back door.* BALLAS *does not see him.* PILLAR *stares questioningly at* STROLL, *who gestures to him that he is ready to go.*)

STROLL: Sorry, Mr Ballas, I have a meeting now–

BALLAS: Well then, go along.

(PILLAR *disappears.* STROLL *hurries out by the back door.* SAVANT *is about to follow.*)

Wait, Alex! Just one more little thing. Tell me, how is Ptydepe actually making out? From the expert's point of view, I mean.

SAVANT: Hard to say. I still have no basis for my statistics, so I can't form any real opinion.

(HELENA *enters by the side door and briskly walks towards the back door.*)

BALLAS: (*To* HELENA) Just a moment!

(HELENA *halts.*)

(*To* SAVANT) What about the results in other organizations?

SAVANT: They're all right, I suppose. Except that wherever Ptydepe has started to be used more widely, it has automatically begun to assume some of the characteristics of a natural language: various emotional overtones, imprecisions, ambiguities. Correct, Nellie?

HELENA: Correct. And you know what? They say that the more one uses Ptydepe the more it gets soiled by these characteristics.

BALLAS: Did you say emotional overtones? But in that case Ptydepe is losing its very purpose!

SAVANT: One could put it that way.

(PILLAR, *unnoticed by* BALLAS, *looks in at the back door, silently beckons to* SAVANT, *who gestures back that he is ready.*)

BALLAS: What can be done about it?

SAVANT: Practically nothing. I'm sorry, Mr Ballas, do you mind if I go now? I have a meeting–

BALLAS: Well then, go along.

(PILLAR *disappears.* SAVANT *hurries out by the back door.* HELENA *is about to follow.*)

Wait, Nellie!

HELENA: What is it, Jan?

BALLAS: Listen, we two have always been able to talk as man to man. Now, tell me quite frankly, I mean really quite frankly, do you get the impression that Ptydepe isn't doing as well as it might be, or, to put it bluntly, that it's sort of got stuck?

HELENA: I do, sweetie.

BALLAS: Thank you, Nellie.

(PILLAR *looks in at the back door.*)

HELENA: May I go now?

BALLAS: Run along.

(PILLAR *disappears.* HELENA *runs out by the back door.* BALLAS *thoughtfully paces up and down. Then sits and again talks towards the secret door.*)

Mr Gross–

GROSS: (*Offstage*) Yes, Mr Ballas.

BALLAS: I hope you aren't taking seriously what occurred

yesterday. You do realize, don't you, it was just a bit of a show for the sake of the others? Listen, why don't I call you Jo. May I?

GROSS: (*Offstage*) But of course, Mr Ballas, I'd be delighted.

BALLAS: I say, old boy–come out of there! You don't want to be doing that sort of work! You! I don't see why you shouldn't carry on as my deputy.

GROSS: (*Offstage*) After what happened?

BALLAS: We must take some risks, damn it! I won't hear of your being abused in this way, Jo! We're having some difficulties at present. Ptydepe isn't doing as well as it might be–

GROSS: (*Offstage*) Yes, I've heard.

BALLAS: The way things are now, I simply need you here, Jo!

(GROSS *emerges from the secret door, scrambling out backwards on all fours.*)

Sit down.

(GROSS *sits down.*)

Where's the enthusiasm we all felt when we were launching Ptydepe! I worked at it as stubbornly as a mule! You know, drank only water, ate only pep pills, went without sleep, just slaved and organized; when the cause was at stake, I was quite ruthless. Well, you remember, don't you?

GROSS: I do remember.

BALLAS: That was the best time of my life! And now see how it's all turned out! This isn't what we wanted, is it?

GROSS: Well, perhaps things will sort themselves out again somehow.

BALLAS: Listen, Jo! You and I, between us, we'll pull things together again! You have your experience, you know how things were done in the past when everything worked; I know how they ought to be done so they'll work in the future; if we two work hand in hand, I'll bet anything you like, we'll hammer out something damn well astonishing! Are you free tonight?

GROSS: Yes.

BALLAS: Good. Let's meet quietly somewhere, have a glass of beer and really think things out! Map out a plan, so we know how to go about it all. Who should I rely on here if not on you, old boy!

GROSS: But I–

BALLAS: (*Cuts in*) And now fetch George and tell him to march back into his cubicle. He's already proved himself in the job and he must see that what we need now above all in the high positions is specialists.

(GROSS *leaves by the back door. Long pause.* BALLAS *searches his pockets, no cigarettes. Looks at his watch.* STROLL *enters by the back door, carrying a folder, and briskly walks towards the side door.*)

Otto!

(STROLL *halts.*)

You still haven't told me about your translations from Ptydepe.

STROLL: So far, I haven't translated anything from Ptydepe.

(SAVANT *enters by the back door, carrying a folder, and walks towards the side door.*)

BALLAS: Alex!

(SAVANT *halts.*)

(*To* STROLL) Why not?

STROLL: Up till now nobody has brought me any authorization from Alex.

BALLAS: Alex! Why do you refuse to authorize translations?

SAVANT: But I can't authorize them without personal registration documents.

(HELENA *enters by the back door, carrying a folder, and walks towards the side door.*)

BALLAS: Nellie!

(HELENA *halts.*)

(*To* SAVANT) You mean in all this time nobody has brought you any documents from Nellie?

SAVANT: That's right.

BALLAS: Nellie! Why do you refuse to issue those damned documents?

HELENA: Oh, for heaven's sake, sweetie! I can't issue them until I've made sure they don't conflict with the findings in the memos, and I can't learn the findings because the blessed memos are written in Ptydepe and, as you damned well know, I'm forbidden to make any translations whatsoever. Hasn't the girl brought my limes yet?

BALLAS: Then why doesn't Otto translate the memos?

STROLL: I can translate only after getting an authorization from Alex!

BALLAS: Then Alex will have to start granting the authorizations!

SAVANT: I can't, if nobody has the documents from Nellie!

BALLAS: Do you hear that, Nellie? You'll have to start giving people the documents regardless!

HELENA: But I'm not permitted to translate!

BALLAS: Why doesn't Otto do the translating?

STROLL: I can translate only after getting an authorization from Alex!

BALLAS: Then Alex will have to start granting the authorizations!

SAVANT: I can't, when nobody has the documents from Nellie!

BALLAS: Do you hear that, Nellie? You'll have to start giving people the documents regardless!

HELENA: But I'm not permitted to translate!

BALLAS: Why doesn't Otto do the translating?

STROLL: I can translate only after getting an authorization from Alex!

BALLAS: Then Alex will have to start granting the authorizations!

SAVANT: I can't, when nobody has the documents from Nellie!

BALLAS: Do you hear that, Nellie? You'll have to start giving people the documents regardless!

HELENA: But I'm not permitted to translate!

BALLAS: I'd like to know who thought up this vicious circle.

STROLL, SAVANT AND HELENA: (*In chorus*) You did, Mr Ballas!

BALLAS: Well, what of it! The situation was entirely different at that time. Then it had a profound significance! But we've progressed since then, and that's why I propose the following simplifications in the procedure of translating all

Ptydepe texts. These will come into effect at once. First: Helena is permitted to issue the personal registration documents without knowing the contents of the memos. Second: Alex is permitted to authorize all translations without the personal registration documents. Third: Otto is permitted to translate without an authorization from Alex. Is that quite clear? The fact that we can afford these measures is one more eloquent proof of the rightness of our path! (*Hands his letter to* STROLL.) And now–translate this for me!

STROLL: (*Reads*) A protest. We, the undersigned staff of the Accounts Department, protest most emphatically against the transfer of our offices to the cellar and we announce hereby that we can no longer work under these deplorable conditions–

BALLAS: (*Interrupts*) That's enough! You may carry on with your work.

(BALLAS *leaves by the back door.* STROLL, SAVANT *and* HELENA *stand about for a moment or two in silence, then the back door opens a crack,* PILLAR *appears and beckons them to follow him. They all leave by the back door. Pause. Then* GROSS *and* GEORGE *enter by the back door.* GEORGE *is livid, frowns, and furiously kicks the coat rack, then the desk, spits, kneels down and climbs on all fours through the secret door into the observation cubicle. After a moment he indignantly throws out* GROSS*'s fire extinguisher.* GROSS *takes it and walks towards the back door. Just then* MARIA *enters by the back door, carrying a paper bag full of limes. When she sees* GEORGE *she halts in surprise.*)

MARIA: Do you realize what would happen to you if anybody saw you here?

GROSS: I'm no longer the Staff Watcher.

MARIA: Oh?

GROSS: Mr Ballas has made me his deputy again.

MARIA: Congratulations!

GROSS: Good gracious, what for? Frankly, I'd rather have remained the Staff Watcher.

MARIA: I know. You'll have to cope with some pretty nasty bits of business now, I expect.

GROSS: Never mind. Well, Maria, good luck to you. And do come and see me in my office someday. (*Slowly starts towards the back door.*)

MARIA: Mr Gross–

GROSS: (*Stops*) Yes?

MARIA: Has anybody translated for you that–you know–the thing you wanted to have translated yesterday?

GROSS: The memorandum? No. And according to current regulations, nobody can. Well, it's probably better that way.

MARIA: Do you think it's a negative one?

GROSS: I've learned always to expect the worst.

MARIA: Was any irregularity found during the audit in your department?

GROSS: Not that I know of. I did take the rubber stamp home a few times, but I took it for reasons of work and not, as some people seemed to suggest, for my children to play with. My little Martin might have played with it at most twice in all that time.

MARIA: If your conscience is clear, you've nothing to worry about. Your innocence will be proved, but you have to fight for it! I believe that if one doesn't give way, truth must always come out in the end.

GROSS: (*Walks to* MARIA, *sadly smiles at her and strokes her cheek.*) What do you know about the world, dear child! Still, I wish you could always stay like this! You're right, one really ought always to stand firm. The trouble is, I've never been very firm, more of an intellectual, always hesitant, always full of doubts, too considerate, a dreamer rather than a man of action–and that's my bad luck.

(*Pause.*)

When I think back, I see that I muddled up many things in my life myself. I often gave in too soon, yielded to threats, and I trusted people too much.

(*Pause.*)

If I ever again have any influence on the course of things, I'll do everything differently. More real deeds and fewer clever words! I've never been sufficiently matter-of-fact, cool-headed, proud, severe and critical–especially with myself.

(*Pause.*)

It may be partly because I belong to an odd, lost generation. We've given ourselves out in small change, we invested the best years of our lives into things which turned out not to be worth it. We were so busy for so long talking about out great mission that we quite forgot to do anything great. In short, we were a mess!

(*Pause.*)

But I believe that now at last I can face all this frankly, without hysteria and without self-pity; that I'll manage to recover from all the upheavals; that I'm still able to forget the past and make a quite new and quite different beginning.

MARIA: (*Moved*) Have you the memo with you?

GROSS: You mean–surely you wouldn't–

MARIA: I'm quite grown up, thank you, Mr Gross. I know what I'm doing. Give it to me!

(GROSS *takes out his memo, hands it to* MARIA, *who reads it with growing excitement.*)

(*Reads*) Dear Sir, the last audit in your department has shown that the allegation of a repeated appropriation of the bank endorsement stamp for improper use is in your case entirely unfounded. On the contrary, we feel obliged to emphasize the very positive findings of the audit, which clearly prove that you have been conscientious and responsible in the directing of your organization and that you therefore merit full confidence. This is further confirmed by your stand against Ptydepe, which has been quite unequivocal from the beginning. Our view of the Ptydepe campaign has always been entirely negative, for we understand it to be a profoundly harmful attempt to place office communications on a confused, unrealistic and anti-human basis. We suggest that you liquidate with the greatest possible resolution and speed any attempt to introduce Ptydepe into your organization, and that you severely punish all those who have been propagating Ptydepe for their own personal advantage and in disregard of the consequences. Wishing you all success in your future work, we remain, yours faithfully, signature illegible.

GROSS: *(After a moment, seriously)* Thank you, Maria. Now at last I have an opportunity to prove that I have more civil courage than I've shown so far. I promise you that this time I shall not give way to anything or anybody, even at the risk of my position!

*(Grabs his fire extinguisher and starts energetically towards the back door.)*

MARIA: *(Shyly bursts out)* I like you–

GROSS: First I must deserve your sympathy, dear child!

*(He leaves by the back door. Pause.)*

GEORGE: *(Offstage)* That was a stupid thing to do, Maria.

MARIA: *(Frightened)* Oh God! Are you there?

GEORGE: *(Offstage)* I came back a moment ago. And I'm not sorry I did. I hope you realize why!

HELENA: *(Offstage)* Listen–what about those limes?

MARIA: *(Softly)* I'm afraid I do.

## SCENE 10

*The Director's office.* BALLAS *is sitting at his desk, vainly searching his pockets for cigarettes.* HANA *is combing her hair.* GROSS *enters energetically by the back door, carrying his fire extinguisher.*

GROSS: Mr Ballas, your era is over! My memorandum has just been translated to me and its contents make it perfectly clear that I'm not only quite innocent as regards the rubber stamp, but above all that I'm the only legitimate director of this organization. Furthermore, I'm requested by this memorandum to make an end of Ptydepe with the greatest possible resolution and speed–

BALLAS: Hana–

HANA: Yes, Mr Ballas?

BALLAS: Isn't it time for you to get your chocolates?

HANA: (*Looks at her watch.*) Oh yes, it is!

BALLAS: Well then, run along! And while you're there get me some cigarettes. The usual.

(HANA *runs out by the back door.*)

Sorry. What did you say?

GROSS: Furthermore, I'm requested by this memorandum to make an end of Ptydepe with the greatest possible resolution and speed and to punish severely all those who were engaged in its introduction for their own advantage. In other words, history has proved me right and I, on the basis of the authority which is rightfully mine–

(PILLAR *looks in at the side door.*)

BALLAS: In a minute, Mr P!

(PILLAR *disappears, leaving the door ajar.*)

What did you say?

GROSS: In other words, history has proved me right and I, on the basis of the authority which is rightfully mine, shall draw due consequences from what has occurred. The way in which you seized the entire organization and forced Ptydepe on it cries out for vengeance. I'm a humanist and my concept–

(HANA *re-enters by back door, carrying a box of chocolates and a packet of cigarettes. Hands the cigarettes to* BALLAS, *puts the chocolates in her shopping bag, sits down and resumes combing her hair.*)

BALLAS: Thanks, Hana. (*Lights a cigarette with gusto.*) What did you say?

GROSS: I'm a humanist and my concept of directing this organization derives from the idea that every single member of the staff is human and must become more and more human. This is why I cannot but fight anyone who tries to spit upon this idea. I place the struggle for the victory of reason and of moral values–

(PILLAR *looks in at the side door.*)

BALLAS: In a minute, Mr P, in a minute!

(PILLAR *disappears, leaving the door ajar.*)

What did you say?

GROSS: I place the victory of reason and of moral values above a peace bought by their loss. And I will carry on to the bitter end a struggle against all the misdeeds you've committed here. I think that under these circumstances it is no longer possible for you to remain in our organization. Kindly move out of my desk!

BALLAS: (*Offering* GROSS *a cigarette*) Have one!

GROSS: I said, kindly move out of my desk!

BALLAS: Do have one, old boy!

GROSS: Move out of my desk!

BALLAS: Let's say after lunch. All right?

GROSS: I'm glad you aren't putting up any resistance. After lunch will be all right.

BALLAS: I don't see why I should put up any resistance.

GROSS: You mean you agree with me?

BALLAS: Of course.

GROSS: (*Astounded, puts the fire extinguisher on the floor.*) Good gracious! How so?

BALLAS: I've seen the light.

GROSS: Have you?

BALLAS: Absolutely. I've come to the conclusion that Ptydepe is really for the birds. I believed in it, I fought for its establishment, but it was all a horrible mistake. Subjectively I meant well, but objectively I did wrong and so now I must accept, whether I like it or not, all the severe consequences of my activity.

(PILLAR *looks in at the side door.*)

One more minute, Mr P!

(PILLAR *disappears, leaving the door ajar.*)

GROSS: Are you being sincere? You ought not to be so calm about it. It's very confusing.

BALLAS: I'm calm, because your severe but just words express what I've been tragically feeling for a long time, and so they fill me with relief that I won't be obliged to continue any longer work which I don't believe in, and that finally all my mistakes will be put right. I wish you all the luck in your liquidation of the disastrous consequences of Ptydepe, and I firmly trust that your work will succeed at least as much as mine has failed. I'll help you to the limits of my humble abilities. (*Offers* GROSS *a cigarette.*) Do have one!

GROSS: No thanks. You seem to have come to your senses.

BALLAS: I have.

GROSS: Perhaps you were indeed sincerely mistaken–

BALLAS: I was.

GROSS: How do you mean, you'll help me?

BALLAS: (*Offering* GROSS *a cigarette*) Are you quite sure you won't have one?

GROSS: Thanks. Not now. How do you mean, you'll help me?

BALLAS: But they're superb!

GROSS: I'm sure they are. How do you mean, you'll help me?

BALLAS: Look, old boy, if you don't take one, I'll be hurt! Well, as your deputy, of course.

GROSS: You must have misunderstood me. I said you'll leave the organization.

BALLAS: You wouldn't want to take such drastic measures, would you?

GROSS: I'm sorry, but I've made up my mind not to give way this time. I don't propose to repeat my old mistakes.

BALLAS: Come, come! Didn't I let you stay on as my deputy?

GROSS: That was different. Rightfully I should have remained the director, and truth was on my side.

BALLAS: I know that too, now!

GROSS: I've known it from the beginning.

BALLAS: It's always easy to be against a thing from the beginning! What is much harder is to be for a thing, even at the risk of getting your teeth kicked in!

GROSS: That doesn't change by one iota the fact that you are the chief culprit and so you must get the severest punishment. You'll simply have to pack up and get out!

BALLAS: And if I don't?

GROSS: You will!

BALLAS: Take it easy, old boy! (*Produces a sheet of paper and shows it to* GROSS.) Recognize this? It's the supplementary order for the introduction of Ptydepe and, if I'm not mistaken, it's signed by you, not by me. Or were you not the Managing Director at the time? Now then, who is the chief culprit?

(PILLAR *looks in at the side door.*)

Yes, Mr P–Give me another minute, will you?

(PILLAR *disappears, leaving the door ajar.*)

Well?

GROSS: That one signature is insignificant. It's nothing in comparison with what you've done.

BALLAS: Trouble is, history knows only such signatures.

GROSS: Besides, it was you who got me to sign it.

BALLAS: I did? I don't seem to remember.

GROSS: By your trick about the authentication of the notebook.

BALLAS: I wouldn't bring that up if I were you.

GROSS: Why not?

BALLAS: Because it's no extenuating circumstance at all. Just the reverse, in fact.

GROSS: I don't know what you're talking about.

BALLAS: Don't you? Well, look here, old boy. If it weren't for that notebook affair, you might have claimed that you signed the order moved by a sincere belief in your principles, which wouldn't have excused your conduct, of course, but would at least have explained it somewhat on humanitarian grounds; while if you do bring up this motive now, you'll be admitting thereby that you signed the order moved merely by petty cowardice, and that to avoid a piddling punishment for the authentication you didn't hesitate to plunge the whole organization into the jaws of its present catastrophe. Do you follow me? If, on the other hand, you hadn't signed the order, you might have pretended that you hadn't quite realized the impropriety of your action regarding the notebook, but your signature proves that you were clearly aware of this and that you panicked, because you were afraid of being punished. As you see, both your errors are intertwined in such an original way that the one greatly multiplies the other. If on top of your guilt in introducing Ptydepe you should now also volunteer an admission of your guilt regarding the notebook, you'd leave nobody in any doubt whatever about the real culprit responsible for all that's happened. Well then, shall we come to an agreement?

GROSS: All right, let's both resign.

BALLAS: As far as I'm concerned, I don't see why I should. (*Pause.*)

GROSS: (*Faintly*) And you would honestly help me in everything?

BALLAS: I'm glad our discussion is at last reaching a realistic level. Of course I would. (*Offers him a cigarette.*) Take one. (GROSS *takes it.* BALLAS *gives him a light.*)

GROSS: You have a great deal of experience. You can work as stubbornly as a mule. Would you also work like a mule against Ptydepe?

BALLAS: I can't do things any other way.

(PILLAR *looks in at the side door.*)

Yes, Mr P. Nearly ready.

(PILLAR *disappears, leaving the door ajar.*)

GROSS: (*Hesitantly*) But somebody has to get the ax. You know how people are–

BALLAS: Leave that to me. (*Calls towards the side door*) Ready, Mr P!

(PILLAR *enters by the side door, followed by* STROLL, SAVANT *and* HELENA, *all three carrying the folders they had in the last scene. They line up in a row and open the folders, as though about to sing in chorus.*)

You may begin.

(PILLAR *gives them a hand signal and they all start solemnly reading.*)

STROLL, SAVANT AND HELENA: (*Together*) Dear Sir! The delegation which, under the leadership of Mr Pillar, now comes to you consists of people who until the very last sincerely believed in Ptydepe and were in the vanguard of its introduction. All the more difficult it is therefore for us, your loyal colleagues, to approach you now as a delegation whose mission it is to warn you against the consequences of any further propagation of Ptydepe. But precisely because we have done much for Ptydepe we feel obliged to be the first to point out to you the insoluble problems connected with its establishment.

BALLAS: (*Gestures them to stop.*) Dear friends. I know only too well, perhaps even better than you, how desperate is the situation we've reached with Ptydepe, and I assure you that it has cost me many a sleepless night. As your former Managing Director I also accept the greatest share of the blame for the whole affair. We meant well, but we did wrong. In short, we sinned and now we must accept, courageously and without any feeling of being sinned against, the full consequences of our activities and with a redoubled energy struggle to remedy the damage we've done. In accordance with directives from the authorities I have taken certain first steps, with which I shall now acquaint you, because they are already specifically aimed towards a bold solution of the very problem which you have now come here to point out to me. First of all, I've resigned as your Managing Director and I've passed this position to the man who, as you'll surely agree, is the best qualified for it, Mr Josef Gross. Mr Gross who, throughout the era of Ptydepe, remained loyal to and even suffered for his convictions. I myself have received with gratitude from the hands of Mr Gross the position of his deputy. I've received it in order above all to have an opportunity to show by diligent work my willingness to serve the new cause and thus to repair all the harm which, with the best of intentions, I committed. And now let me give the platform to Mr Gross.

GROSS: (*Embarrassed*) What can I add? I'm not angry with you. I know that you meant well. The proof of it is also this, your delegation, which comes in the name of reason and of moral values. Well, we should let bygones be bygones. Let us lose no more words over it. What is at stake now is the future. (STROLL, SAVANT *and* HELENA *look questioningly at* PILLAR. *He gestures for them to turn the page. They begin to read further.*)

STROLL, SAVANT AND HELENA: (*Together*) We are sorry, but we cannot be satisfied with such a brief explanation. We threw our whole lives into the struggle for the wrong thing and we want to know who was responsible and who took advantage of it. We were deceived and we have the right to know who has deceived us.

GROSS: (*Softly to* BALLAS) Will you answer this point?

BALLAS: (*Softly to* GROSS) Yes. (*Louder*) Friends! We are all guilty.

HELENA: (*At* PILLAR*'s signal*) That is only a hollow phrase!

STROLL: (*At* PILLAR*'s signal*) We want to know the actual persons!

SAVANT: (*At* PILLAR*'s signal*) The names.

BALLAS: All right then, I'll tell you. I'm sure you've all noticed that for some time now there has been prowling about our offices a mysterious, silent man whose real function in our organization has never been known to us. I myself have come to know this man very well, having been under his direct and constant surveillance. Inexhaustible was the well of methods by which he has been forcing us to do things we disagreed with. He pried into every nook and cranny, was always present, always subtly disguised in the cloak of inconspicuousness and of silent participation. And it is no accident that this grey eminence of Ptydepe, so diligently trying never to be publicly compromised in any way, has penetrated today–when the cause he served with such sycophancy is quite lost–to the head of your delegation, abusing your honest trust and averting from himself all suspicion by assuming the mask of a critical attitude towards Ptydepe.

(PILLAR, *growing more and more desperate, turns from* STROLL *to* SAVANT, *from* SAVANT *to* HELENA, *but they all turn away from him. Dead silence.* PILLAR *runs in panic across the room, but stops at the back door.*)

PILLAR: (*Shouts*) Death to all artificial languages! Long live natural human speech! Long live Man!

(PILLAR *runs out by the back door. An embarrassed pause. Then somebody knocks on the back door. All turn towards the sound. Pause. More knocking. Quizzical looks. More knocking.*)

GROSS: Come in.

(COLUMN *enters by the back door.*)

BALLAS: Welcome, Mr C! Come in! This is Mr Column.

(COLUMN *bows to them, then sits in* PILLAR*'s place. General relief.*)

GROSS: Now then, let me conclude. What is at stake is the future. I appeal to you to put all your best efforts into the struggle for the re-establishment of natural human language, of our beloved mother tongue–

BALLAS: (*Interrupts*) Wait a minute, Jo! Our colleagues are surely tired by now. We can talk tomorrow about what happens next. Now, why don't we all go and have lunch together. Who's in favour?

(STROLL, SAVANT, HELENA, COLUMN *and* HANA *at once raise their hands.*)

STROLL: That's an idea!

SAVANT: Bravo!

HELENA: Hurrah!

BALLAS: Let's all meet in a quarter of an hour at the Translation Centre!

(STROLL, SAVANT *and* HELENA *hurry out by the back door.*)

Well, that's that. Are you quite comfortable, Mr C?

(COLUMN *nods, walks to the desk, begins to collect the papers lying on it and to shove them in his pockets.* BALLAS *crosses to the fire extinguisher hanging on the wall and takes it down. Then* BALLAS *and* COLUMN *leave by the side door.*)

GROSS: Things do seem to be moving rather fast.

HANA: Mr Gross–

GROSS: There was nothing else I could do. An open conflict would have meant that I'd be finished. This way, as the Managing Director, I can at least salvage this and that.

HANA: Mr Gross–

GROSS: Anyway, who knows, maybe this–Ballas–will turn out to be quite a good man after all. If I use him in the right place–

HANA: Mr Gross–

GROSS: What is it?

HANA: May I go and get my lunch?

GROSS: Run along.

(HANA *hastily takes her knife and fork and hurries out through the back door.* GROSS *halts in the centre and sadly stares ahead.* BALLAS *and* COLUMN *enter by the side door, both carrying their knives and forks, and walk towards the back door.*)

(*To himself*) Why can't I be a little boy again? I'd do everything differently from the beginning.

BALLAS: You might begin differently, but you'd end up exactly the same–so relax!

(BALLAS *and* COLUMN *leave by the back door.* GROSS *lingers dejectedly for a second longer, then takes his fire extinguisher, hangs it in its original place, takes his knife and fork from the drawer and slowly walks out by the back door.*)

## SCENE II

*The Ptydepe classroom. All four clerks are back in their chairs, including* THUMB. LEAR *is lecturing.*

LEAR: The basic mistake of Ptydepe was its uncritical overestimation of the significance of redundancy. Redundancy turned into a veritable campaign, it became the slogan of the day. But it was overlooked that side by side with a useful redundancy, which indeed lowered the danger of incorrect interpretations of texts, there existed also a useless redundancy, consisting merely in a mechanical prolongation of texts. In the pursuit of maximum redundancy some eager clerks inserted within Ptydepe words–already quite long enough, thank you – even further so-called 'empty texts', thus blindly increasing the percentage of redundancy, so that the length of inter-office communications grew out of all proportion and sense.

(BALLAS *and* COLUMN *enter by the back door, carrying their knives and forks, cross the room;* BALLAS *pats* LEAR *appreciatively on the shoulder, then both leave by the side door.*)

Let me give you an example. I've heard of a case where a brief summons to military HQ filled thirty-six typed pages single space.

(THUMB *giggles.*)

Another disastrous manifestation is to be seen in certain stylistic habits which came into being during the Ptydepe era. The straining after maximum dissimilarity between what preceded and what followed within a given text, out of which the habit grew, was limiting more and more the possibilities for the further continuation of texts, until in some instances either they could continue only in one specific direction, so that the authors lost all influence over what they were trying to communicate, or they couldn't be continued at all.

(GROSS *enters by the back door, carrying his knife and fork, starts towards the side door, but when he hears* LEAR, *he stops and listens.*)

All these mistakes have served as a sound lesson in the creation of the new synthetic language – Chorukor – which no longer attempts to limit the unreliability of a text by a strenuous pursuit of words as dissimilar from each other as possible, but, on the contrary, achieves this by a purposeful exploitation and organization of their similarity: the more similar the words, the closer their meaning; so that a possible error in the text represents only a slight deviation from its sense.

(GROSS *hurries out through the side door.*)

This method has many advantages, among them the fact that Chorukor is very easy to learn. Often it is enough to know only one word from within a certain radius of meaning in order to guess many other words of that group. We can do that unaided and without any further study.

THUMB: (*Raises his hand.*) Sir!

LEAR: Yes?

THUMB: (*Gets up.*) Would you please demonstrate this to us with an example? (*Sits down.*)

LEAR: Certainly. Monday becomes in Chorukor 'ilopagar', Tuesday 'ilopager', Wednesday 'ilopagur', Thursday 'ilopagir', Friday 'ilopageur', Saturday 'ilopagoor'. Now, what do you think Sunday is? Well?

(*Only* THUMB *raises his hand.*)

Well, Mr Thumb?

THUMB: (*Gets up.*) Ilopagor. (*Sits down.*)

LEAR: Correct, Mr Thumb. You get an A. It is easy, isn't it?

(THUMB *nods.*)

There you are! And at the same time the danger of an error can be entirely disregarded. For example, if a typist makes a mistake and instead of 'ilopageur' writes in the announcement of a meeting 'ilopager', the subject of the meeting is not at all distorted thereby. The most that can happen is that the staff will meet on Tuesday, instead of on Friday, and the matter under consideration will thus even be expedited.

## SCENE 12

*The Secretariat of the Translation Centre.* MARIA *is standing dejectedly by her desk.* BALLAS *and* COLUMN *are there, both with their knives and forks. Noise of a party offstage can be heard, as in Scene 6.* MARIA *begins to sob.* BALLAS *looks at her.*

BALLAS: I'm sorry. I've promised Mr Gross that I shall work like a mule and I don't want to break my promise by compromising on my very first day. What's going on next door?

MARIA: (*Sobbing*) It's Mr Wassermann's birthday, so his colleagues are giving him a party.

BALLAS: Paul Wassermann? Do you hear that, Mr C? It's Paul's birthday!

(BALLAS *and* COLUMN *start towards the side door. Just then* GROSS *runs in by the back door, holding his knife and fork in his hand.*)

GROSS: (*Excitedly*) Mr Ballas!

BALLAS: Yes?

GROSS: What on earth does this mean?

BALLAS: What?

GROSS: Another artificial language is being taught here!

BALLAS: Chorukor.

GROSS: But we agreed, didn't we, that office communications are again to be conducted in the mother tongue!

BALLAS: I don't recall we agreed anything of the sort.

GROSS: But my memorandum states quite clearly–

BALLAS: As far as I remember, it states nothing about what language is now to be used here. Making an end of Ptydepe doesn't mean that we must automatically give up all attempts at finally introducing some precision and order into office communications. If we did, we would be–so to speak–throwing out the baby with the bathwater. Am I not right, Mr C?

(COLUMN *nods.*)

GROSS: But I understood that–

BALLAS: You understood wrong. It is evident that you've lived for too long in an isolation which tragically marked you through the loss of a living contact with reality. I don't want to meddle in the business of the Managing Director, but when I see that you're clearly fumbling and could easily come into conflict with the opinion of most of our staff, then I'm sorry but I have to interfere.

GROSS: Look, wouldn't it make things easier if you carried on as the Managing Director and I as your deputy?

BALLAS: Not on your life! I've been foolish enough to try that once already and I don't propose to do it again! Let's each do what suits him best. I have certain organizational talents which I can put to excellent use as your deputy, while you can better bear the weight of responsibility connected with the position of the Managing Director. (*To* COLUMN) They're still at it over there! Let's go!

(BALLAS *and* COLUMN *leave by the side door. The noise of the party grows louder, then quiets down.*)

MARIA: Mr. Gross–

GROSS: Yes?

MARIA: You didn't tell me the Watcher had come back.

GROSS: Well?

MARIA: He saw and heard everything!

GROSS: Everything? What?

MARIA: That I translated your memo.

GROSS: Well?

MARIA: He told on me and I was fired on the spot for translating an important Ptydepe text before passing my exams.

GROSS: But the use of Ptydepe has been cancelled–

MARIA: Mr Ballas said that's beside the point. A rule is a rule, he said. What guarantee is there, he said, that I wouldn't some day make an improper translation from Chorukor as well. He said he had promised you to work like a mule and he didn't want to break his promise the very first day by compromising.

GROSS: What are you going to do?

MARIA: Well, I hate to bother you, but couldn't you perhaps reverse his decision? Or perhaps at least put in a kind word for me?

GROSS: Dear Maria! We're living in a strange, complex epoch. As Hamlet says, our 'time is out of joint'. Just think, we're reaching for the moon and yet it's increasingly hard for us to reach ourselves; we're able to split the atom, but unable to prevent the splitting of our personality; we build superb communications between the continents, and yet communication between man and man is increasingly difficult.

(*Short pause. Noise of the party.*)

In other words, our life has lost a sort of higher axle, and we are irresistibly falling apart, more and more profoundly alienated from the world, from others, from ourselves. Like Sisyphus, we roll the boulder of our life up the hill of its illusory meaning, only for it to roll down again into the valley of its own absurdity. Never before has Man lived projected so near to the very brink of the insoluble conflict between the subjective will of his moral self and the objective possibility of its ethical realization. Manipulated, automatized, made into a fetish, Man loses the experience of his own totality; horrified, he stares as a stranger at himself, unable not to be what he is not, nor to be what he is.

*(Again a short pause. Noise of the party.)*

*(Turns directly to* MARIA *and continues with urgency:)* Dear Maria! You can't begin to guess how happy I would be if I could do for you what you've just asked me to do. The more am I frightened therefore that in reality I can do next to nothing for you, because I am in fact totally alienated from myself: the desire to help you fatefully encounters within me the responsibility thrust upon me–who am attempting to salvage the last remnants of Man's humanity–by the permanent menace to our organization from the side of Mr Ballas and his men; a responsibility so binding that I absolutely may not risk the loss of my position, on which it is based, by any open conflict with Mr Ballas and his men.

*(Pause. The noise offstage culminates in unintelligible singing which changes into cheers.)*

VOICES: *(Offstage)* Hip, hip, hurrah!

*(Cheers culminate in laughter which, however, soon dies down. The party is over. While* GROSS *continues speaking,* STROLL, SAVANT, HELENA, HANA, BALLAS, COLUMN, LEAR, THUMB *and three clerks enter by the side door.* GEORGE *scrambles out of the secret door. All have their knives and forks. All stand in the background, waiting for* GROSS *to join them to go to lunch.)*

GROSS: Besides, there is no point in further complicating my already complicated situation by taking too tragic a view of your prospects. Let's try to be quite matter-of-fact about it, shall we? You're still young, you've got your whole life ahead of you, you have lost nothing so far. Just think! How many people today are able to say with any degree of honesty they have a brother with a theatre group? A minuscule minority! For all we can tell, one day you might come to be thankful to Mr Ballas for a career as a famous actress. What matters now is that you must not lose your hope, your love of life and your trust in people! Chin up, my girl! Keep smiling! I know it is absurd, dear Maria, but I must go and have lunch. So–goodbye! Be good!

(*He joins the others in the background. Pause. They all look at* MARIA.)

MARIA: (*Softly*) Nobody ever talked to me so nicely before.

(*They all slowly leave in a solemn, funeral-like procession by the back door, clutching their knives and forks.* MARIA *takes her bag, collects her things, puts on her new hat, looks about for the last time and then–happy–she also leaves.*)

# THE INCREASED DIFFICULTY OF CONCENTRATION

# CHARACTERS

DR EDUARD HUML, social scientist
VLASTA HUML, his wife
RENATA, his mistress
BLANKA, his secretary
DR ANNA BALCAR, social scientist
KAREL KRIEBEL, technician
EMIL MACHAL, surveyor
MR BECK, supervisor

# ACT ONE

*Huml's flat: a cross between a living room and a hall. A small staircase left leading up to the bedroom. There are three doors downstairs: the left door, leading to the study; the back door, to the kitchen, the bathroom and all other parts of the flat; the right door, equipped with a peep-hole, is the main entrance. Upstage, a mirror and a commode with a cactus on it. Downstage, a dining table with four chairs around it. Throughout, the audience should be prevented from distinguishing the objects currently displayed on the table; their view can be partially obscured by a flower stand, for example. To the right, an easy chair flanked by a small table with telephone.*

*For a moment the stage is empty, the back door is open; then* MRS HUML, *wearing a dressing-gown over her dress, enters by the back door. She carries a tray with breakfast for two: cups, saucers, tea-pot, rolls, butter. Setting the table, she calls towards the bedroom.*

MRS HUML: Breakfast!

(*When she has finished the table,* MRS HUML *pours the tea, sits down and begins to eat, while the door upstairs opens and* HUML *enters in his pyjmas, dishevelled, obviously just out of bed, leisurely descends, sits down opposite* MRS HUML, *spreads a napkin in his lap and also starts eating. Longish silence is finally interrupted by* MRS HUML.)

Well?

HUML: Have we some honey?

MRS HUML: Failed again, I bet.

HUML: Couldn't help it.

MRS HUML: Why?

HUML: The atmosphere wasn't right.

MRS HUML: Where did you go?

HUML: Flicks. Cartoons.

MRS HUML: What an idea! And then?

HUML: She went on telling funny stories and jokes, it just didn't seem right. Have we some honey?

MRS HUML: And you couldn't steer the conversation to more serious subjects, I suppose.

HUML: I tried. But every time she'd cut in with some new story. She was full of fun and games, that's all. Nothing I could do about it. Have we some honey?

MRS HUML: In the cupboard.

(HUML *puts down his napkin, gets up and shuffles out by the back door, leaving it open. Pause.*)

HUML: (*Offstage*) Can't find it –

MRS HUML: (*Calling towards the back door*) On the top shelf – (*Longish pause.*)

HUML: (*Offstage*) Where?

MRS HUML: Oh, for heaven's sake! (*Jumps up, runs out by the back door. Offstage*) And what's this?

(*Shortly after, the left door slowly opens and* HUML *quietly backs in, apparently hoping his exit from the study will not be noticed. He is fully dressed and spruced up. Carefully, he pushes the door almost shut, then quickly tiptoes to the back door and calls softly through it.*)

HUML: Come!

(RENATA, *wearing a coat, appears in the door.* HUML *grabs her hand and leads her swiftly towards the right door, looks around stealthily, then kisses* RENATA'*s cheek.*)

(*Whispers*) Bye, kitty-cat.

RENATA: (*Whispers*) Bye. And don't you forget!

(HUML *peers through the peephole, then quietly opens the door and lets* RENATA *out; quickly closes door, runs back, closes the back door, after which he ambles to the left door, quietly opens it and holds it open. Presently,* MISS BALCAR *and* KRIEBL *enter, wearing lab coats, carefully carrying Puzuk between them. Puzuk is a complicated piece of machinery, faintly reminiscent of a cash register and/or a calculator. It is furnished with a keyboard, various push buttons, a small crank on one side, an eyepiece not unlike that of a microscope, a red and a green bulb, a small loudspeaker, and a long cord with a plug.* MISS BALCAR *and* KRIEBL *place Puzuk gently on the table,* HUML *closes the left door.*)

KRIEBL: (*To* HUML) Where's the socket?

HUML: There – behind the cactus.

(KRIEBL *crosses to back wall, trailing the cord, sticks plug into socket.* MISS BALCAR *sits down in the easy chair.* KRIEBL *returns, sits at Puzuk and begins to fiddle with its machinery.* HUML *also sits down, examining the apparatus with some curiosity.*)

So that's what he's like!

MISS BALCAR: Nice, isn't he?

HUML: Nice. May I ask how he works?

MISS BALCAR: Well, we fed him with some basic information about you which had been placed at our disposal, he processed it, and on the basis of it he's now going to ask you his first question. You're going to give him an honest answer, he'll process your answer – together with other data concerning your environment, researched for him by Mr Machal – after which he'll proceed with his next question to you. He'll go on in this way until the sum total of the received information forms a coherent pattern inside him.

HUML: How interesting! He sort of does your work for you, doesn't he?

MISS BALCAR: At a certain stage –

HUML: That's what I meant – at a certain stage –

(KRIEBL *is still fiddling with Puzuk, worrying the keyboard, turning the crank, peering into the eyepiece, etc.* MISS BALCAR *stares at him.*)

MISS BALCAR: Anything wrong, Mr Kriebl?

KRIEBL: He felt rather cool, so Machal and I massaged his control panel a bit to warm him up to the right degree.

MISS BALCAR: And what about the electrodes?

KRIEBL: Functioning. We can start –

MISS BALCAR: Splendid! Now, put down – (*Dictating*) Eduard Huml, 1928 – beginning of interview 15:25 – first question. (*Calls*) Silence, please!

(KRIEBL, *having typed the data on the keyboard, turns the crank, peers into the eyepiece, and presses a button. The loudspeaker gives out a soft rumbling.* KRIEBL *stares closely at his watch; general suspense. Suddenly, the upstairs door opens and* MACHAL *appears, wearing a lab coat, with a pencil stuck behind his ear.* KRIEBL *again quickly presses a button and turns the crank. The rumbling stops.* MACHAL *takes no notice of anybody, slowly descends, halts, counts the steps, produces from his pocket a grubby slip of paper on which he notes the ascertained number. Having finished, he slowly crosses to* KRIEBL *and hands him the slip of paper.*)

KRIEBL: Thanks, Emil –

(KRIEBL *smooths out the slip of paper on the table, then slides it into Puzuk.* MACHAL *ambles out by the left door.*)

MISS BALCAR: Ready now?

KRIEBL: Ready.

MISS BALCAR: (*Calls*) Silence, please!

(KRIEBL *again turns the crank, presses a button, Puzuk begins to rumble. Once more,* KRIEBL *stares closely at his watch; general suspense. After a while, Puzuk's red light goes on.*)

Red!

(KRIEBL *quickly presses a button and turns the crank. The light goes out and the rumbling stops. Awkward pause.*)

He's overheated. You must have massaged him too hard –

KRIEBL: We massaged him just right; more likely it's a stuck switch.

MISS BALCAR: What shall we do?

KRIEBL: He must cool off a bit. (*To* HUML) Have you a fridge?

HUML: Yes. In the kitchen –

(KRIEBL *unplugs Puzuk's cord and together with* MISS BALCAR *carries Puzuk out by the back door, which has meanwhile been opened by* HUML. HUML *follows, leaving door open. Pause.*)

(*Offstage*) Will he get in?

KRIEBL: (*Offstage*) Do you mind if I take out the milk bottles for a moment?

HUML: (*Offstage*) Not in the least –

(*Shortly after, they all return by the back door, slowly cross to the table, sit down as before and wait. Longish uneasy pause.*)

MISS BALCAR: Hope he won't get too cold in there –

KRIEBL: He'll make himself heard when he's cold!

MISS BALCAR: Let's hope so –

*(Longish uneasy pause.)*

KRIEBL: *(To* HUML) Fond of fruit?

HUML: How did you know?

KRIEBL: I saw your supplies in the kitchen –

HUML: My mother lives in the country, so she sends us some occasionally –

KRIEBL: Good for you –

*(Longish uneasy pause.)*

MISS BALCAR: *(To* KRIEBL) What about giving him an electric shock?

KRIEBL: Better not. That usually gives him stray thoughts. And also the condensor is likely to get troublesome then –

*(Longish uneasy pause.)*

*(To* KRIEBL) You come from the country?

HUML: Yes.

KRIEBL: Mountains?

HUML: How did you know?

KRIEBL: The plums your mother sent you grow only in high altitudes.

HUML: Yes, they are indeed high-altitude plums.

*(Longish uneasy pause.)*

MISS BALCAR: *(To* KRIEBL) When did you oil him last?

KRIEBL: Day before yesterday.

MISS BALCAR: Day before yesterday?

KRIEBL: That's right.

MISS BALCAR: So that in fact he's been freshly oiled –

KRIEBL: Right.

*(Longish uneasy pause.)*

HUML: *(To* MISS BALCAR) May I ask you something?

MISS BALCAR: By all means –

HUML: The questions I'm going to be asked by the instrument –

MISS BALCAR: Puzuk –

HUML: I mean Puzuk – have they a specific investigational objective?

MISS BALCAR: What do you mean?

HUML: I'd be interested to know whether this is a matter of a specific case to which my testimony is somehow related, or just a sort of – how shall I put it – complex investigation – sort of preventive evidence –

MISS BALCAR: Why the alternatives? Our investigation is complex precisely because it is concerned with a specific case.

HUML: Oh! I see! And can you tell me who is your subject?

MISS BALCAR: Who? You, of course.

HUML: Me?

*(Just then, Puzuk's sharp siren starts wailing offstage.)*

KRIEBL: What did I tell you! Now he's cold!

(MISS BALCAR *and* KRIEBL *jump up and run out by the back door, leaving it open,* KRIEBL *starts to follow. Before he gets to the door,* RENATA *enters by the back door, wearing Mrs Huml's apron, and carefully carrying a tray with lunch: two plates with steaming stew, a pot of mustard, a basket with bread, glasses, beer, knives and forks. She begins setting the table.* HUML *crosses to table and helps* RENATA. *Then they both sit down and start eating. Longish pause, finally interrupted by* RENATA.)

RENATA: You're not just trying to jolly me along, are you?

HUML: Not in the least. I want to put an end to it, I really do. Only you've got to try and understand it's not an easy matter. We've lived together for ten years, she has nobody but me, she can't imagine her life without me – some beer?

RENATA: Just a drop –

(HUML *pours beer for* RENATA *and himself, then continues.*)

HUML: Prospectively, she rather counts on my parting with you and living again only with her – well, you know how it is, women are terribly sensitive about these things; in any case, it's going to be a blow for her.

RENATA: I've never even suggested you shouldn't do it tactfully, that goes without saying, doesn't it?

*(Pause. They go on eating.)*

HUML: Why don't you take some mustard –

RENATA: Sorry, I loathe mustard –

*(Pause. They go on eating.)*

Listen, Eddi –

HUML: Yes?

RENATA: Glad I've come?

HUML: You know I am –

RENATA: Why don't you say something tender to me?

HUML: You know my imagination doesn't work that way –

RENATA: A man who's in love always finds a way to express what he feels!

HUML: I think you're attractive –

RENATA: That's not much, is it?

HUML: I'm very fond of you –

RENATA: Is that all?

HUML: Sorry, kitty-cat, I'm really no good at using big words! Which doesn't mean, however, that I don't feel anything –

RENATA: If you felt something big, no words would seem big enough to you! (*Excitedly*) After all, we can part, just say the word!

HUML: Starting that again, are you!

RENATA: I'm a fool, I really am!

(RENATA *throws down her knife and fork, jumps up in great agitation, runs out sobbing by the left door and slams it.* HUML *finishes his bite, gets up, crosses to the left door, tries it; it is locked. He hesitates, then addresses the locked door.*)

HUML: Renata – (*Pause.*) Kitty-cat – (*Pause.*) Come on! (*Pause.*) Remember the Dolomites! In that old kiln?

(*He waits a while. As there is no response from* RENATA, *he shrugs and walks back. Just then,* BLANKA *enters by the back door, closes it, crosses to the table, sits down, takes shorthand pad and pencil and gets ready for dictation.*)

Where did we stop?

BLANKA: (*Reads*) 'Various people have at various times and in various circumstances various needs – '

HUML: Ah! Yes – (*Begins to pace thoughtfully to and fro, while dictating to* BLANKA, *who takes it down in shorthand.*) – and thus attach to various things various values – full stop. Therefore, it would be mistaken to set up a fixed scale of values, valid for all people in all circumstances and at all times – full stop. This does not mean, however, that in all of history there exist no values common to the whole of mankind – full stop. If those values did not exist, mankind would not form a unified whole – full stop. Yet, as a rule, each man – each period – each social group – has its own scale of values, by which the basic, universal values are in a certain way made more concrete – full stop. At the same time, an individual scale of values is always somehow related to other – more general – scales of values – for instance, to those belonging to a given period – which form a sort of framework, or background, to the individual scales – full stop. Would you mind reading me the last sentence?

BLANKA: (*Reads*) 'At the same time, an individual scale of values is always somehow related to other, more general, scales of values, for instance, to those belonging to a given period, which form a sort of framework, or background, to the individual scales.'

HUML: That's pretty good. Let's go on. Among the most basic values of presentday man one can include, for example, work – in other words – the opportunity to do that which would enable man to fulfil himself completely, to develop his own specific potentialities, his relationships with other people, his moral principles – certain convictions regarding his concept of the world, his faith in something to which he can commit his life – full stop. Got it?

BLANKA: Yes.

HUML: Good. And now a new paragraph, please. The state in which man finds himself after he has satisfied one of his particular needs – i.e. when he has achieved a particular value – is called happiness – full stop. However, since – as we have already said – people have – (*Stops, ponders, then turns to* BLANKA.) Blanka –

BLANKA: Yes, Dr Huml?

HUML: That Rudy of yours – is he your first love?

BLANKA: Yes.

HUML: How old is he?

BLANKA: Eighteen.

HUML: Eighteen? Really? (*Pause. He becomes dreamy.*) Eighteen!

When I was eighteen! Good God! I was devouring Hegel, Schopenhauer, Nietzsche, writing essays on metaphysics, editing a student magazine, I was hopelessly in love with a medical student, Ann Gluecksmann – by the way, you remind me of her a little – and in addition, I still managed to frequent the Pygmalion Bar daily and play football for the Liberal Youth Club twice a week! What a strange time that was – rather nice – (*Pause.*) Where did we stop?

BLANKA: (*Reads*) 'However, since, as we have already said, people have – '

HUML: (*Again begins to pace thoughtfully to and fro while dictating*) However, since – as we have already said – people have a great variety of needs and thus consider a great variety of things to be of value – the content of a state of happiness is also extremely varied – full stop. This is why, in spite of the fact that we all have our own precise image of what is happiness, we find it very hard to agree on a particular definition of happiness which would be satisfactory for all – full stop. New paragraph –

BLANKA: Excuse me a moment – (*Gets up and walks towards the back door.*)

HUML: Ah! The water's boiling!

(BLANKA *exits by the back door,* HUML *follows, the door stays open. Pause.*)

MRS HUML: (*Offstage*) And what's this?

HUML: (*Offstage*) There's honey in that?

(MRS HUML *enters by the back door, wearing a dressing-gown over her dress, sits down at table and continues with her breakfast. Shortly after,* MR HUML *shuffles in by the back door, dishevelled, carrying a jar of honey. He, too, sits down at table and goes on with his breakfast. To start with, he dabs honey on a roll. Pause.*)

MRS HUML: Oh well, another opportunity missed!

HUML: Look, it's not the last time I'm going to see her – she's supposed to drop in today, I'll give it another try –

MRS HUML: One time she's full of fun, next time you're sorry for her, another time you're not feeling well – listen, be honest, aren't you perhaps postponing the whole thing on purpose?

HUML: Why on earth should I do that?

MRS HUML: Maybe you actually love her –

HUML: You know very well I don't love her! I only find her sexually exciting, and even that far less than at the beginning.

MRS HUML: Let's hope so! And what do you say to her when she asks if you love her?

HUML: When possible, I try to change the subject. Want some?

MRS HUML: Quite right! Would you put some on my roll?

HUML: (*Dabs honey on her roll.*) Of course, she got me up against the wall a few times, so I couldn't help giving her a positive answer.

MRS HUML: But it didn't come from your heart, did it?

HUML: No. Here you are – (*Passes her the roll.*)

MRS HUML: Listen, Eddi –

HUML: Mmnn –

MRS HUML: Promise me you'll finally wind it up in some reasonable way. We just can't go on like this! It makes me suffer more than you think. Most of all in the evenings when I sit at home, mending your socks or your underpants – and all the time I know you're with her, having fun, spending our money, driving her about in our car, kissing her –

(*Pause. They continue their breakfast.*)

I'm sure you'll think I'm being silly, but do you know what bothers me most at those moments?

HUML: What?

MRS HUML: The idea that you might just then be sleeping with her!

HUML: You know very well that I don't sleep with her so often; after all, we have nowhere to go. We usually end up by kissing; at the very most I might touch her breasts a bit. Pass me a roll, will you –

MRS HUML: (*Passing him a roll*) I hope you aren't making it all up just to calm me down! Does it ever occur to you what it's like for me, having to pretend in front of others that I don't know anything, to put up with their meaningful glances and ignore them, having to play the silly housewife who doesn't know what's going on! Besides, if it's not worth your while to break it off on my account, you ought to do it for your own sake – just look at yourself! Can't you see the way you're slipping? Do you read anything at all any more?

HUML: More butter?

MRS HUML: Finish it, if you like.

HUML: I told you, didn't I, I want to do it in stages –

MRS HUML: I know your blessed stages, so far you haven't budged!

HUML: What do you mean? Only last night I began to prepare the ground –

MRS HUML: Did you? How?

HUML: Well, to start with, I didn't kiss her neck as I usually do –

MRS HUML: You kiss her neck? You're never told me that!

HUML: She likes it and it excites me too in a way.

MRS HUML: And then? Did you tell her you still love me?

HUML: For a start, I said I like you as the companion of my life.

MRS HUML: Well, that's at least something. What did she say?

HUML: She insisted I should divorce you.

MRS HUML: I hope you didn't promise her any such thing!

HUML: She was so insistent, I had to agree – on the surface. But deep down I kept my own counsel and I didn't commit myself to anything definite. Listen, Vlasta, hate to mention it, but it's almost half past –

MRS HUML: Is it? Goodness! Here I go on gossiping and now I might be late for work! (*Jumps up, finishes her tea standing, runs out by the back door. Offstage*) Are you staying home for lunch?

HUML: Yes.

MRS HUML: (*Offstage*) Well, come out here! I'll show you where it is.

(*Short pause. Then* HUML *slowly rises and shuffles out by the back door. Pause.*)

(*Offstage*) It's stew. Leave it in the pot and then just put it on the stove as is. Wait until it's warm, then dish it out and shove the pot back in there –

(MISS BALCAR *and* KRIEBL *enter by the back door, carefully carrying Puzuk between them. They are followed by* HUML, *fully dressed and spruced up.* MISS BALCAR *and* KRIEBL *place Puzuk on the table.* KRIEBL *plugs in the cord; all sit down as before;* KRIEBL *fiddles with Puzuk.*)

MISS BALCAR: Hope the mixture in his capillaries didn't freeze up –

KRIEBL: No – his siren wouldn't have worked, would it? We can start –

MISS BALCAR: Splendid! Now, put down – (*Dictating*) Eduard Huml, 1928 – beginning of interview 15.55 – first question. (*Calls*) Silence, please!

(KRIEBL, *having typed the data on the keyboard, turns the crank, peers into the eyepiece, and presses a button. The loudspeaker gives out a soft rumbling.* KRIEBL *stares closely at his watch; general suspense. Suddenly* BECK, *in an overcoat, enters by the left door. All turn towards him.* KRIEBL *again quickly presses a button and turns the crank. The rumbling stops.* BECK, *paying no attention to anybody, angrily stalks to and fro. Longish pause. All follow his movements with some embarrassment. At last,* MISS BALCAR *produces a small box of chocolates our of her pocket, offering them to* BECK.) Chocolate?

(BECK *has noticed* MISS BALCAR*'s gesture, but chooses to ignore it.* MISS BALCAR *waits for a moment, then, embarrassed, replaces the box in her pocket.* BECK *goes on pacing about. Longish uneasy pause.* MISS BALCAR *nervously glances at* BECK *a few times, hesitates, then asks:*)

Anything wrong, Mr Beck?

(BECK *gives* MISS BALCAR *a black look, turns and exits by the back door, slamming it.* HUML *looks questioningly at* MISS BALCAR, *but she quickly turns to* KRIEBL.)

Ready now?

KRIEBL: Ready.

MISS BALCAR: (*Calls*) Silence, please!

(KRIEBL *again turns the crank, presses a button, Puzuk begins to rumble. Once more,* KRIEBL *stares closely at his watch. General suspense. After a while, Puzuk's red light goes on.*)

Again red!

(KRIEBL *quickly presses a button and turns the crank. The light goes out and the rumbling stops. Awkward pause.*)

He shouldn't have stayed so long in the fridge –

KRIEBL: Hasn't been there so long.

MISS BALCAR: Well, what's the matter with him?

KRIEBL: The mixture in his capillaries may have frozen, that's all. He'll have to get warmed up. (*To* HUML) Have you an oven?

HUML: Yes.

(KRIEBL *unplugs Puzuk's cord and together with* MISS BALCAR *carries Puzuk out by the back door, which has meanwhile been opened by* HUML. *Pause.*)

(*Offstage*) In there – second door on the left.

KRIEBL: (*Offstage*) Perfect fit!

(*Just then,* HUML *and* BLANKA *enter by the right door, both a bit out of breath.* HUML *holds* BLANKA *by the hand, leads her to the table and seats her at her place.* BLANKA *is somewhat excited, straightens her hair.* HUML *is embarrassed.*)

HUML: I'm sorry – it was just a sudden impulse – I mean, a sort of joke, really – I'm so sorry, do forgive me –

BLANKA: Promise me it won't happen again!

HUML: You have my word!

(*Short pause.* BLANKA *has calmed down, takes shorthand pad off the table and reads.*)

BLANKA: However, just as the various values man wants to achieve are open to various valuations –

HUML: Ah! Yes –

(*He begins to pace thoughtfully to and fro, while dictating to* BLANKA *who takes it down in shorthand.*)

– to various valuations from various points of view – so is the activity man puts forth in order to achieve those values – full stop. Basically, one can say there exist two kinds of activity – a positive one – for instance, the struggle for justice – and a negative one – for example, scheming – full stop. At the same time, the moving force of every activity is that which might be described as ambition – in the broadest sense of the word – full stop. Regarding ambition, one must again distinguish between two kinds – dash – I mean colon –

BLANKA: Colon?

HUML: Yes, colon: a healthy ambition and an unhealthy one – full stop. By healthy ambition we understand a really fruitful, profound interest in a definite object – man's natural desire to fulfil himself within the sphere of this interest – full stop. On the other hand, when a desire to use one's resources does not stem from inner motives, but is merely a means towards achieving certain superficial values – such as power, money publicity, etc. – we talk of unhealthy ambition – full stop. (*Halts, ponders, then turns to* BLANKA.) Listen, Blanka, what do you actually think of me?

BLANKA: Who, me?

HUML: Yes, you –

BLANKA: That you're very well educated, Dr Huml –

HUML: Do be serious, please!

BLANKA: I'm being serious –

HUML: Naughty little thing, aren't you? (*Looks at his watch.*) Let's finish at least this paragraph. Where did we stop?

BLANKA: (*Reads*) 'But is merely a means towards achieving certain superficial values – such as power, money, publicity, etc. – we talk of unhealthy ambition.'

HUML: (*Again begins pacing thoughtfully to and fro, while dictating to* BLANKA) Whilst positive activity stems above all from healthy ambition, negative activity stems mostly from unhealthy ambition – full stop. Naturally, the above is only a general scheme and as such presupposes some deviations – as, for example, when negative activity stems from healthy ambition, or – on the contrary – when unhealthy ambition leads to positive activity – full stop. Got it?

BLANKA: Yes.

HUML: Well, that'll be all for today. Thank you very much.

BLANKA: Pleasure, I'm sure.

(*She shoves shorthand pad and pencil into her briefcase which has been lying on the table, closes briefcase, gets up.*)

HUML: Tomorrow at nine again, all right?

BLANKA: Yes, Dr Huml.

HUML: And don't forget to give that message to Mr Pittermann –

BLANKA: If I don't get hold of him, I'll leave it with Mrs Blaha –

HUML: OK.

(BLANKA *just stands, waiting for something.* HUML *is at a loss. Awkward pause.*)

BLANKA: May I have my coat?

HUML: Good gracious!

(HUML *runs towards the back door, but before he can leave, the doorbell rings.* HUML *halts, turns to* BLANKA.)

Would you mind – there – in the wardrobe –

(BLANKA *exits by the back door.* HUML *crosses to the right door, peers through the peep-hole, then opens.* BLANKA *stands outside the door, wearing a coat and carrying her briefcase.*)

BLANKA: Good morning –

HUML: Good morning, Blanka, do come in –

BLANKA: Am I not too early?

HUML: Not at all, I'm glad you're here already now, I'm expecting someone at twelve, so we'll have to cut it short a bit. May I –

BLANKA: Thanks –

(HUML *helps* BLANKA *out of her coat, carries it out by the back door, returns at once.* BLANKA *has meanwhile taken a shorthand pad and pencil out of her briefcase. She puts briefcase on table and sits down in her place.*)

HUML: Well, what's the news?

BLANKA: They've mended the lift.

HUML: Finally! And what about the heating, working all right now?

BLANKA: Not yet. And how do you feel, Dr Huml?

HUML: Thanks, almost back to normal, still a bit shaky, you know, that's all. I've been out already a few times, as a matter of fact, I might drop in at the Institute day after tomorrow – (*Pause.*) Well, ready?

BLANKA: I'm ready –

HUML: OK. Write down – Chapter 5 – Regarding Values – Introduction. (*He begins to pace thoughtfully to and fro, while dictating to* BLANKA, *who takes it down in shorthand.*)

BLANKA: Is that a title?

HUML: Yes. By a value we mean that which satisfies some human need – semicolon – the structure of values thus always reflects the structure of human needs – full stop. We distinguish material values – for example, food, clothes, houses, etc. – from spiritual values – for instance, particular ideas, or pieces of knowledge, relationship to other people, artistic experience, etc. – full stop. Various people have at various – (*Suddenly stops and turns to* BLANKA.) I wonder if you realize what we've forgotten.

BLANKA: Put the kettle on for coffee?

HUML: Correct!

(BLANKA *gets up and exits by the back door, leaving it open. At that moment,* RENATA *enters irritably by the left door, wearing* MRS HUML*'s apron.*)

RENATA: The Dolomites! The Dolomites! That's all you can talk to me about!

HUML: Come on, kitty-cat, pull yourself together! (HUML *walks over to* RENATA, *puts his arms lightly around her and begins soothingly to kiss her cheeks, forehead, hair. To start with,* RENATA *resists a little, but gradually gives in. They end up locked in a long, passionate kiss.* RENATA *then gently frees herself – she is smiling now – and throws her arms around* HUML*'s neck.*)

RENATA: You know what I dreamed about last night?

HUML: What?

RENATA: That we got married in a mosque!

HUML: That's absurd –

RENATA: Well, you see, that's the sort of dreams I have!

(*She kisses* HUML, *then releases him, takes him by the hand and leads him up the stairs towards the bedroom. She stops at the door and turns to him.*)

This is our kiln!

HUML: Our mosque –

(RENATA *kisses* HUML *once more and they both exit by the upstairs door, closing the door behind them. Just then,* MISS BALCAR *and* KRIEBL *enter by the back door, followed by*

HUML. HUML *closes the door, all three slowly cross to the table, sit down as before and wait. Longish uneasy pause.*)

MISS BALCAR: Will he let us know if he gets too hot?

KRIEBL: The siren functions normally –

(*Longish uneasy pause.*)

(*To* HUML) I've got an aunt in the country.

HUML: Oh?

KRIEBL: I spend my summer holidays with her. It's not in the mountains, but there are lakes –

HUML: How nice –

(*Longish uneasy pause.*)

RENATA: (*To* KRIEBL) Won't it do him some harm, the way we keep moving him about?

KRIEBL: No – he's used to it, isn't he?

(*Longish uneasy pause.*)

HUML: (*To* MISS BALCAR) I realize that just now asking questions is your job rather than mine –

MISS BALCAR: Go on, you may ask anything you like –

HUML: You said I was the subject of your inquiry –

MISS BALCAR: That's right.

HUML: I'd be interested to know in what sense precisely, I mean – how far –

MISS BALCAR: Completely.

HUML: As I see, there's an anthropological aspect to your work – which means I'll surely find myself on familiar ground! Besides, it's rather logical that you feel you must get to know a person in the round if you want to understand his actions –

MISS BALCAR: Are you familiar with anthropology?

HUML: Well, anthropology is not exactly my field, but I do work in social sciences –

MISS BALCAR: Really? These questions have been ignored here in recent years. Therefore the need to fill in the gap is all the more pressing.

HUML: I believe there are some facts one might be able to lean on; the rest of the world has been dealing with the problem of man for years –

MISS BALCAR: We're aware of that. Particularly the so-called synthetic anthropology, as it has been developed in the United States, is very closely related to our own research. Naturally, we are trying to learn from foreign experiments, even though in principle we don't propose simply accepting their results in a mechanistic way.

HUML: Well, that's clear enough, you have your own specific requirements. And how far do you lean on the results concerning the subject of man arrived at by other scientific disciplines?

MISS BALCAR: We lean on them a great deal, but actually only in sort of negative way. You see, for the various specialized sciences, man represents no more than a particular function or a general category – be it as a highly developed mammal, as a maker, or as a psychological prototype – and thus in each case their concept of man depicts no more than one particular, partial characteristic – which is moreover always shared by many other individuals as well. On the other hand, we are concerned with the man in the round, a man whose complexity has not been simplified, whose human uniqueness has been preserved. This means working on a qualitatively new level where we cannot get by with a simple accumulation of what is already here – rather, on the contrary, we must start at the point where the individual specialized sciences end.

HUML: Well, this is indeed a modern approach to the subject! What's more, your results might have a really broad application. If, for example, you managed to find a way to shape human individuality scientifically, it would be of the greatest importance not only to yourselves, but to the whole of society –

MISS BALCAR: Most certainly! If nothing else, it might open a way to a rationally organized limiting of such phenomena as, for example, alienation.

(*Suddenly,* BECK, *in his overcoat, enters by the back door. He takes no notice of anybody, angrily crosses to the upstage wall, halts, turning back on the others. All watch him with some embarrassment. After a while he speaks up without turning.*)

BECK: Tomorrow I'm going fishing and that's that!

*(Awkward pause.)*

MISS BALCAR: Surely, you don't mean that, Mr Beck! What would we do without you? You do know how much we need you – *(Awkward pause.* BECK *does not react.)*

But who would direct our whole research work? Not one of us has anywhere near your qualifications –

*(Awkward pause.* BECK *does not react.)*

Really, you couldn't do that to us, Mr Beck – *(Awkward pause. Suddenly* BECK *turns and snaps.)*

BECK: You heard me!

*(Beck stalks energetically out by the left door and slams it.* HUML *looks questioningly at* MISS BALCAR, *but she quickly turns to* KRIEBL.)

MISS BALCAR: Do you know where Mrs Huml works?

KRIEBL: Where?

MISS BALCAR: In a toy shop!

KRIEBL: *(To* HUML) Oh?

*(Just then, Puzuk's sharp siren starts wailing offstage.)*

What did I tell you! Now he's hot!

(MISS BALCAR *and* KRIEBL *jump up and run out by the back door.* HUML *follows. All of a sudden, the telephone starts ringing and goes on for quite a while. At last,* HUML *runs in by the upstairs door, wearing only his trousers and shirt, with a towel around his neck. He reaches the telephone and picks up the receiver.)*

HUML: *(Into the telephone)* Yes, speaking. *(Pause.)* Is it absolutely necessary? You see, I've been ill – may I ask who's calling? *(Pause.)* I see – I see – I'll be here – not at all – *(Slowly he replaces the receiver, ponders for a moment, then shakes his head in puzzlement and slowly returns upstairs. Shortly after,* MISS BALCAR *and* KRIEBL *enter by the back door, carefully carrying Puzuk between them. They are followed by* HUML, *fully dressed and spruced up.* MISS BALCAR *and* KRIEBL *place Puzuk on the table.* KRIEBL *plugs in the cord; all sit down as before;* KRIEBL *fiddles with Puzuk.)*

MISS BALCAR: Hope his insulators haven't burned out –

KRIEBL: No – there'd be smoke coming out of him, wouldn't there? We can start –

MISS BALCAR: Splendid! Now, put down – (*Dictating*) Eduard Huml, 1928 – beginning of interview 16:32 – first question. (*Calls*) Silence, please! (KRIEBL, *having typed the data on the keyboard, turns the crank, peers into the eyepiece, and presses a button. The loudspeaker gives out a soft rumbling.* KRIEBL *stares closely at his watch; general suspense. After while, Puzuk's green light goes on.*)

Splendid! It's green!

KRIEBL: About time!

(*Out of Puzuk's loudspeaker issues an effeminate voice.*)

PUZUK: Tell me –

(*Pause. Suspense.*)

Tell me –

(*Pause. Suspense.*)

Tell me please –

(*Pause. Suspense.*)

Karel?

KRIEBL: (*To Puzuk*) What is it?

PUZUK: May I have a little rest?

## ACT TWO

*Huml's flat: The same as in Act One. Again the stage is empty. Offstage the sound of water filling up a receptacle. When, judging by the sound, the receptacle is full, the sound ceases and* HUML, *wearing a suit, enters by the back door, with a small watering-can full of water. He slowly crosses to the cactus on the commode upstage and beings to water it with care. Then, sound of key turning in the right door and* MRS HUML *enters, wearing an overcoat, carrying a bulging shopping bag and under her arm a table lamp.*

HUML: Hello!

MRS HUML: Hello! Well?

HUML: (*Finishes watering, puts can behind commode, walks over to* MRS HUML *and takes lamp from her.*) Let me see –

MRS HUML: (*Puts bag on table and exhausted, sinks into a chair.*) Did you talk to her?

HUML: Handy, isn't it? How much?

MRS HUML: Hundred and fifty.

HUML: Not bad – (*Lamp in hand, exits by the left door. Offstage*) I'd better put in a stronger bulb –

(*Pause. He returns by the left door, having left lamp in the study and having taken off his jacket. He is putting on his dressing-gown over his shirt; closes door.*)

Have we a stronger bulb?

(*Short pause.*)

MRS HUML: You are a horrible man!

HUML: What's the matter?

MRS HUML: It would be too much for you to say one kind word to me!

HUML: Well, thank you very much, you found a wonderful lamp – (*Pause.*) I'm awfully pleased with it – (*Pause.*) It's nice that you're home again –

MRS HUML: Oh, skip it!

HUML: Well, what do you want, for heaven's sake?

(*He notices a newspaper sticking out of the shopping bag, pulls it out, crosses to the easy chair, sits down, makes himself comfortable and begins to glance through the paper. Pause.*)

MRS HUML: I asked a question –

HUML: (*Without looking up*) So did I –

MRS HUML: Why don't you look for yourself! You know where we keep the bulbs –

(*Pause.* HUML *is reading.*)

You never kiss *me* on the neck!

HUML: (*Looks up, surprised*) What did you say?

MRS HUML: I said, you never kiss me on the neck –

HUML: I've kissed you enough during my lifetime!

MRS HUML: But not on the neck, with me that never excited you! Make no mistake, we women remember that sort of thing very well!

HUML: Should you stop speaking for womankind and see about starting dinner? (*Again turns to his paper.*)

(MRS HUML *gapes at him for a while, then gets up excitedly, grabs her shopping bag off the table.*)

MRS HUML: I'm a fool, I really am!

(MRS HUML, *offended, walks out by the back door.* HUML *looks after her, for a moment remains sitting, then slowly gets up and with the paper open in his hands shuffles towards the back door. He halts at the threshold and speaks towards backstage.*)

HUML: Vlasta, dear – (*Pause.*) You know I didn't mean it that way – (*Pause.*) Remember the Alps? In that old mill?

(*Pause, then* MRS HUML *returns by the back door tying an apron over her dress.*)

MRS HUML: The Alps! The Alps! That's all you can talk to me about!

HUML: Come on, kitty-cat, pull yourself together! (HUML *approaches* MRS HUML, *puts his hands on her shoulders from behind, pulls her towards himself and gives her a long kiss on her neck.* MRS HUML *half closes her eyes and smiles happily. Then gently feels herself.*)

MRS HUML: You see! I need so little to be happy –

HUML: I had no idea it meant so much to you –

HUML: What would you like for dinner? There's cauliflower, or sausages – or I could make you an omelette, if you like –

HUML: Sausages would be just fine –

MRS HUML: And during dinner you'll tell me how it went! I can hardly wait –

(MRS HUML *hastens out by the back door.* HUML *stands for a while pondering, newspaper in hand, then shuffles up the stairs to the bedroom and exits by the upstairs door. Just then,* BLANKA *enters by the back door, carefully carrying small tray with two cups of coffee. She puts it on the table, sits down in her place, takes a cup and stirs.* HUML *enters by the back door, fully dressed, carrying small bowl with biscuits, leaves door ajar, crosses to table and offers* BLANKA *a biscuit.* BLANKA *takes one.*)

BLANKA: Thank you –

HUML: (*Puts bowl on table, sits down, stirring his coffee. Longish pause.*) Are you going to see Pittermann today?

BLANKA: If I can get hold of him –

HUML: Well, if you do see him, please tell him to send me – perhaps via you – his comments on the editorial plan, I'd like to have another look at them –

BLANKA: I'll tell him –

(*Pause. Both sip their coffee.*)

We can go on working –

HUML: Why don't you finish your coffee –

BLANKA: No, really –

HUML: All right? Well, where did we stop?

BLANKA: (*Takes shorthand pad and pencil from table and reads:*) 'To agree on a particular definition of happiness which would be satisfactory for all.'

HUML: Ah, yes! Now – new paragraph. When one particular need of a man has been satisfied – it actually ceases thereby – full stop. However, man is – to coin a phrase – in constant need of further needs – for the moving force of his life is not that state in which all his needs have been satisfied, but the process of continually satisfying them – man's effort towards their gratification – full stop.

(HUML *gets up and begins to pace thoughtfully to and fro, while slowly dictating to* BLANKA. *Now and then he halts at the table and takes a sip of coffee.* BLANKA *takes down his dictation in shorthand and she too occasionally takes a sip of her coffee.*) There exist situations – for example in some advanced western countries – in which all the basic human needs have been satisfied and still people are not happy – they experience feelings of depression, boredom, frustration, etc. – full stop. In these situations man begins to desire that which in fact he perhaps does not need at all – he simply persuades himself he has certain needs which he does not have – or he vaguely desires something which he cannot specify and thus cannot strive for – full stop. Hence, as soon as man has satisfied one need – i.e. achieved happiness – another so far unsatisfied need is born in him so that every happiness is always simultaneously a negation of happiness, because –

(HUML *halts near* BLANKA *and stares at her.* BLANKA *does not realize what is going on, thinking he is merely searching for a precise formulation. Longish pause. Suddenly,* HUML *leaps towards* BLANKA, *falls on his knees, grabs her shoulders and tries to kiss her.* BLANKA *is startled and cries out.*)

BLANKA: Oh!

(*A short struggle ensues,* HUML *attempting to put his arms around* BLANKA *and kiss her;* BLANKA *resists; finally she gives him a push;* HUML *loses his balance and falls down.* BLANKA *jumps up.*) You should be ashamed of yourself, Dr Huml!

(BLANKA, *alarmed, runs out by the back door;* HUML *looks sheepishly after her for a moment, then quickly gets up and follows her out by the right door. From behind the door his receding voice is heard.*)

HUML: (*Calling offstage*) Blanka! Blanka! Blanka – listen to me!

RENATA: (*Offstage*) Does she ever dust in here?

HUML: (*Enters by the back door, crosses to table, sits down.*) I'm sure she does –

(*Shortly after* HUML, RENATA *enters by the back door, she is putting on* MRS HUML's *dressing-gown over her dress.*)

RENATA: Don't I remind you of her?

HUML: A bit –

RENATA: And you don't mind?

HUML: I do –

(RENATA *takes off the dressing-gown, takes it out by the back door, returns at once, closes the door, crosses to the easy chair, sits down, lights a cigarette. Short pause.*)

RENATA: And what do you say to her when she asks if you love her?

HUML: When possible, I try to change the subject. What about some lunch, kitty-cat? There's some stew –

RENATA: Listen, Eddi –

HUML: Mmnn –

RENATA: Promise me you'll finally wind it up in some reasonable way! We just can't go on like this! It makes me suffer more than you think. Most of all in the evenings when we're together, driving around in your car, having fun, kissing each other – and all the time I know that in a while it'll be all over, you'll go back to her, to the warm family hearth, where meanwhile she's been mending your socks or your underpants; she'll give you a bite to eat, she'll bring your pyjamas, you'll turn on the radio softly and then you'll both climb into one huge bed and stay there the whole night – (*Pause.*) I'm sure you'll think I'm being silly, but do you know what bothers me most at those moments?

HUML: What?

RENATA: The idea that you'll be sleeping with her after you go home –

HUML: You know very well that I now sleep with her only very rarely –

RENATA: I hope you aren't making it all up just to calm me down! Does it ever occur to you what it's like for me, always having to keep secrets, to hide, to pretend in front of others that I don't know you, having to come to you like a thief! If it's not worth your while to break it off on my account, you ought to do it for your own sake – just look at yourself! Can't you see the way you're slipping?

HUML: I told you, didn't I, I want to do it in stages. What about some lunch?

RENATA: I know your blessed stages, so far you haven't budged!

HUML: What do you mean? Only this morning I began to prepare the ground.

RENATA: Did you? How? Did you tell her you love me?

HUML: For a start, I said I find you sexually exciting.

RENATA: Well that's at least something. What did she say?

HUML: She insisted I should part with you. What about some lunch?

RENATA: I hope you didn't promise her any such thing!

HUML: She was so insistent, I had to agree – on the surface. But deep down I kept my own counsel and I didn't commit myself to anything definite.

RENATA: Really? And then? Did you suggest to her you want a divorce?

HUML: I said you were rather counting on it – prospectively. What about some lunch? There's some stew –

RENATA: I'll have a look –

(RENATA *gets up and exits by the back door.* HUML *slowly follows her. At the door he meets* RENATA, *who has just returned, wearing a coat.* HUML *turns and walks with her towards the right door.*)

Well, can I count on you discussing it with her this evening?

HUML: And what if she asks me why I didn't tell her before, right when I started with you?

RENATA: Just tell her you're very sorry, but for a long time you saw it as only a passing affair – not really worth mentioning –

HUML: But that's exactly what she minds most about the whole thing –

RENATA: Don't worry, you'll find a way!

(*The doorbell rings.* HUML *starts.*)

HUML: They're here! (*Grabs* RENATA *and drags her back to the back door.*) Wait in the bathroom, I'll fetch you in a minute –

(HUML *pushes* RENATA *out by the back door, and hastens to the right door, first peers through the peep-hole, then opens.* MISS BALCAR *enters first.* KRIEBL *and* MACHAL *follow, each carrying two vast suitcases;* BECK *is the last to enter. All wear overcoats.*)

MISS BALCAR: Dr Huml?

HUML: Yes. Come in –

MISS BALCAR: We phoned –

HUML: Yes, I've been expecting you –

MISS BALCAR: This is Mr Kriebl, our technician; Mr Machal, our surveyor; I'm Dr Balcar – and this is Mr Beck, our supervisor –

HUML: How do you do –

MISS BALCAR: The boys will have to unpack their instruments and set them up –

HUML: Instruments?

MISS BALCAR: That's right. Where can they go so they won't be too much in our way?

HUML: Well, perhaps there – to the study –

(KRIEBL *and* MACHAL, *carrying their suitcases, exit by the back door.* HUML *crosses to* MISS BALCAR.)

Allow me –

MISS BALCAR: Thank you –

(HUML *helps* MISS BALCAR *out of her coat and turns to* BECK.)

HUML: Won't you take off your coat?

(BECK *makes a disparaging gesture.* HUML, *puzzled, takes Miss Balcar's coat out by the left door and instantly returns.* MISS BALCAR *makes herself comfortable in the easy-chair.* HUML *offers a chair to* BECK *who does not react, but instead begins to stalk thoughtfully to and fro, still in his overcoat.* HUML *uneasily sits down. Short pause.*)

MISS BALCAR: I'm so glad you've agreed to spare us some of your time –

HUML: It's my duty, isn't it?

MISS BALCAR: Most people don't quite see our work that way –

HUML: They're governed by all sorts of prejudices, I suppose –

MISS BALCAR: I'm afraid so.

(*Short awkward pause.* MISS BALCAR *glances nervously at* BECK *who is still pacing around, hesitates for a moment, then produces a small box of chocolates out of her pocket, offering them to* BECK.)

Chocolate?

(BECK *has noticed* MISS BALCAR*'s gesture, but chooses to ignore* *it.* MISS BALCAR *waits for a moment, then, embarrassed, replaces the box in her pocket. Pause.*)

HUML: May I ask what are the instruments you've brought with you?

MISS BALCAR: Apart from a variety of measuring equipment, it's mainly Puzuk.

HUML: Puzuk?

MISS BALCAR: We call him that. It's a small automatic calculator, model CA–213, suitably adapted to our particular needs, of course.

HUML: I had no idea you were so modernized –

(*Short awkward pause.* MISS BALCAR *again nervously glances at the pacing* BECK, *hesitates, then asks:*)

MISS BALCAR: Anything wrong, Mr Beck?

(BECK *gives* MISS BALCAR *a black look, turns and exits by the left door, slamming it.* HUML *looks questioningly at* MISS BALCAR, *but she quickly turns to him.*)

Is your wife out?

HUML: Yes. She has a job.

MISS BALCAR: Oh? Where?

HUML: She's the manager of a toy shop.

MISS BALCAR: Is she really? How nice! When I need any toys I'll get in touch with her.

HUML: But of course! She'll be delighted to help you. Have you children?

MISS BALCAR: No.

(*Short pause. Then* MACHAL, *wearing a lab-coat, enters by the back door, a pencil stuck behind his ear. He takes no notice of anybody, slowly climbs the stairs, halts outside the bedroom, pulls a plumb-line from his pocket and lowers it all the way to the floor, taking care the string remains free of the stairs. After the plumb-line has settled, he hoists it and replaces it in his pocket, produces a grubby slip of paper on which he scribbles some notes. Then he exits by the upstairs door. Short pause.*)

HUML: It's the bedroom – up there –

MISS BALCAR: That's right.

HUML: I'm sorry, but –

MISS BALCAR: Yes?

HUML: You didn't make quite clear on the telephone –

MISS BALCAR: We purposely provide beforehand only the vaguest information. You see, people might prepare themselves, and that would affect the authenticity of their testimony.

HUML: Ah! Yes – I see –

MISS BALCAR: Wait a minute –

*(She listens concentratedly. From offstage a sort of faint rumbling. She calls towards the back door)*

Mr Kriebl?

KRIEBL: (*Offstage*) What is it?

MISS BALCAR: Why does he rumble?

KRIEBL: (*Offstage*) Doesn't want to say. Got a bit cold in the suitcase, I suppose –

MISS BALCAR: But he always gets sweaty in the suitcase –

KRIEBL: (*Offstage*) We've got a new case.

MISS BALCAR: You'll let me know when you're ready, won't you?

KRIEBL: Won't be long –

(*Short pause.*)

HUML: You're carrying somebody around in a suitcase?

MISS BALCAR: (Smiles.) Of course not. We're talking about Puzuk. He's very sensitive, you know. It's always hard to make him feel acclimatized. Yet, his condition is terribly important to us. When he feels right, our work literally flies along. On the other hand, when he's being difficult it makes a lot of complications for us. The most sensitive thing about him are the little relays. Their performance is affected even by the weather – pressure, temperature, humidity – all influence them. When it's raining, or when there's fog we prefer to stay away from fieldwork altogether –

(*Just then the left door opens and* KRIEBL, *in his lab-coat, appears.*)

KRIEBL: We can start –

MISS BALCAR: Splendid!

(MISS BALCAR *quickly gets up and exits with* KRIEBL *by the left door. As soon as they are gone,* HUML *jumps up, runs to the back door, opens it and softly calls:*)

HUML: Renata –

RENATA: (*Offstage, softly*) Took you ages –

HUML: Get ready –

(HUML *leaves the back door open and swiftly exits by the left door which he carefully leaves ajar.*)

MRS HUML: (*Offstage*) Wait until it's warm, then dish it out and shove the pot back in there. Have some bread with it; there's beer in the fridge –

HUML: (*Offstage*) Shall I leave some for you?

(MRS HUML *hastily enters by the back door, wearing her dress and carrying a make-up case.*)

MRS HUML: Finish it if you like. I'll get something for dinner –

(HUML *ambles in by the back door, dressed in his pyjamas, dishevelled, with Mrs Huml's coat over one arm, in the other hand her shopping bag.* MRS HUML *crosses to the mirror, spreads the contents of her case on the commode and hastily puts on her lipstick, mascara and powder, and combs her hair.* HUML *stands nearby with her coat and bag and waits. Pause.*)

And did you suggest to her you want to part with her?

HUML: I said you were rather counting on it – prospectively –

MRS HUML: You really said that? And then?

HUML: What d'you mean, 'then'?

MRS HUML: I mean, how did you go on preparing the ground?

HUML: Well, I didn't laugh at a whole lot of her jokes, for example, and altogether I was more reserved –

MRS HUML: You're not just trying to jolly me along, are you?

HUML: Not in the least. I want to put an end to it, I really do. Only you've got to try and understand it's not an easy matter. We've been having an affair for over a year, she has nobody but me, she can't imagine her life without me, she promises herself a lot from our relationship – she rather counts – prospectively – on my divorcing you and marrying her – well, you know how it is, women are terribly sensitive about these things; in any case, it's going to be a blow for her.

MRS HUML: I've never even suggested you shouldn't do it tactfully. That goes without saying, doesn't it?

HUML: And what do I say if she asks me why I didn't tell her right away, before she began to really count on me?

MRS HUML: Just tell her you're very sorry, but it was a misunderstanding, that you saw it as only a passing affair.

HUML: But that's exactly what she keeps suspecting –

MRS HUML: Don't worry, you'll find a way!

(*Pause.* MRS HUML *is combing her hair.*)

HUML: Listen, Vlasta –

MRS HUML: Yes?

HUML: You wouldn't like to settle the whole thing with her yourself, would you? After all, you're not so deeply involved in this relationship –

MRS HUML: For heaven's sake, what would that look like! Nonsense! You have a word with her today and that's that! (*Finishes her make-up, cleans her comb, swiftly throws all her make-up things into the case.*) Dictating today?

HUML: Yes.

MRS HUML: Scripts?

HUML: No, that thing for the VCA.

(MRS HUML *shoves the make-up case into her shopping bag, held by* HUML, *who then helps her into her coat.*)

MRS HUML: Shall I buy that table lamp for you?

HUML: Would you?

(MRS HUML *is dressed, takes her shopping bag from* HUML, *surveys herself in the mirror, makes sure her keys are in the bag, then crosses to the right door, accompanied by* HUML. *At the door she halts and turns towards* HUML.)

MRS HUML: Well, bye – and I'm keeping my fingers crossed for you!

(*She offers* HUML *her cheek; he kisses it.*)

HUML: Bye –

(MRS HUML *exits.* HUML *shuts the door, stretches, looks at his watch, then leisurely shuffles out by the back door, leaving it open. Offstage* HUML*'s singing is heard, interrupted by sounds of his washing: splashing of water, sighing, brushing of teeth, etc. After a while, sounds suddenly stop. The right door opens and* HUML *and* BLANKA, *both out of breath, enter.* HUML *is fully* *dressed and spruced up. He holds* BLANKA *by the hand, leads her to the table, seats her at her place.* BLANKA *is somewhat excited, straightens her hair.* HUML *is embarrassed.*)

I'm sorry – it was just a sudden impulse – I mean, a sort of joke, really – I'm so sorry – do forgive me –

BLANKA: Promise me it won't happen again!

HUML: You have my word!

(*Short pause.* BLANKA *has calmed down, takes her shorthand pad from the table and reads*:)

BLANKA: 'So that every kind of happiness is always simultaneously a negation of happiness, because – '

HUML: Ah, yes! Now – new paragraph –

BLANKA: Shall I cross out 'because'?

HUML: Do.

(*He begins to pace thoughtfully to and fro, while slowly dictating to* BLANKA, *who takes it down in shorthand.*)

Happiness is thus – on the one hand – in the exact meaning of the term – something very unstable, transient, mutable – on the other hand, however, it is also – as a general state – something very permanent – because man always desires to be happy – it is, therefore, a sort of ideal – towards which human activity rises again and again – an ideal which, however, can never in fact be fully attained by man – full stop. Therefore, happiness is not something given once and for all – we keep losing it and we keep having to strive for it again and again – full stop. (*Halts, ponders, then turns to* BLANKA.) Blanka –

BLANKA: Yes, Dr Huml?

HUML: What sort of memories have you of your childhood?

BLANKA: Nice ones –

HUML: So have I. My childhood is forever bound up with the countryside where I grew up and with the people around me.

BLANKA: So is mine –

HUML: I still carry it all inside me – the Rapid River, the elms above the dam, which we used to climb as boys so many times – Black Pond in which old Vavra drowned his wife – the pine trees, the firs, and all that flint under foot, the purple prunus and the juniper – gossamer, after the fields had been ploughed – old Danek, whose cow rolled over and smothered his goat one Easter – Rosie, the miller's daughter, who could make such marvellous mouth music – the little chapel at the crossroads, all those melancholy autumn walks through the oak woods right under the Castle – anyway, all the means nothing to you, nothing at all – (*Pause. He is still dreaming.*)

BLANKA: Well, shall we go on? You said you were short of time –

HUML: (*Does not respond, but watches* BLANKA *for a moment, then asks:*) Are you a virgin?

BLANKA: What?

HUML: I said, are you a virgin?

BLANKA: I beg your pardon!

HUML: It's kindly meant, I ask as your friend –

BLANKA: No, I'm not.

HUML: That's what I thought! Well – let's go on. Where did we stop?

BLANKA: (*Reads:*) 'Therefore, happiness is not something given once and for all – we keep losing it and we keep having to strive for it again and again.'

HUML: (*Once more starts thoughtfully pacing and dictating*) Particularly in the present world – distinguished by the gigantic development of communications – the attainment of happiness is becoming an increasingly difficult task – full stop. Man's effort to achieve satisfaction of his needs – that is, to attain specific values – directly or indirectly characterizes all human activity – full stop. Yet, as the different values man wants to attain can be viewed from different angles – brackets – for example, from the angle of the observer's individual scale of values, or from a broader angle, i.e. that of a particular period – end of brackets – sorry, how did it go before the brackets?

BLANKA: (*Reads:*) 'Yet, as the different values man wants to attain can be viewed from different angles – '

HUML: Cross out what's inside the brackets –

BLANKA: All of it?

HUML: All of it.

(HUML *halts near* BLANKA *and stares at her.* BLANKA *does not realize what is going on, thinking he is merely searching for a precise formulation. Longish pause. Suddenly,* HUML *leaps towards* BLANKA, *falls on his knees, grabs her shoulders and tries to kiss her.* BLANKA *is startled and cries out.*)

BLANKA: Oh!

(*A short struggle ensues,* HUML *attempting to put his arms around* BLANKA *and kiss her.* BLANKA *resists, finally she gives him a push,* HUML *loses his balance and falls down.* BLANKA *jumps up.*)

You should be ashamed of yourself, Dr Huml! (BLANKA, *alarmed, runs out by the right door.* HUML *looks sheepishly after her for a moment, then quickly gets up and follows her out by the right door. From behind the door his receding voice is heard.*)

HUML: (*Calling, offstage*) Blanka! Blanka! Blanka! – listen to me!

(*Short pause. The upstairs door slowly opens and* HUML *appears in the bedroom door, shirt opened at the neck, tie loose, jacket in his hand. He stretches a bit and leisurely descends the stairs, while putting on his jacket, buttoning his shirt and straightening his tie. After him* RENATA *appears in the door, slightly dishevelled, zipping up her dress. She too walks down, crosses to the mirror and tidies herself in front of it, ignoring him, who stands silently, sheepishly, nearby. When she finishes at the mirror,* RENATA *crosses to the easy chair, sits down and lights a cigarette. She seems distant and avoids looking at* HUML, *who watches her and is beginning to get slightly nervous. Longish uneasy pause.*)

RENATA: You're just overworked, that's all!

HUML: Mmnn –

(*Longish uneasy pause.*)

RENATA: About time something happened!

HUML: Mmnn –

(*Longish uneasy pause.*)

RENATA: What you need is to get away from it all. Physical work. Change of diet. Fresh air. What does she actually give you for dinner?

HUML: Well – all sorts of things – sausages – omelettes –

RENATA: Do you ever eat any carrots?

HUML: Not really –

RENATA: No – this way it'll never work!

(*Pause.* HUML *surreptitiously glances at his watch, crosses to table, picks up the things left over from lunch and from his coffee with* BLANKA *on tray, carries it to the back door, puts it on the commode, opens the door, takes the tray out, returns at once, shuts the door and remains standing by the commode, watching* RENATA *rather unhappily.* RENATA *ignores him and goes on smoking.*)

HUML: Listen, Renata –

RENATA: Yes?

HUML: You wouldn't like to settle the whole thing with her yourself, would you? After all, you're not so deeply involved in this relationship –

RENATA: For heaven's sake, what would that look like! Nonsense! You have a word with her today, and that's that! (*Longish uneasy pause.*)

HUML: (*Becoming more nervous, again surreptitiously glances at his watch*) Listen, Renata –

RENATA: Yes?

HUML: I'm expecting some chaps –

RENATA: Who?

HUML: Don't know, they rang me up, they didn't want to say on the phone what it's all about, but it appears to be rather important, most likely they're from – you know –

RENATA: You think so?

HUML: I'd rather they didn't meet you here –

RENATA: In other words, you're throwing me out! May I at least finish my cigarette?

HUML: I mean it for your own sake, too –

(RENATA *extinguishes her cigarette, gets up and coldly exits by the back door, leaving it open.* HUML *is visibly relieved, crosses to the right door and peers out through the peep-hole.*)

RENATA: (*Offstage*) Where's my coat?

HUML: Just outside the door –

(*He starts towards the back door.* HUML *stops at the mirror and hastily tidies himself up. Just then, the doorbell rings. He rushes to the right door, peers through the peep-hole and opens.* RENATA *stands outside, wearing her coat.*)

RENATA: Give us a kiss!

(HUML *kisses* RENATA*'s cheek.*)

Well?

BLANKA: (*Wearing her coat, enters by the back door.*) Good morning –

HUML: Let me introduce – Miss Blanka, our secretary – Renata, my sister-in-law –

(RENATA *and* BLANKA *shake hands, short awkward pause, then* BLANKA *takes her briefcase from the table and crosses to the right door.*)

(*To* BLANKA) Well, again many thanks for your patience – your co-operation – your punctuality –

BLANKA: Quite all right. Goodbye –

HUML: Goodbye –

(HUML *opens the right door for* BLANKA. *She exits.* HUML *walks over to* RENATA.)

RENATA: Goodbye –

What was that?

HUML: She takes my dictation –

RENATA: Let's hope so! Well?

HUML: Won't you take off your coat?

RENATA: Failed again, I bet.

HUML: Couldn't help it.

RENATA: Why?

HUML: The circumstances weren't right. She was a bit irritable and in rather a hurry to get to work. Won't you take off your coat?

RENATA: Another opportunity missed! (RENATA *takes off her coat, helped by* HUML, *who then slowly recedes towards the back door, followed by* RENATA.)

HUML: Look, it's not the last time I'm going to see her, I'll give it another try the evening –

RENATA: Evening! Evening! Again another evening! Listen, be honest, aren't you perhaps postponing the whole thing on purpose?

HUML: Why on earth should I do that? (*Disappears with the coat by the back door.*)

RENATA: Maybe you actually still love her –

HUML: (*Offstage*) You know very well I stopped loving her long ago! I just like her as a friend, a housewife, a companion of my life –

RENATA: (*Has meanwhile followed* HUML *out by the back door offstage.*) Some housewife! Does she ever dust in here? (MISS BALCAR *and* KRIEBL *enter by the back door, carefully carrying Puzuk between them. They are followed by* HUML. MISS BALCAR *and* KRIEBL *place Puzuk on the table.* KRIEBL *plugs in the cord; all sit down as before;* KRIEBL *fiddles with Puzuk.*)

MISS BALCAR: Hope his insulators haven't burned out –

KRIEBL: No – there'd be smoke coming out of him, wouldn't there? We can start –

MISS BALCAR: Splendid! Now, put down – (*Dictating.*) Edward Huml, 1928 – beginning of interview 16:32 – first question. (*Calls:*) Silence, please! (KRIEBL, *having typed the data on the keyboard, turns the crank, peers into the eyepiece, and presses a button. The loudspeaker gives out a soft rumbling.* KRIEBL *stares closely at his watch; general suspense. After a while, Puzuk's green light goes on.*)

Splendid! It's green!

KRIEBL: About time!

(*Out of Puzuk's loudspeaker issues an effeminate voice.*)

PUZUK: Tell me –

(*Pause. Suspense.*)

Tell me – (*Pause. Suspense.*)

Tell me, please –

(*Pause. Suspense.*)

Karel?

KRIEBL: (*To Puzuk*) What is it?

PUZUK: May I have a little rest?

KRIEBL: But you haven't done a stroke of work yet!

PUZUK: I got so tired from all this moving about –

KRIEBL: All right, go on then, for all I care –

(KRIEBL *quickly presses a button and turns the crank. The light goes out.*)

MISS BALCAR: Doesn't seem to be feeling very well today, does he?

KRIEBL: Just showing off, that's all.

MISS BALCAR: (*To* HUML) Sometimes he's like a child –

KRIEBL: The other day, he was just as awkward, I got a bit tired of it, so I simply shoved him into the garage for a couple of hours, turned off the light and made him solve several hundred differential equations. You should have seen him afterwards – he was killing himself to please me! It's a question of upbringing, too, you know!

MISS BALCAR: That's what I say – like a child –

(*Longish uneasy pause.*)

KRIEBL: (*To* HUML) I wouldn't mind buying some of those high-altitude plums for the children –

HUML: Take as many as you like – free of course – I wouldn't hear of taking money for them –

KRIEBL: Well, if I may – thanks –

(*Longish uneasy pause.*)

HUML: (*To* MISS BALCAR) I'm sorry to keep bothering you with questions –

MISS BALCAR: Goodness no, it's a pleasure to discuss our work with you –

HUML: You do understand, don't you, it's sort of professional interest on my part – in a way –

MISS BALCAR: I quite understand. After all, we're really colleagues – so to speak –

HUML: Precisely. I'd be interested to know more about the exact procedure you use in shaping human personality –

MISS BALCAR: Well, we proceed from the following, altogether logical, proposition: if men are related by the general aspects of their personalities, they must necessarily, on the other hand, be differentiated by those aspects which are particular and random. In other words, the gravitational focus of human individuality does not lie in any aspects which can be established as predictable, but, on the contrary, in those which defy all laws, all norms, and thus constitute precisely the vast and neglected sphere of coincidence.

HUML: It sounds convincing. But how can one cope with this sphere – scientifically, I mean?

MISS BALCAR: That's exactly where Puzuk plays such an important part. He simply compares the quantum of all the possible relationships from among all the pieces of information about a particular individual which we've fed into him, or which he has acquired on his own – he compares these concurrently with the laws and norms of all the scientific disciplines previously fed into his memory – in order to eliminate all those relationships which an existing scientific discipline can establish as predictable. Simultaneously, he rejects those elements which he'd already encountered with other individuals and which, therefore, could be considered potentially predictable. Thus he gradually arrives at a certain comprehensive structure of maximally random relationships – and in fact this is already – basically – a sort of condensed model of human individuality.

HUML: How very original! Indeed, both the theory and the practical application – I must say –

*(Just then, the left door opens and* MACHAL *appears in his lab-coat, pencil behind his ear. All turn towards him.)*

KRIEBL: *(To* MACHAL*)* What's the matter?

MACHAL: Have you seen the safety bolt of the moisture meter?

KRIEBL: You usually keep it in your sandwich bag.

MACHAL: It's not there.

KRIEBL: I don't know, then –

(MACHAL *stands about for a while, emptily staring ahead, then slowly turns and starts out, as* KRIEBL *addresses him.)*

Emil –

(MACHAL *stops short at the door, turns towards* KRIEBL, *who quickly gets up, crosses to* MACHAL, *whispers to him some instructions, while pointing towards the back door,* MACHAL *nods, understands, agrees.* KRIEBL *pats his head in a friendly manner,* MACHAL *dodges at once, apparently unable to tolerate this sort of endearment.* KRIEBL *returns to his place,* MACHAL *exits by the left door, leaving it open, instantly returns, carrying a string bag, again leaves the left door open, ambles towards the back door, paying no attention to anybody.*)

MISS BALCAR: (*To* MACHAL.) Have you weighed the bedclothes yet?

MACHAL: (*Halts at the back door, standing with his back to the room, after a moment grumbles*:) What?

MISS BALCAR: I said, have you weighed the bedclothes yet?

MACHAL: (*Without turning*) I'm measuring the moisture of the walls –

MISS BALCAR: I see –

MACHAL: (*Short pause.*) (*Still facing the door, grumbles*) All this fuss and bother – (*Exits by the back door.*)

(*Short pause.*)

HUML: (*To* MISS BALCAR) Do you mind my asking just one more question – how do you select your subjects – I mean – today, for example, why did you call on me of all people, why not somebody else?

MISS BALCAR: Entirely superficial reasons –

HUML: Oh? Such as?

MISS BALCAR: We called on you – same way we called on many others – simply because your name begins with an H, and your house has an odd number.

HUML: I'm afraid I'm not responsible for my name, nor for the number of my house! Matter of pure coincidence, isn't it?

MISS BALCAR: The more random the key to our selection of samples, the more representative the sample – depending on its size, that is –

HUML: So, as far as you're concerned, I represent nothing but a random sample here, is that it?

MISS BALCAR: That's right.

HUML: I see –

MISS BALCAR: We can't help proceeding this way in the first stage. I'm afraid, we haven't been able to call on everybody so far –

(*Just then,* MACHAL *enters by the back door, carrying the string bag full of plums.* KRIEBL *winks at him, exuding agreement and thanks.* MACHAL, *paying no attention to anybody, shuffles out by the left door. Pause.*)

(*To* KRIEBL) Shall we have another try?

KRIEBL: Why not –

MISS BALCAR: (*Calls*:) Silence, please!

(KRIEBL *turns the crank, presses a button, Puzuk begins to rumble.* KRIEBL *stares closely at his watch; general suspense. Suddenly,* BECK *in his overcoat enters by the left door. All turn towards him.* KRIEBL *again quickly presses a button and turns the crank. The rumbling stops.* BECK, *ignoring everybody, angrily stalks upstage and plants himself there facing the wall, his back to the room. All watch him with some embarrassment. After a while, he speaks up without turning.*)

BECK: Tomorrow I'm going fishing and that's that! (*Awkward pause.*)

MISS BALCAR: Surely, you don't mean that, Mr Beck! What would we do without you? You do know how much we need you –

(*Awkward pause.* BECK *does not react.*)

But who would direct our whole research work? Not one of us has anywhere near your qualifications –

(*Awkward pause.* BECK *does not react.*) Really, you couldn't do that to us, Mr Beck –

(*Awkward pause. Suddenly* BECK *turns and snaps*:)

BECK: You heard me!

(BECK *stalks energetically out by the right door and slams it.* HUML *looks questioningly at* MISS BALCAR, *but she quickly turns to* KRIEBL.)

MISS BALCAR: Ready now?

KRIEBL: Ready.

MISS BALCAR: (*Calls*) Silence, please!

(KRIEBL *again turns the crank, presses a button, Puzuk begins to rumble. Once more,* KRIEBL *stares closely at his watch; general suspense. Suddenly the left door opens and* MACHAL *reappears, wearing earphones; they are connected to an instrument he carries in his arms. All turn towards him.* KRIEBL *again quickly presses a button and turns the crank. The rumbling stops.* MACHAL *shuffles to the right wall, pulling out of his pocket a funnel, connected to the instrument by a flexible tube, presses the funnel against the wall and listens with great concentration to whatever goes on inside his earphones. Pause.*)

KRIEBL: (*To* MACHAL) Did you find the safety bolt of the moisture meter?

(*Pause.* MACHAL *does not respond, removes the funnel from the wall, lets it drop, so that it hangs on its tube; produces from his pocket a grubby slip of paper on which he laboriously notes the measurements; then crosses to the back wall, presses the funnel against it and again listens.*)

(*Raising his voice somewhat.*) Did you find the safety bolt of the moisture meter?

(MACHAL *does not respond, removes the funnel from the wall, lets it drop down, makes another entry; then crosses to the left wall, presses the funnel against it and again listens.*)

(*Raising his voice still more*) I say, Emil, did you find the safety bolt of the moisture meter?

(*Pause.* MACHAL *does not respond, removes the funnel from the wall, lets it drop down, and makes an entry.*)

MISS BALCAR: He can't hear you –

KRIEBL: I suppose not –

(MACHAL, *having finished, slowly crosses to* KRIEBL *and hands him the slip of paper.*)

Thanks, Emil –

(KRIEBL *smooths out the slip of paper on the table, then slides it into Puzuk.* MACHAL, *carrying the instrument and trailing the funnel, ascends towards the bedroom. On the stairs he trips over the tube, falls down, for a while does not move, then slowly gets up, grumbles, mounts the stairs, stumbles on the last step, exits by the upstairs door. Short pause.*)

MISS BALCAR: Ready now?

KRIEBL: Ready.

MISS BALCAR: (*Calls:*) Silence, please!

(KRIEBL *once more turns the crank, presses a button, Puzuk begins to rumble.* KRIEBL *stares closely at his watch. General suspense. After a while, Puzuk's red light goes on.*)

Again red!

(*Just then, the red light goes out and the green light goes on.*)

No – it's green!

KRIEBL: About time!

(*Out of Puzuk's loudspeaker issues an effeminate voice. There is a short pause after each question. Puzuk's red and green lights alternately keep flashing on and off.*)

PUZUK: Which is your favourite tunnel? Are you fond of musical instruments? How many times a year do you air the square? Where did you bury the dog? Why didn't you pass it on? When did you lose the claim? Wherein lies the nucleus? Do you know where you're going and do you know who's going with you? Do you piss in public, or just now and then?

(*Short pause. Puzuk's loudspeaker emits only a soft rumbling.* HUML *gets up energetically.*)

HUML: What's the meaning of this?

(HUML *bangs the table and angrily stalks towards the back door. Just as he reaches it, the door is flung open, disclosing* BLANKA.)

BLANKA: You should be ashamed of yourself, Dr Huml!

(BLANKA *slams the door shut.* HUML *for a moment freezes in astonishment, then swiftly turns and crosses to the right door. Just as he reaches it, the door is flung open disclosing* MACHAL.)

MACHAL: Have you seen the safety bolt of the moisture meter?

(MACHAL *slams the door shut.* HUML *for a moment freezes in astonishment, then swiftly turns and crosses to the left door. Just as he reaches it, the door is flung open disclosing* RENATA.)

RENATA: Do you ever eat any carrots?

(RENATA *slams the door shut.* HUML *for a moment freezes in astonishment, then swiftly turns and runs up towards the bedroom. Just as he reaches the upstairs door, the door is flung open, disclosing* BECK.)

BECK: Tomorrow I'm going fishing and that's that!

(BECK *slams the door shut.* HUML *for a moment freezes in astonishment, then swiftly turns and runs down again to the back door. Just as he reaches it, the door is flung open, disclosing* MRS HUML.)

MRS HUML: You're not just trying to jolly me along, are you?

(MRS HUML *slams the door shut.* HUML *for a moment freezes in astonishment, then swiftly turns and runs to the table.*)

KRIEBL: Give me your high-altitude plums!

MISS BALCAR: Dr Huml?

PUZUK: Which is your favourite tunnel? How many times a year do you air the square? Why didn't you pass it on? Wherein lies the nucleus? Do you piss in public, or just now and then?

(HUML *runs over to the left door, in which* BLANKA *appears.*)

BLANKA: Have you seen the safety bolt of the moisture meter?

(BLANKA *disappears;* HUML *rushes up to the the upstairs door, in which* MACHAL *appears.*)

MACHAL: You should be ashamed of yourself, Dr Huml!

(MACHAL *disappears;* HUML *rushes down to the back door, in which* RENATA *appears.*)

RENATA: Do you ever eat any jolly plums?

(RENATA *disappears;* HUML *runs to the right door, in which* BECK *appears.*)

BECK: Tomorrow I'm going carroting and that's that!

(BECK *disappears;* HUML *runs to the left door, in which* MRS HUML *appears.*)

MRS HUML: You're not just trying to jolly along the fish, are you?

(MRS HUML *disappears;* HUML *runs back to the table.*)

KRIEBL: Dr Huml?

(HUML *turns to* MISS BALCAR, *who gets up.*)

MISS BALCAR: Give me your high-altitude plums!

(*Suddenly all the characters appear on the stage. All, including* KRIEBL *and* MISS BALCAR, *begin variously to criss-cross from one door to another, while repeating together with Puzuk, over and over their questions and demands, addressed to* HUML. *Their movements and speech become faster and faster, their voices louder, so that the end impression of this scene is an ever-increasing acoustic and visual chaos.* HUML *keeps desperately rushing among them, as though seeking some sort of haven.*)

MRS HUML: You're not just trying to jolly along the fish, are you? You're not just trying to jolly along the fish, are you? (*Etc.*)

BECK: Tomorrow I'm going carroting and that's that! Tomorrow I'm going carroting and that's that! (*Etc.*)

RENATA: Do you ever eat any jolly plums? Do you ever eat any jolly plums? (*Etc.*)

MACHAL: You should be ashamed of yourself, Dr Huml! You should be ashamed of yourself, Dr Huml! (*Etc.*)

BLANKA: Have you seen the safety bolt of the moisture meter? Have you seen the safety bolt of the moisture meter? (*Etc.*)

KRIEBL: Dr Huml? Dr Huml? (*Etc.*)

MISS BALCAR: Give me your high-altitude plums! Give me your high-altitude plums! (*Etc.*)

PUZUK: Which is your favourite tunnel? Are you fond of musical instruments? (*Etc.*)

(*When the uproar becomes intolerable, Puzuk emits his well-known siren-type wail. At once, the tumult ends;* KRIEBL, MISS BALCAR *and* HUML *resume their places at the table, all the other characters instantly disappear.*)

HUML: What's the meaning of this?

MISS BALCAR: (*To* KRIEBL) Switch him off!

(KRIEBL *presses a button and turns the crank. The lights which have been flashing until now go out, the rumbling stops.* HUML *sits down again. Awkward pause.*)

That's all we needed! (*To* KRIEBL.) A short, I suppose, wasn't it?

KRIEBL: Shouldn't think so. More likely a stray electric impulse.

MISS BALCAR: Blast! (*To* HUML) Those are the so-called stray thoughts – at such moments he's quite unaware of what's happening inside him. (*To* KRIEBL) From the start I had a notion he wasn't somehow feeling all right today! Are you going to try and locate that damn impulse?

KRIEBL: I'd like to, but I can't – the union, you know. But I'll see a chap I know in the workshop, he'll fix it for me in a jiffy – for a bottle of booze, that is.

(MACHAL *enters by the upstairs door, all turn towards him; he pays no attention to them, slowly descends, while removing the earphones from his ears, still carrying the instrument with the funnel.*)

Emil –

MACHAL: What is it?

KRIEBL: We'll be packing up now –

(MACHAL *carries the instrument out by the back door, leaving it open, returns and together with* KRIEBL, *who has meanwhile unplugged the cord, carries out Puzuk by the left door. Pause.*)

MISS BALCAR: I'm so sorry we've troubled you for nothing today. May we drop in again after the weekend?

(*Pause.* HUML *stares quizzically at* MISS BALCAR.)

HUML: Listen, where do you work, actually?

MISS BALCAR: Well, formally, we're attached to the Institute of Sociology, we even use their premises, but in fact we are a more or less independent research group.

HUML: Oh, I see –

MISS BALCAR: Why do you ask?

HUML: No special reason –

(*Pause.*)

MISS BALCAR: May we come after the weekend?

(*Pause.*)

Dr Huml –

(*Pause.*)

May we come back after the weekend?

HUML: What?

MISS BALCAR: I wondered – may we trouble you once more – when Puzuk is all right again –

HUML: I'm sorry, but I think it'd be no use –

MISS BALCAR: Why? I mean, to us it'd be of great use!

HUML: I'm afraid, it wouldn't – not even to you.

MISS BALCAR: I don't follow you!

HUML: Look, I've no doubt you mean well, I respect the enthusiasm with which you've committed yourself to this project, but as a man who has devoted many years to professional work in the social sciences – try as I may – I can't take the whole matter seriously –

MISS BALCAR: What do you mean?

HUML: I mean I can't take the whole matter seriously.

MISS BALCAR: But why?

HUML: What I've just seen, as well as what you've told me about your work, has been quite enough to convince me that from the point of view of science the whole project is nothing but an unfortunate mistake. And I hope you'll see that my conscience as a scientist wouldn't allow me to co-operate on a project which I'm absolutely sure is thoroughly mistaken.

MISS BALCAR: But you talked quite differently before –

HUML: That was a little misunderstanding –

MISS BALCAR: Besides, such a sweeping statement would have to be substantiated!

HUML: Nothing easier, if you really care to know. For example, it should be enough to point out the rather obvious fact that things which from one angle appear as predictable may from another angle appear as coincidental, and vice versa; because predictability and coincidence are no absolute categories, nor are they any objectively existing and differentiated spheres of reality – their extent depends merely on the chosen viewpoint, or angle. It can't be helped, from the scientific point of view everything is always to some extent predictable, while science itself is but a gradual disclosing of this predictability; what we call coincidental is either that which lies beyond the radius of predictability, or simply that which so far we've been unable to establish as predictable. In other words, your endeavour to isolate the element of coincidence and use it as a means of shaping human individuality bears no relationship to science whatsoever. Moreover, it is bound to miss its goal completely. Why? Because it replaces reality – i.e. an objective totality – with a chimera of one of its specific relative and wholly subjective aspects. Science is able merely to keep reaching up towards the totality of a unique personality. It can do this within the limits of that which – at a given moment – it is capable of illuminating and describing as predictable. It can never reach beyond these limits, because man, as an objective totality, fundamentally contains the dimensions of infinity. And I'm afraid the key to a real knowledge of the human individual does not lie in some greater or lesser understanding of the complexity of man as an object of scientific knowledge. The only key lies in man's complexity as a subject of human togetherness, because the limitlessness of our own human nature is so far the only thing capable of approaching – however imperfectly – the limitlessness of others. In other words, the personal, human, unique relationship which arises between two individuals is so far the only thing that can – at least to some extent – mutually unveil the secret of those two individuals. Such values as love, friendship, compassion, sympathy and the unique and irreplaceable mutual understanding – or even mutual conflict – are the only tools which this human approach has at its disposal. By any other means we may perhaps be able more or less to explain man, but we shall never understand him – not even a little – and therefore we shall never arrive at a basic knowledge of him. Hence, the fundamental key to man does not lie in his brain, but in his heart.

(MISS BALCAR *begins to cry softly.*)

(*Surprised*) Why are you crying? (MISS BALCAR *goes on crying.* HUML *is baffled. Pause.*) I didn't mean to hurt you –

(MISS BALCAR *goes on crying. Pause.*)

It was just my private opinion –

(MISS BALCAR *goes on crying. Pause.*)

It never occurred to me you'd take it personally –

(MISS BALCAR *loudly sobs.* HUML *watches her for a moment in some embarrassment, then he quickly approaches her, takes her gently in his arms and begins to stroke her hair.* MISS BALCAR *does not resist, on the contrary – still crying – she rests her head on* HUML*'s chest.*)

Just forget everything I said!

MISS BALCAR: It's my whole life –

HUML: I'm sure I was wrong – perhaps I didn't quite understand your explanation –

MISS BALCAR: (*Tearfully*) It's all I have in the whole world!

HUML: I do apologize, I'm sincerely sorry –

MISS BALCAR: (*Crying*) You've humiliated me terribly! How bad and malicious you all are! You don't understand anything – anything at all –

HUML: Calm yourself, please –

MISS BALCAR: How I hate you for what you've done to me!

(HUML, *still stroking* MISS BALCAR'*s hair, begins to kiss her gently on her tearful eyes, cheeks, lips, and on her hair.*)

HUML: (*Whispers*:) There, there, don't cry – I was being cruel – cynical – I'm ashamed of myself – (MISS BALCAR *presses herself closer to* HUML, *still loudly sobbing. There follows prolonged, passionate kissing.* KRIEBL *and* MACHAL *enter by the left door, both dressed in their overcoats, and carrying the large suitcases.* KRIEBL *also carries the string bag full of plums.* MISS BALCAR *and* HUML *jump apart. Embarrassment.*)

MISS BALCAR: Well, many thanks – thank you – both of you. See you tomorrow then. Good bye!

KRIEBL: Goodbye –

MACHAL: Goodbye –

(KRIEBL *and* MACHAL *exit by the right door,* HUML *hesitantly walks out by the back door, instantly returns, carrying* MISS BALCAR'*s coat, helps her to put it on.* MISS BALCAR *buttons it up and pulls it straight; crosses to* HUML, *throws her arms around his neck and gently covers his face with kisses; then she strokes his hair and starts towards the right door.* HUML *stands in the middle of the room, rather nonplussed.* MISS BALCAR *opens the door, stops at the threshold and turns to* HUML.)

MISS BALCAR: May I ring you up tomorrow?

HUML: (*Surprised*) Yes – of course –

MISS BALCAR: Will you have some time for me?

HUML: Certainly –

MISS BALCAR: Say something nice to me before I go!

HUML: Kitty-cat –

MISS BALCAR: I don't like that –

HUML: Dearest –

MISS BALCAR: That's a bit better –

HUML: Darling –

(MISS BALCAR *runs over to* HUML, *gives him a kiss, runs back, smiling happily, stops at the door and again turns.*)

MISS BALCAR: My name's Anna –

HUML: Well – bye, Anna –

MISS BALCAR: Bye, Eddi!

(MISS BALCAR *exits by the right door, closing it.* HUML *stares after her for a while in utter bewilderment, then shakes his head, sighs deeply, looks at his watch, looks around the room, ambles to the commode, reaches behind it, pulls out a small watering-can and shuffles out by the back door. Off stage, sound of water filling up a receptacle. When, judging by the sound, the receptacle is full, the sound ceases, and* MRS HUML *enters by the back door. She is wearing an apron over her dress, and carries a tray with dinner for two: plates, sausages, mustard, two glasses, a bottle of wine, a basket with bread, knives and forks. Setting the table, she calls towards the bedroom:*)

MRS HUML: Dinner!

(*When she has finished the table,* MRS HUML *pours some wine into the glasses, sits down and begins to eat, while the upstairs door opens and* HUML *enters, wearing a dressing-gown over his shirt and trousers. He is slightly dishevelled, obviously having just had a nap, leisurely descends, sits down opposite* MRS HUML, *spreads a napkin in his lap and also starts eating. Longish silence is finally interrupted by* MRS HUML.) Well?

# AUDIENCE
A one act play

# CHARACTERS

FOREMAN
VANEK

*The foreman's office. A door, left, and next to it a framed diploma hanging on the wall. Right, a wardrobe and filing cabinet, on top of which are several empty beer bottles. On the rear wall a large amateurish painting of Svejk and the publican Palivec, with the inscription 'Lot of good beer, lot of good cheer'. In the centre of the stage, an office desk and three chairs, the desk covered with papers and more beer bottles; also a few glasses. A crate of beer stands next to the desk. Along the walls, and especially in the corners of the room, a motley of discarded bits of machinery, an ancient radio, a broken hat-stand, a pile of old newspapers, rubber boots, etc. The curtain goes up to reveal the* FOREMAN *sitting with his head resting on his folded arms on top of the desk, snoring loudly. After a while there is a knock at the door. The* FOREMAN *immediately awakes.*

FOREMAN: Come in . . .

(VANEK *enters, dressed in a padded working jacket and gumboots.*)

VANEK: Good morning.

FOREMAN: Oh, it's you, Mr Vanek. Come in, come in. Take a seat.

(VANEK *sits down, looking timid and uncertain.*)

Want a beer?

VANEK: No, thank you very much.

FOREMAN: Why not? Do you good . . .

(*He takes a bottle of beer from the crate, opens it and pours two glasses, one of which he pushes in front of* VANEK. *He drinks his own straightaway.*)

VANEK: Thank you.

(*The* FOREMAN *pours himself another glass. There is a short silence.*)

FOREMAN: Well, tell me, how're things?

VANEK: Thank you, fine . . .

FOREMAN: They've got to be, haven't they?

VANEK: Well . . .

(*Silence.*)

FOREMAN: What're you doing today? Rolling barrels?

VANEK: Helping to roll . . .

FOREMAN: That's better than rolling, isn't it?

VANEK: Yes, it is . . .

(*Silence.*)

FOREMAN: Who *is* rolling today then?

VANEK: Serkezy* . . .

FOREMAN: He came to work?

VANEK: Yes, just now . . .

FOREMAN: Drunk?

VANEK: Well, yes, a little . . .

(*Silence.*)

FOREMAN: Come on, Mr Vanek, you're not drinking. Why aren't you drinking?

VANEK: Thank you, but I'm not much of a beer drinker . . .

FOREMAN: Is that so? Never mind, we'll teach you to drink beer all right. You'll soon get used to it around here. We all drink it around here, it's a . . . sort of tradition . . .

VANEK: Yes, I know.

(*Silence.*)

FOREMAN: And you mustn't be depressed.

VANEK: I am not depressed . . .

(*Silence.*)

FOREMAN: Well, and how're things?

VANEK: Sorry? What things did you have in mind?

FOREMAN: Things, you know . . . In general . . .

VANEK: Oh. Thank you, not too bad . . .

(*Silence.*)

FOREMAN: How do you like it here?

VANEK: I like it . . .

FOREMAN: Could be worse, eh?

VANEK: Oh, yes, undoubtedly . . .

*Serkezy, though he never actually appears on stage, is also mentioned in Dienstbier's *Reception*, where he is referred to as the prison's dope expert and expert tattooer.

(*The* FOREMAN *opens another bottle and pours himself a beer.*)

FOREMAN: Got to get used to everything in this life. Right?

VANEK: Yes, you do . . .

(*Silence.*)

FOREMAN: Come on, then, drink up.

(VANEK *finishes his beer and the* FOREMAN *pours him another.*)

VANEK: No more for me, thank you.

FOREMAN: Oh, balls . . . You haven't had none yet . . .

(*Silence.*)

What about the others? You get on with them all right, do you?

VANEK: Oh yes, thank you, I get on with them.

FOREMAN: Well, you take my advice and don't get too pally with any of 'em. I don't trust a soul, and that's the truth. People can be real bastards and no mistake. Real bastards. Take my word for it. Just do your job and keep your distance. It's no good getting too pally . . . specially in your case.

VANEK: I understand.

(*Silence.*)

FOREMAN: What was it you used to write, if you don't mind me asking?

VANEK: Plays. Stage plays.

FOREMAN:, Plays, you say. Like for the theatre?

VANEK: That's right.

FOREMAN: Is that so? Theatre plays. See here, why don't you write one about our brewery. You could write about Bures, for a start. You know him?

VANEK: Yes, I know him.

FOREMAN: He's a right charlie, he is.

VANEK: Yes, I suppose so.

(*Silence.*)

FOREMAN: And don't be depressed.

VANEK: I am not depressed . . .

(*Silence.*)

FOREMAN: I bet you never thought it would happen, did you?

VANEK: What was that?

FOREMAN: Well, that you'd be rolling barrels in a brewery, that's what.

VANEK: No, I can't say I did.

FOREMAN: Funny, isn't it?

VANEK: Yes, I suppose you might call it that.

FOREMAN: You might call it that. You might and all.

(*Silence.*)

Did you say you were helping to roll barrels today?

VANEK: That's right . . .

FOREMAN: But you rolled yesterday, I saw you myself.

VANEK: That's because Serkezy wasn't here yesterday . . .

FOREMAN: That's it then, is it? Yes, that makes sense, don't it . . .

(*Silence.*)

Tell you something, Mr Vanek, we never had a writer here before, and that's a fact. Had all kinds of odds and sods, but never a writer. Take Bures . . . know what he did before he came here? He was a gravedigger, he was. That's how he learned to knock 'em back in the first place, and then he came here. Now *he* could tell you stories, he could, and no mistake.

VANEK: I know . . .

FOREMAN: What did you use to write those plays about anyway?

VANEK: Mainly about bureaucrats . . .

FOREMAN: Bureaucrats, eh? You're not pulling my leg or anything . . . So that's what they were . . .

(*Silence.*)

You had your tea break yet?

VANEK: No, not yet . . .

FOREMAN: Well, why don't you go a bit later, then. Just tell them at the gate that you've been to see me.

VANEK: Thank you . . .

VANEK: What you keep thanking me for all the time?

(*Silence.*)

You know something, I take my hat off to you.

VANEK: You do? Whatever for?

FOREMAN: Must've been bloody hard for you . . . sitting at home all your life, I mean, nice and cosy and warm . . . sleeping late in the morning and all . . . And now this! I don't mind

telling you, I take my hat off to you.
(*Silence.*)
'Scuse me.
(*The* FOREMAN *gets up and goes out.* VANEK *quickly pours the rest of his beer into the foreman's glass. The* FOREMAN *returns, buttoning up his flies, and sits down again.*)
You must've known all them actresses since you wrote for the theatre.

VANEK: Yes, I knew most of them . . .

FOREMAN: Like Bohdalov* . . . did you know her?

VANEK: Oh yes . . .

FOREMAN: *Personally*, I mean . . . Did you know her personally?

VANEK: Yes, I did. Personally.

FOREMAN: Tell you what, why don't you ask her down here for a beer one of these days . . . We could get Bures to come as well . . . Have a bit of fun like . . . What d'you say?

VANEK: Well . . .
(*Silence.*)

FOREMAN: Don't be depressed.

VANEK: I am not depressed . . .
(*The* FOREMAN *opens another bottle and pours himself a beer. A short silence.*)

FOREMAN: That young lad on the separator . . . know who I mean?

VANEK: Mlynarik?

FOREMAN: That's him. Well, you be careful what you say in front of him.
(*Silence.*)
How about Gott?† You know him too, do you?

*Jirina Bohdalova is a popular stage and television actress in Czechoslovakia.
†Karel Gott is a successful popular singer, one of the few who could move relatively freely across the border to the West and back under the Soviet regime. He has made numerous recordings in Czechoslovakia, Germany, and Austria. It may be of interest that Milan Kundera calls Gott an exponent of 'music minus memory, the music in which the bones of Beethoven and Ellington, the dust of Palestrina and Schoenberg, lie buried' (*The Book of Laughter and Forgetting* [New York, Knopf, 1981], p. 181).

(*Silence.*)

FOREMAN: Pity you weren't here four, five years ago. Had a good crowd here in them days. Things just ain't what they used to be, and that's a fact. Lot of fun we had four, five years ago . . . used to meet in the malt shop . . . me, Charlie Maranek – he's left, went some time ago – Johnnie Peterka and the girls from the bottling plant . . . many a time we didn't go home till the morning. And the work got done and all. You ask Johnnie Peterka, see what he says about it . . .

VANEK: I know, he told me . . .

(*Silence.*)

FOREMAN: Those plays of yours . . . good money, was it?

VANEK: It varied . . .

FOREMAN: You made five thousand a year, at least, didn't you? At least five?

VANEK: That depends how many performances there are, how much it's played. Sometimes you earn a lot, other times nothing . . .

FOREMAN: What? Nothing for the whole month?

VANEK: Oh, maybe several months . . .

FOREMAN: You surprise me. So it's not all wine and roses, is it? Like everything else . . .

VANEK: No, it's not . . .

FOREMAN: Funny isn't it, when you come to think of it . . .

VANEK: Yes, I suppose so.

FOREMAN: It is and all.

(*Silence.*)

Here . . . you're not drinking.

VANEK: Oh yes . . .

(*The* FOREMAN *opens a bottle and pours beer for both of them. A short silence.*)

FOREMAN: Listen . . . I'll tell you something . . . in confidence like, all right? If there was someone else sitting in my place, you wouldn't be working here, I guarantee you that . . .

VANEK: Did you have difficulties, then?

FOREMAN: Did I! You bet your gumboots I did . . .

VANEK: I am very grateful . . .

FOREMAN: I don't want to boast, that's not my style, you understand . . . but why shouldn't I help somebody when I can? That's the way I am . . . even today. People ought to help one another, that's my philosophy. I help you out of a hole, you help me out of one, isn't that so?

VANEK: That's right . . .

(*Silence.*)

FOREMAN: Had your tea break yet?

VANEK: No, I haven't . . .

FOREMAN: Well, you go later . . . Tell them at the gate you've been to see me.

VANEK: Thank you . . .

FOREMAN: Don't keep thanking me all the time.

(*Silence.*)

I'm telling you, nowadays no one wants to pull anyone's chestnuts out of the fire, and that's a fact.

VANEK: I know . . .

(*Silence.*)

FOREMAN: Important thing is we should all stick together . . .

VANEK: Yes, I agree . . .

FOREMAN: I don't know what *you* think, but I always say there's nothing like a good crowd . . .

VANEK: Yes . . .

FOREMAN: Why aren't you drinking? Wine is more your cup of tea, I suppose.

VANEK: Well . . .

FOREMAN: You'll soon get used to beer around here . . . We all drink it, you know . . . it's a sort of tradition . . .

VANEK: Yes, I know . . .

(*Silence.*)

FOREMAN: Gott, now, he's doing all right these days, isn't he?

VANEK: I think so, yes . . .

(*Silence.*)

FOREMAN: You married?

VANEK: Yes, I am.

FOREMAN: Any kids?

VANEK: No, we don't have children.

(*Silence.*)

FOREMAN: Still, I take my hat off to you.

VANEK: Oh, really . . .

FOREMAN: Take my word for it. Must be bloody hard . . .

(*Silence.*)

'Scuse me . . .

(*The* FOREMAN *gets up and goes out.* VANEK *quickly pours the rest of his beer into the foreman's glass. The* FOREMAN *returns, buttoning up his flies, and sits down again.*)

How old is she, then?

VANEK: Who?

FOREMAN: Bohdalova, I mean . . .

VANEK: Oh . . . about forty-three, I imagine . . .

FOREMAN: You don't say . . . She don't look it . . .

(*Silence.*)

Everything will turn out all right, you'll see . . . If we only stick together, so to speak, if we all muck in and help one another . . . as I always say, there's nothing like a good crowd. (*He opens another bottle and pours himself a glass.*) Pity you weren't here five years ago. A good crowd in them days. But today? Don't trust nobody nowadays . . .

(*Silence.*)

Who's this Kohout, anyway?

VANEK: Kohout? Which Kohout?

FOREMAN: I heard a feller called Kohout came to visit you . . .

VANEK: That's a colleague of mine . . .

FOREMAN: Another writer?

VANEK: That's right. Why?

FOREMAN: Oh, I just asked . . .

(*Silence.*)

Take it from me, Vanek, I have my problems too . . .

VANEK: Oh . . .?

FOREMAN: Why do you think I'm stuck in this dump? But I don't suppose that interests you . . .

VANEK: Oh, it does . . .

FOREMAN: You know what I was supposed to do?

VANEK: What was that?

FOREMAN: I was to work as a foreman in the big brewery in Pardubice.

VANEK: Really?

FOREMAN: There you are – and look where I ended up. Funny, isn't it?

VANEK: Why didn't you get the job?

FOREMAN: Let's forget it . . .

(*Silence.*)

You married?

VANEK: Yes . . .

FOREMAN: Got kids?

VANEK: No . . .

(*Silence.*)

FOREMAN: Look, you can say it's none of my business, but you should tell that Holub of yours to stop visiting you . . .

VANEK: You mean my colleague, Kohout . . .

FOREMAN: And what did I say?

VANEK: Holub . . .

FOREMAN: Look, it may be none of my business . . . I don't know the man from Adam . . . don't know nothing about him . . . but I'm telling you for your own good . . .

VANEK: Now, really, I . . .

FOREMAN: For Christ's sake, you're sipping that beer like it was brandy!

VANEK: I told you I'm not used to beer . . .

FOREMAN: Oh, come off it . . .

VANEK: No, really . . .

FOREMAN: Maybe you don't think I'm good enough for you . . . not your sort of drinking partner . . .

VANEK: Not at all . . .

FOREMAN: After all, I'm no Gott, am I . . . I'm just an ordinary common or garden brewery foreman . . .

VANEK: You're a professional just like Gott, just a different profession. Tell me, why didn't you go to Pardubice?

FOREMAN: Never mind . . .

(*The* FOREMAN *opens another bottle and pours himself a glass. A short silence.*)

Everything will be all right, Vanek. Never fear, I shan't let you go. You're a quiet, hard-working man, you work regular hours and you don't moan and grouse like the rest of the men, you're not always asking for a rise, either . . . With the shortage of labour, it isn't easy . . .

VANEK: I'm very grateful to you . . .

FOREMAN: *And* you're a decent sort of chap. I know, I can tell one when I see one. I can tell a crook as soon as look at him. That Mlynarik, now, the young one on the separator, know who I mean?

VANEK: Yes, I know . . .

FOREMAN: Him I had taped the minute he showed up here. He's mean all right . . . got to watch your step with him . . .
(*Silence.*)

VANEK: Why didn't you go to Pardubice?

FOREMAN: Never mind . . .
(*Silence.*)
I'm telling you Vanek, you can rely on me. I shan't leave you in the lurch . . .

VANEK: Thank you . . .

FOREMAN: But I got to know that *I* can rely on you . . . see what I mean? . . . that you won't do me dirt. I got to know you're dependable . . .

VANEK: I'll do everything I can to give satisfaction in my work . . .

FOREMAN: After all, I didn't have to tell you, did I? Come to think of it, I *oughtn't* to have told you. Anyone else in my place . . .

VANEK: Forgive me, but what shouldn't you have told me?

FOREMAN: About this Holub,* of course . . .

VANEK: Kohout . . .

*Miroslav Holub (born 1923), a distinguished Czech scientist, is also a well-known poet whose work is available in English. The confusion of the names of Kohout and Holub provides linguistic humour in Czech which gets lost in translation: the foreman mixes up not only writers but also bird species (Kohout means rooster and Holub means pigeon in Czech).

FOREMAN: Look, I don't know what kind of a man he is, and I don't care . . . nothing to do with him . . . he can go and take a running jump . . . It's you I'm worried about, ain't it . . . You've got quite a cushy job here . . . helping to roll empty barrels . . . Nobody takes a blind bit of notice of you. This Kohout won't give you a job, now, will he? If I can't keep you on, that is. Will he?

VANEK: Hardly . . .

FOREMAN: There you are. So why don't you be sensible . . . (*Silence.*)

VANEK: Excuse me . . .

FOREMAN: Yes, what is it?

VANEK: Surely I can . . .

FOREMAN: What can you do?

VANEK: Don't take this amiss, but surely I can choose my own friends . . .

FOREMAN: Choose your own friends? I should think so! Be friends with who you bloody well like. That's your inalienable right. Nobody's going to tell you what to do. Mustn't stand for that – you're a man and not a mouse. It's a matter of principle.

VANEK: I knew you'd understand.

FOREMAN: He'll see that, won't he, this Kohout? That you're going to make up your own mind about who to be friends with.

(*The* FOREMAN *opens another bottle and pours himself a beer. A short silence.*)

VANEK: Excuse me . . .

FOREMAN: Yes?

VANEK: I'll have to be going . . .

FOREMAN: Whatever for?

VANEK: They'll be looking for me down in the cellars . . .

FOREMAN: Oh, fuck the cellars . . . They can do without you for a bit . . . and anyway, Serkezy is down there. Just sit tight and drink your beer.

(*Silence.*)

You don't give a damn why I didn't go to Pardubice, do you?

VANEK: I *would* like to know . . .

FOREMAN: You mean it?

VANEK: I mean it. *Why* didn't you go to Pardubice?

FOREMAN: You know what they did? They said I'd gone halves with a publican on five hundred hectolitres of surplus export beer. How do you like that? I don't have to tell you that wasn't the way it was at all, only that bastard . . . that Mlynarik from the separator . . . you know the one I mean . . .?

VANEK: Yes, I know . . .

FOREMAN: I'm only telling you so you can see what kind of people we have here these days. I don't trust a soul, and that's a fact. People are proper bastards, believe you me. Just do your work and don't have much to do with anyone, that's my advice . . . specially in your case.

VANEK: Yes, I understand . . .

(*Silence.*)

FOREMAN: Had your tea break yet?

VANEK: Not yet, no . . .

FOREMAN: You go later, just tell 'em at the gate you've been to see me . . .

VANEK: Thank you.

FOREMAN: And don't keep thanking me!

(*Silence.*)

'Scuse me.

(*The* FOREMAN *gets up and goes out.* VANEK *quickly pours the rest of his beer into the foreman's glass. The* FOREMAN *returns, buttoning his flies, and sits down at his desk.*)

When're you going to bring her?

VANEK: What?

FOREMAN: Why, Bohdalova, of course.

VANEK: Oh . . . I'll ask her one of these days . . .

FOREMAN: How about inviting her for Saturday?

VANEK: *This* Saturday?

FOREMAN: Well, why not?

VANEK: I don't know if she'll have time . . .

FOREMAN: Oh, come on, she'll make time for you, won't she?

**VANEK**: Actors are very busy people, you know . . . their engagements are often planned a long time in advance . . . it's not easy to make new arrangements at short notice . . .

**FOREMAN**: Of course, if you don't think we're good enough for her down here . . . don't invite her.

**VANEK**: Oh no, that's not it at all . . .

**FOREMAN**: Don't let me talk you into anything . . . I just thought we could all have a bit of fun together . . .

**VANEK**: Yes, I see . . .

(*Silence.*)

**FOREMAN**: Don't be depressed.

**VANEK**: I'm not depressed . . .

(*Silence.*)

**FOREMAN**: Listen here, Ferdinand . . . you *are* Ferdinand, aren't you . . .

**VANEK**: Yes, that's right . . .

**FOREMAN**: Listen, Ferdinand, I've been meaning to have a chat with you . . .

**VANEK**: Yes, I know . . .

(*Silence.*)

**FOREMAN**: Why aren't you drinking?

**VANEK**: I've told you I'm not a beer drinker . . .

**FOREMAN**: Here everybody drinks beer . . .

**VANEK**: I know . . .

(*Silence.*)

**FOREMAN**: Listen, Ferdinand . . . You don't mind me calling you Ferdinand, do you?

**VANEK**: No, I don't mind.

**FOREMAN**: How would you like to be a warehouseman? That wouldn't be a bad job for you, now would it? After all, you're an intelligent chap . . . and honest, so why not? You're not going to spend the rest of your natural rolling barrels with gypsies. You'd be in a warm place and you'd shut up shop at lunchtime, say you was clearing up . . . and you could think up some more jokes for those theatrical plays of yours, in peace and quiet. You could even have a snooze, if you felt like it. What do you say to that, eh?

VANEK: Do you think I could . . .?

FOREMAN: Why not?

VANEK: I'm not in a position to pick and choose, but if such an opportunity did present itself, I'd naturally welcome it. I do believe I am reasonably tidy, and I can type . . . I know one or two foreign languages . . . Come to think of it, it *is* pretty chilly in that cellar, and if you're not used to it . . .

FOREMAN: There you are, then . . . Know anything about bookkeeping?

VANEK: I'm sure I could learn . . . I once took a course in economics . . .

FOREMAN: Is that right? Know anything about bookkeeping?

VANEK: I'm sure I could learn . . .

FOREMAN: You'd be in a warm place . . . you could shut up shop over lunch . . . you're not going to go on rolling barrels with gypsies for ever.

VANEK: Well, if it is possible . . .

(*Silence.*)

FOREMAN: I can tell a crook as soon as look at him. You're an honest man, Vanek, and so am I, so why shouldn't we stick together. What do you say?

VANEK: Yes, of course . . .

FOREMAN: So you agree . . .?

VANEK: Naturally . . .

FOREMAN: If not, you've only got to say so. Maybe you don't fancy going into partnership with me . . . maybe you don't think much of me, eh? Or have you got other plans?

VANEK: No, nothing like that . . . you've done a great deal for me and I'm most grateful . . . especially if this warehouse thing came off. I'll do my utmost to do a good job . . .

(*The* FOREMAN *opens another bottle and pours beer out for both of them.*)

FOREMAN: Shall we drink to it then?

VANEK: Right . . .

(*They drink.*)

FOREMAN: Bottoms up!

(VANEK *drinks up, with an effort. The* FOREMAN *immediately*

*refills his glass. A short silence.*)
You mustn't be depressed.

VANEK: I am not depressed . . .
(*Silence.*)

FOREMAN: Look here, Ferdinand . . .

VANEK: Yes . . .?

FOREMAN: We're pals, right?

VANEK: Yes, we are pals . . .

FOREMAN: You're not just saying it?

VANEK: No . . .

FOREMAN: You trust me, then?

VANEK: Of course I trust you.

FOREMAN: All right, I'll tell you something . . . but keep it to yourself, understand?

VANEK: I understand . . .

FOREMAN: Can I depend on that?

VANEK: You can depend on it.

FOREMAN: Right, then . . . (*He lowers his voice.*) They come here and ask about you . . .

VANEK: Who do?

FOREMAN: Who do? What d'you mean 'who do'? *They* do, of course.

VANEK: Really?

FOREMAN: Would I be telling you?

VANEK: Do you think that my job here at the brewery is in jeopardy?
(*Silence.*)
Are they insisting that I be dismissed?
(*Silence.*)
Or are you having trouble because you took me on?
(*Silence.*)

FOREMAN: All right, I'll tell you . . . but it's strictly between you and me, understand?

VANEK: I understand . . .

FOREMAN: Can I depend on it?

VANEK: You can depend on it.

FOREMAN: Well, then, if anyone else was in my place, you

wouldn't be working here, I guarantee you. How about that, Ferdie?

VANEK: Yes, I see . . . I'm very grateful to you . . .

FOREMAN: I'm not telling you this so you should thank me . . .

VANEK: I know you're not . . .

FOREMAN: I just want you to know how things are . . .

VANEK: Thank you . . .

(*Silence.*)

FOREMAN: 'Scuse me . . .

(*The* FOREMAN *gets up with some difficulty and goes out.* VANEK *quickly pours the rest of his beer in the foreman's glass. The* FOREMAN *returns, buttoning his flies, and sits down again.*)

Did you have it off with her?

VANEK: With who?

FOREMAN: With Bohdalova, of course.

VANEK: I? Of course not.

FOREMAN: Honest?

VANEK: Yes . . .

FOREMAN: I think you're a stupid nit, then.

(*Silence.*)

VANEK: Excuse me . . .

FOREMAN: What is it?

VANEK: I'll have to be going . . .

FOREMAN: Whatever for?

VANEK: They'll be looking for me down in the cellars.

FOREMAN: Fuck the cellars . . . They can do without you for a bit . . . and anyway Serkezy is down there. Just sit tight and drink your beer.

(*Silence.*)

Listen, Ferdinand . . . you *are* Ferdinand, aren't you?

VANEK: Yes, that's right . . .

FOREMAN: Listen, Ferdinand . . . you don't mind me calling you Ferdinand, do you . . .?

VANEK: I don't mind . . .

FOREMAN: Hang on, hang on . . . I'd rather you told me if you mind . . . don't want to offend you, do I?

VANEK: Why should I be offended?

FOREMAN: With you a man never knows what's what . . . you don't say anything . . . Gawd knows what you're thinking . . . you just keep saying 'yes, of course' and 'thank you' . . .

VANEK: I was brought up that way . . .

FOREMAN: And I'm just an uneducated brewery yokel. That's what you meant, wasn't it? Don't tell me you didn't . . .

VANEK: I didn't mean that at all . . .

FOREMAN: No, come on, be honest . . . let's put our cards on the table . . .

VANEK: Honestly, I don't have a low opinion of you . . . quite the contrary . . .

FOREMAN: So we're pals?

VANEK: Yes . . .

FOREMAN: You trust me . . .?

VANEK: I trust you.

FOREMAN: Well, listen here, then . . . I know one of them what comes here asking about you . . . we went to school together, him and me . . . good friend of mine. His name is Tonda Masek, a decent sort, at least he's done all right by me . . .

VANEK: You're lucky, aren't you . . .

FOREMAN: No, listen, you mustn't think he pulls a lot of weight because he doesn't, but he has been helpful to me once or twice and I might need him again one o' these days . . . and anyway, as I said, he's a good lad. So you see I couldn't just drop him in it, could I . . . You see that, don't you?

VANEK: Yes, I see . . .

(*Silence.*)

FOREMAN: What're you staring at me for?

VANEK: I wasn't staring at you.

FOREMAN: Why don't you tell me what you're thinking . . .? Come on, tell me . . .

VANEK: I wasn't thinking anything . . .

FOREMAN: Come off it, I know what you're thinking. What you don't know is that if I hadn't promised to do it, they'd have found someone else, and that would be worse because he'd hardly be as decent about it as I've been. I'm a fair-minded sort of bloke, that's what I am, unlike others I could mention. That's my philosophy, even today. And that's where you've been lucky, if you want to know. Because people are proper bastards, they are. You don't think anyone else would've been so bloody daft as to tell you all this, do you? When was you born? Where do you think you're living?

VANEK: I appreciate your frankness . . .

FOREMAN: Have you any idea what risk I'm taking by being so decent to you? What happens if you rat on me?

VANEK: I'm not going to tell anybody . . .

FOREMAN: So you'll write about it. Put it in one of those plays of yours . . . they'll confiscate it and I'll be ruined . . .

VANEK: Don't worry, I'm going to keep it to myself . . .

FOREMAN: Honest?

VANEK: Honest . . .

(*The* FOREMAN *opens another bottle and pours himself a beer. A short silence.*)

I say . . .

FOREMAN: What?

VANEK: Should it come off . . . I mean that job in the warehouse . . . what about old Mr Sustr?

FOREMAN: Well, what about him?

(*Silence.*)

Come to think of it . . . funny, isn't it?

VANEK: I suppose so . . .

FOREMAN: It is and all . . .

(*Silence.*)

VANEK: I say . . .

FOREMAN: What?

VANEK: About that warehouse . . . you really think they'll allow it? After all, they must know I'd be in a nice warm place . . .

FOREMAN: They know sweet Fanny Adams . . .

(*Silence.*)

You married?

VANEK: Yes . . .

FOREMAN: Any kids?

VANEK: No . . .

FOREMAN: I've got three, I have . . .

(*Silence.*)

VANEK: You might possibly argue that I'd have less contact with the other employees . . .

FOREMAN: Listen, Ferdinand . . .

VANEK: That's what they're after, isn't it . . . That I shouldn't have contact with people . . .

FOREMAN: *Listen*, Ferdinand . . .

VANEK: That would be a convincing argument, wouldn't it . . .?

FOREMAN: Listen, Ferdinand . . .

VANEK: Yes . . .?

FOREMAN: You play poker?

VANEK: No, I don't play . . .

FOREMAN: I do . . . we had a regular session every Thursday, not half bad that was . . . and what do you know? I had to give it up on account of that Lojza Hlavacek . . .

VANEK: Oh . . .?

FOREMAN: So don't think I've got such a cushy life, either . . .

(*Silence.*)

Listen, Ferdinand . . .

VANEK: Yes . . .?

FOREMAN: Ever met my old woman?

VANEK: No, I haven't . . .

(*Silence.*)

FOREMAN: Tell you something, Ferdinand . . .

VANEK: Yes . . .?

FOREMAN: It's all a bloody mess . . .

VANEK: I know . . .

FOREMAN: Shit! What do *you* know . . . You're in clover. Writing those plays of yours . . . rolling barrels . . . and the world can go hang! What have you got to grouse about? And you know what – they're scared of you, that's what.

VANEK: Oh come, I hardly think so . . .

FOREMAN: That's God's truth. But what about me? Who cares what happens to me? Nobody. Does anyone make out reports about me? Not on your life. They can yell at me to their heart's content. Got me cornered, haven't they? But you – you're in clover.

(*Silence*.)

Listen, Ferdinand . . .

VANEK: Yes . . .?

FOREMAN: You won't forget about Bohdalova, will you? You *will* bring her along? Say you'll bring her along . . .

VANEK: Don't worry . . . I'll phone her today and arrange everything . . .

FOREMAN: Do you think she'll come?

VANEK: I'll do my level best . . .

FOREMAN: You and she are friends, isn't that right?

VANEK: Yes, we are . . .

FOREMAN: Hang on, hang on . . . you said you were friends . . .

VANEK: Yes, that's right . . .

FOREMAN: No, hang on . . . are you friends or not?

VANEK: But yes, we are . . .

FOREMAN: So what's the snag?

(*Silence*.)

Damn it all, she can choose her own friends.

VANEK: Of course she can . . .

FOREMAN: That's her inalienable right, that is.

VANEK: Of course it is.

FOREMAN: A matter of principle, that's what it is.

(*Silence*.)

Anyway, who needs to know that *you* brought her here. She can come as a gesture of solidarity with the working class, can't she? There's nothing wrong with that.

VANEK: I think so too.

FOREMAN: So you'll bring her, then?

VANEK: I'll do my level best. I'll call her today . . . after all, we're friends. There's nothing wrong with that.

(*Silence*.)

FOREMAN: Listen, Ferdinand . . .

VANEK: Yes . . .?

FOREMAN: You've no idea how fed up I am with it all . . .

VANEK: I know . . .

FOREMAN: You know bugger all. I bet you're saying to yourself:

bloody fool, let him talk . . .

VANEK: No I'm not . . .

FOREMAN: Why aren't you drinking?

VANEK: I am . . .

FOREMAN:, Had your tea break yet?

VANEK: No, not yet . . .

FOREMAN: To hell with your tea break . . . forget it . . .

VANEK: I'm not really hungry anyway . . .

FOREMAN: I may be a fool, but I'm fair-minded.

VANEK: That's right, so you are.

FOREMAN: I wanted to have a word with you . . .

VANEK: I know . . .

FOREMAN: People are proper bastards, they really are. Why aren't you drinking?

VANEK: I am . . .

FOREMAN: Had your tea break yet?

VANEK: No, not yet . . .

FOREMAN: Oh you, you're in clover . . .

VANEK: I'm most grateful to you . . .

FOREMAN: It's all a bloody mess . . .

(*He opens another bottle and pours himself a glass. A short silence.*)

Listen . . .

VANEK: Yes?

FOREMAN: You don't mind me calling you Ferdinand?

VANEK: I don't mind . . .

FOREMAN: You've only got to tell me if you do . . .

VANEK: No, I don't really . . .

FOREMAN: Good, I'm glad you don't mind . . .

VANEK: On the contrary, I like it. I am delighted we have been drawn closer together.

FOREMAN: 'I'm delighted we've been drawn closer together', 'I appreciate your frankness' – why do you keep talking like that? . . . like . . . like a . . .

VANEK: Like a book?

FOREMAN: That's it . . .

VANEK: Does it irritate you . . .?

FOREMAN: It don't irritate me . . . I'm delighted we've drawn closer together . . . Shit!

VANEK: I beg your pardon?

FOREMAN: Shit, I said.

(*Silence.*)

VANEK: Excuse me . . .

FOREMAN: What is it?

VANEK: I'll have to be going . . .

FOREMAN: Whatever for?

VANEK: They'll be looking for me in the cellars . . .

FOREMAN: Fuck the cellars . . . They can do without you for a bit . . . and anyway, Serkezy is down there. Just sit tight and drink.

VANEK: No, seriously . . . they'll be annoyed.

FOREMAN: Oh, I see . . . I bore you, that's what it is . . . I know . . . Gott and Bohdalova, they're better company, aren't they? . . .

VANEK: No, I enjoy talking to you, I just don't want to have any trouble . . . it isn't worth it . . . especially now that I have the prospect of that job in the warehouse . . .

FOREMAN: You really mean that . . . that you enjoy talking to me?

VANEK: Really.

FOREMAN: You're not just saying it?

VANEK: No . . .

(*The* FOREMAN *opens another bottle and pours himself a glass. A short silence.*)

FOREMAN: Ferdinand . . .

VANEK: Yes?

FOREMAN: You know what's the worst about all this?

VANEK: No, what?

FOREMAN: I'm damned if I know what to tell 'em every bloody week. What do I know about you . . . you tell me that . . . next to nothing, right? I hardly see you, day in day out . . . and as for the tittle-tattle I sometimes hear . . . that you slip off to the lab whenever you want to take a rest from work . . . that you've been seen a couple of times in town with Marge from the bottling plant . . . that the boys from Maintenance helped repair your central heating – I ask you, is that any good? So what am I supposed to tell 'em every bloody week?

VANEK: I'm sorry, but I hardly think I can help you there . . .

FOREMAN: But that's just it – you can. If only you wanted to . . .

VANEK: Help you? How can I?

FOREMAN: You're an intellectual, aren't you? You know all about politics and things. And you write, don't you? Who should know better what it is they want than you? Tell me that.

VANEK: Oh really, you don't think that I . . .?

FOREMAN: Listen, Ferdinand, in that warehouse you'll have plenty of time to spare – what harm would it do if you put it on paper for me once a week . . . Don't I deserve it? I'll see you don't come to any harm. You'll be nice and cosy in there . . . you can even take beer in with you . . . as much as you like. Writing comes natural to you, it'll be child's play. That Tonda Masek is a decent sort . . .I've known him since we were boys . . . and he really needs it. Can't leave him in the lurch, can we. Didn't we say we'd stick together? That we were going to be pals? Didn't we drink to that? Go on, you tell me, did we or didn't we?

VANEK: Yes, I know, but . . .

FOREMAN: It's all up to you now, Ferdinand. If only you do your bit, everything's going to turn up trumps. You help me, I help him, he'll do me a good turn and I'll do you one – we'll all benefit. Hang it all, we're not going to make life difficult for one another, are we now?

(*Silence.*)

What're you staring at me for?

VANEK: I wasn't staring at you.

(*Silence.*)

FOREMAN: Like this, you'll be able to decide exactly what you want 'em to know about you . . . you must admit, that can't be bad . . .

VANEK: Yes, I know . . .

(*Silence.*)

FOREMAN: You'd like to be in that warehouse, wouldn't you? Nice and cosy and warm, and plenty of time to spare . . .

VANEK: That would be wonderful . . .

(*Silence.*)

FOREMAN: Well then, what's the snag?

(*Silence.*)

VANEK: Look here . . .

FOREMAN: What is it?

VANEK: I'm truly most grateful to you for everything you've done for me . . . I appreciate it all the more because I know how rare such an attitude is nowadays . . . you have, so to speak, saved my bacon, for I don't honestly know what I would have done without your help . . . and that job in the warehouse would be an even greater boon to me than you realize . . . but I . . . please don't misunderstand what I am going to say, but I just can't . . . I can't inform on myself . . .

FOREMAN: Inform . . . inform? Who's talking about informing?

VANEK: It's not myself I am worried about . . . it wouldn't do *me* any harm . . . but there's a principle involved. How can I be expected to participate in . . .

FOREMAN: In what? Go on, just say it! What can't you participate in?

VANEK: In something I have always found repugnant . . .

(*A short, tense silence.*)

FOREMAN: I see. So you can't, eh. You can't. I like that. Now you've really shown your true colours, haven't you. A fine pal *you've* turned out to be. (*He gets up and starts to pace the room in great agitation.*) And what about me? Going to drop me right in it, aren't you? Let me stew in my own juice. Doesn't matter about *me* being a right bugger. Never mind about me, *I* can be allowed to wallow in the slime, I'm just an ordinary brewery yokel – but a fine gentleman like you can't participate. I can soil my hands as much as I like, as long as the gentleman stays clean. The gentleman has principles. Everything else can go hang. Just so he keeps his lilywhite soul. Putting principles before people. That's you lot all over . . .

VANEK: Who do you mean – you lot . . .?

FOREMAN: Who do I mean? You bloody intellectuals, that's who.

Who else? Fine gentlemen, spouting fine words. *You* can afford to, because you always come out on top, you're *interesting*, you always know how to wriggle out of things, you're on top even when you're down, but an ordinary bloke like me can work his bloody fingers off to the bone and what 'as he got to show for it – sweet Fanny Adams, that's what – no one to turn to, everybody does him down, everybody gives him the boot, everybody has a go at him, he leads a bloody miserable life, and then what – a gent like you comes along and says he has no principles. You'd take a nice cushy job in a warm warehouse from me, wouldn't you, but a bit of the dirt I've got to wade through every day, that you won't. You're a clever lot, you are – *very* clever, oh yes, you know what's what all right, you can take good care of your bloody selves. Principles! I'm not surprised you hang on to your bleeding principles – they come in handy, don't they, you know how to make a mint out of 'em, you do, they give you a living – but what about me? Nobody gives *me* a hand, nobody is scared of me, nobody writes about me, nobody gives a blind bit of notice what *I* do, I'm just about good enough to shovel the muck out of which your principles can grow, I'm good to find you cosy warm spots for you to play the hero in, and what do I get for all that – nothing but a raspberry. One fine day *you* will go back to your actresses, you'll boast about the time you worked here rolling barrels, showing off what a fine big he-man you are – but what about me, eh? What about me? I ain't got nowhere to go back to, have I? Where can I go? Who'll take any notice of me? Who cares what I do? What has life to offer me? What about *my* future?

(*He slumps down on his desk, puts his head on* VANEK*'s shoulder and begins to sob. After a while he calms down, looks up at* VANEK *and says softly:*)

Ferdinand . . .

VANEK: Hm . . .

FOREMAN: You a pal?

VANEK: Yes, I am.

FOREMAN: Go and fetch her, would you – *now* . . . bring her here, please . . .

(*Silence.*)

Tell her, 'Jirinka, I've got a pal over there, just an ordinary brewery yokel, he is, but fair-minded . . .'

(*Silence.*)

I'll get you that job in the warehouse, I promise – and you don't have to make out any reports either – just do this for me . . .

(*Silence.*)

You *will* do it for me, won't you? I know you will. Just for one evening . . . everything will be all right then, everything will be different, I'll at least know I haven't lived for nothing, that this fucking life hasn't been completely wasted . . . You *will* go and fetch her, won't you?

(*Silence. Then the* FOREMAN *grabs* VANEK *by his lapels and starts shouting in his face.*)

If you don't . . . if you don't bring her here – I just don't know . . . I don't know *what* I'll do . . . I . . . I . . . I think . . .

(*The* FOREMAN *breaks down and cries softly, again resting his head on* VANEK*'s shoulder. Silence; after a while the* FOREMAN*'s sobs subside and he begins to snore loudly.* VANEK *waits a little, then gently removes the* FOREMAN*'s head from his shoulder, allowing it to rest on top of the desk, gets up and goes to the door. He turns round, stands hesitating for a while and then says to the sleeping* FOREMAN*:*)

VANEK: Don't be depressed . . .

(VANEK *goes out. A little later there is a knock on the door. The* FOREMAN *wakes instantly and having had a short nap, is completely sober. He behaves exactly as he did at the beginning of the play. He has evidently forgotten everything that happened.*)

FOREMAN: Come in . . .

(VANEK *enters, buttoning his flies.*)

Oh, it's you, Mr Vanek. Come in, come in. Take a seat.

(VANEK *sits down.*)

Want a beer?

(VANEK *nods; the* FOREMAN *takes a bottle from the crate, opens it and pours two glasses, one of which he pushes in front of* VANEK. VANEK *drinks it straight away*.)

Well, tell me, how're things?

VANEK: It's all a bloody mess.

# UNVEILING

## CHARACTERS

**VERA**
**MICHAEL**
**FERDINAND VANEK**

*Vera's and Michael's apartment*

*Vera's and Michael's apartment. It consists of a large living room, extending into a step-up dining area upstage. A serving window connects the dining area with the kitchen behind the stage. Stage right, there is a door leading into a hallway; stage left, a large fireplace; at the centre of the stage stands an antique table, surrounded by soft, modern seats. A mass of sundry antiques and curious objects decorates the room – for example, there is an art-nouveau marquee, a Chinese vase, a limestone baroque angel, an inlaid chest, a folkloristic painting on a glass pane, a Russian icon, old hand-mortars and grinders, and so on; a niche in the wall houses a wooden Gothic Madonna; a rococo musical clock adorns the fireplace, and Turkish scimitar hangs above it. The dining area is furnished in a 'rustic style', with a wooden farm-cart wheel on the wall; the floor is covered with a thick, shaggy carpet, on it lie several Persian mats and, near the fireplace, a bear skin with a stuffed head: downstage left stands a filigreed wooden confessional. The room also has a hi-fi stereo and a drinks trolley, standing near the fireplace and holding various bottles, glasses, ice cubes, as well as a bowl with stuffed oysters. As the curtain rises,* VANEK* *is standing at the door, evidently having just come in.* VERA *and* MICHAEL *are facing him.* VANEK *is holding a bouquet of flowers behind his back.*

VERA: We're so glad that you've made it –
MICHAEL: We were afraid that you might not make it any more –
VERA: We've been looking forward to seeing you so much –
MICHAEL: What can I get you? A whisky?
VANEK: All right –

(MICHAEL *steps over to the drinks trolley and starts preparing*

*In the original Czech version the Vanek-figure here was called Bedrich (Frederick in Czech). At this stage, however, when Ferdinand Vanek has become a well-known character, the editor feels free to rename Bedrich in accordance with his meaning in the play.

*three whiskies;* VANEK *is momentarily at a loss about what to do, then he hands the flowers to Vera.*)

VERA: Oh, they are lovely! (*She takes the bouquet and looks at it.*) And you never forget – (*She smells it.*) What a beautiful aroma! Thank you, Ferdinand –

(VERA *walks upstage and puts the flowers into a vase;* VANEK *looks around the apartment with curiosity. A short pause.*)

VANEK: It looks different here somehow –

VERA: I hope so! Michael has poured a lot of sweat into it! You know how he is when he gets involved in something: He won't let go till he has everything just the way he's planned it –

MICHAEL: I only finished the thing the day before yesterday: we haven't had anybody over yet, so this actually is sort of an unveiling. Ice?

VANEK: All right –

(VERA *comes back downstage; the surprised* VANEK *is still looking around.*)

Where did you get all this?

MICHAEL: It wasn't easy, as you can imagine. I did have a few contacts among the antique dealers and collectors. I had to establish a few more. The most important thing was not to give up when I wasn't able to get my hands on what I wanted the first time around –

VERA: He did quite a job on this, didn't he?

VANEK: I guess so –

VERA: I confess that even I didn't think it would come out this well! When you want to give your place some character, it's not enough merely to like old things – you have to know how to get them and how to present them and how to integrate them with your modern furnishings – but, it so happens that Michael is really good at that – that's why you won't find a single goof here –

(*Michael hands the glasses to* VERA *and* VANEK, *then he takes his glass, raises it, and turns to* VANEK.)

MICHAEL: Welcome, Ferdinand –

VERA: We've missed you –

MICHAEL: As I was working on this, I thought about you often – what you were going to say when you saw it all.

VANEK: Well, cheers –

*(They all drink; a short pause.)*

MICHAEL: Of course, if I didn't have Vera's full support, it would have never come out like this. And it wasn't just a matter of support and understanding either, she gave me direct assistance in this, too! Take that Turkish scimitar there – how do you like it?

VANEK: It's nice –

MICHAEL: And how does it fit in with everything here?

VANEK: Very well –

MICHAEL: You see, and it's something that Vera found on her very own, and she even put it up there, too – all the while not knowing that this was exactly the thing I had in mind for that spot over the fireplace! Isn't that awesome?

VANEK: That's great –

*(A short, awkward pause.)*

VERA: Have a seat –

VANEK: Thank you –

*(They all sit down in the soft seats. A short pause,* VANEK *is looking around again;* VERA *and* MICHAEL *watch him with satisfaction;* VANEK *eventually notices the confessional.)*

What's that?

MICHAEL: It's what you see – a confessional –

VANEK: Where did you get that?

MICHAEL: You won't believe how lucky I was. I heard that they were going to liquidate a church that'd been closed down, so I dropped everything and jumped in the car. And this is the result. I managed to get it out of the sexton for three hundred –

VANEK: That's all?

MICHAEL: Not bad, is it? Pure baroque!

VANEK: What are you going to do with it?

MICHAEL: What do you mean, what are we going to do with it? You don't like it?

VANEK: Well, I do –

MICHAEL: Isn't that a fantastic object, we're really happy about it, aren't we, Vera?

VERA: It really is a superb piece of craftsmanship, I'd say that Michael really got another one of his steals there –

(*A short pause.*)

What do you think of the dining area?

VANEK: (*Turns around*) It's cosy –

VERA: Wasn't that a nice idea – to do it so simply – as if on a farm –

VANEK: Mmn –

(*A short pause.*)

MICHAEL: Do you know what I like best here?

VANEK: What?

MICHAEL: This Gothic Madonna! I needed one that would fit into that niche, and they were all either bigger or smaller –

VANEK: And there was no way to enlarge the niche?

MICHAEL: But that's just what I didn't want to do. It strikes me that it's got the perfect dimensions the way it is –

VERA: See, that's Michael! He'd rather wear out his feet than simply enlarge the thing!

(*pause.*)

MICHAEL: And what about you? When are you going to get started?

VANEK: On what?

MICHAEL: On your place –

VANEK: I don't know –

MICHAEL: You should finally do something about it! You can't go on living out of boxes for ever –

VANEK: I don't even pay any attention to it any more –

MICHAEL: If you don't feel like tackling it yourself, why doesn't Eva do something about it? She has plenty of time on her hands –

VERA: I think Eva actually needs to get involved in something like that – it would be a good way to get her back on her feet –

MICHAEL: We would gladly come to the rescue if she found she couldn't handle something –

VERA: Michael has tons of experience with this now – he'd tell her what to do – where to start – what she'd need –

MICHAEL: I'd tell her who's got what – where to go and who to see –

VERA: That's true, Ferdinand. Why don't you put Eva in charge of it anyway?

VANEK: It's not really Eva's cup of tea –

VERA: We know that, but if you were to waken her interest somehow –

MICHAEL: Damn it, you have to do something about that home of yours –

VERA: You know, Michael and I think that a person lives the way a person lives. When you have what we call a place with character, your whole life suddenly – like it or not – acquires a certain face, too – a sort of new dimension – a different rhythm, a different content, a different order – isn't that so, Michael?

MICHAEL: She's right, Ferdinand! One really shouldn't be indifferent to what one eats, one shouldn't be indifferent to what one eats on, and what one eats with, what one dries oneself with, what one wears, what one takes a bath in, what one sleeps on. And once any of these things starts to matter, you'll find that something else suddenly matters, too, and then another thing gets you, and so a whole sort of a chain of things develops – and if you head down that road, what else can it mean but that you're upgrading your life to another, higher level of culture – and that you raise yourself to a kind of higher harmony – which then in effect translates itself into your relationships with other people! You tell him, Vera!

VERA: That is a fact, Ferdinand! If the two of you were to put a little more effort into the way you live, I'm sure that things would get smoother in your marriage, too –

VANEK: But things are smooth –

VERA: Ferdinand!

VANEK: But really –

VERA: You don't like to talk about it, I know. But you know, Michael and I have been talking about the two of you a lot lately; we've been thinking about you a lot – and we really care about how you two live!

MICHAEL: We're only trying to help, Ferdinand!

VERA: You're our best friend – we like you a lot – you have no idea how happy we'd be for you if your situation finally got resolved somehow!

VANEK: What situation?

VERA: Let's just drop it. Shouldn't I light the fire?

VANEK: Not for me –

MICHAEL: So I'll put on some music, all right?

VERA: Michael has just brought a ton of new records from Switzerland –

VANEK: Maybe later, perhaps?

(*Pause; then suddenly the musical clock on the mantelpiece breaks into a period tune, startling* VANEK. *After a while, the clock falls silent. Pause.*)

VERA: So tell us – how is everything with you?

VANEK: Well, you know – nothing's changed –

VERA: Is it true that you've got a job in a brewery now?

VANEK: Yes –

VERA: That's horrible!

(*Pause. Then* VERA *points at the drinks trolley.*)

Michael, would you –

MICHAEL: Oh yeah –

(MICHAEL *takes the bowl with oysters off the trolley and stands it in front of* VANEK.)

VERA: Help yourself –

VANEK: What is it?

MICHAEL: That's Vera's specialty: sautéed groombles –

VANEK: Groombles? I never heard of this –

VERA: We've really become very fond of them lately, Michael has just brought a whole box of them from Switzerland –

MICHAEL: Because Vera really knows how to make them –

VERA: What you have to do is to watch for the precise moment, when they've just stopped puffing up and before they start falling –

MICHAEL: Taste one!

(VANEK *takes one oyster and, using a spoon, begins to scoop out its contents. He concentrates on the taste;* VERA *and* MICHAEL *watch him tensely.*)

So what do you think?

VANEK: It's good –

MICHAEL: Isn't it?

VANEK: You went to all the trouble of making this just for me?

VERA: We're having our unveiling today, right?

VANEK: It sort of reminds me of blackberries a little bit –

VERA: That may be because I put in a few drops of woodpeak to help the taste –

VANEK: Drops of what?

MICHAEL: Woodpeak –

VERA: That's my original contribution –

VANEK: Really?

MICHAEL: An excellent idea, isn't it? I can't help it, but Vera's really got a talent for cooking. A week doesn't go by without her making some novelty – and she always uses her imagination to improve it. Take this Saturday for example – what was it that we had now? Oh yeah, the liver with walnuts! And it was such a delicacy; anyway, would you ever think of putting woodpeak on groombles?

VANEK: Never –

MICHAEL: See what I mean!

(VANEK *puts away the empty oyster shell and wipes his mouth with a napkin.*)

VERA: Well, it's a joy cooking for Michael! He knows how to appreciate and praise even the most modest idea, and when something turns out well, he really gets off on it. If he just stuffed everything in like a mechanical pie-eater, not even knowing what it is that he's swallowing, then I probably wouldn't have so much fun with it either –

VANEK: I can understand that –

MICHAEL: But there's even more to it than that. When you know that an interesting dinner, some small gourmet surprise, is waiting for you at home, you look that much more forward to getting there and you have that much less reason to go bar-hopping with your buddies. Maybe it'll strike you as being petty, but I think that these things also represent a kind of cement that holds a family together and helps to create that important feeling that you've got something to back you up at home. Don't you think?

VANEK: Yes, of course –
*(pause.)*

VERA: How's Eva doing? Has she learned to cook anything yet?

VANEK: She's always cooked –

VERA: Granted, but how!

VANEK: I pretty much like her cooking –

VERA: Because you got used to it already. Don't get offended, but those pepper steaks she made when we were over that time before Christmas – it was before Christmas, wasn't it?

VANEK: Yeah –

VERA: Don't get offended, but they were dreadful! Do you remember, Michael?

MICHAEL: How could I forget!

VANEK: Eva was a little nervous that time –

VERA: I'm sorry, but something like that should never ever happen to a cook! What does she cook for you usually anyway?

VANEK: We tend to have cold dinners –

VERA: Even on Saturdays?

VANEK: Sometimes we have something warm, too – breaded cutlets, for example –

MICHAEL: Listen, Ferdinand, it's none of my business, but why don't you send Eva to some of those courses? She has plenty of time on her hands –

VERA: Eva? Come on! You think Eva would take any courses?

MICHAEL: Well, that's true –

VERA: If she did learn how to cook though, it would immediately boost her self-confidence – but she won't see the connection. She's floating around somewhere, God knows where –

VANEK: I think her cooking's fine –

VERA: Ferdinand!

VANEK: Really, I –

MICHAEL: You don't like to talk about it, I know. But you know Vera and I have been talking about the two of you a lot lately, we've been thinking about you a lot – and we really care about how you two live!

VERA: We're only trying to help, Ferdinand!

MICHAEL: You're our best friend – we like you a lot – you have no idea how happy we'd be for you if your situation finally got resolved somehow!

VANEK: What situation?

MICHAEL: Let's just drop it. Shouldn't I light the fire?

VANEK: Not for me –

VERA: So I'll put on some music, all right? Michael has just brought a ton of new records from Switzerland –

VANEK: Maybe later, OK?

(*Pause. Then suddenly the musical clock on the mantelpiece breaks into a period tune, startling* VANEK. *After a while, the clock falls silent. Pause.*)

MICHAEL: So what do you actually do there, in that brewery?

VANEK: I draw beer –

MICHAEL: Into barrels?

VANEK: Yes –

MICHAEL: That's got to be pretty rough, doesn't it?

VANEK: It's not that bad –

(*Pause.*)

MICHAEL: Are we going to show Pete to Ferdinand?

VERA: A little later, Michael, he might still wake up right now –

VANEK: How is Pete doing?

MICHAEL: He's fantastic! I'd only been gone to Switzerland for ten days, but when I got back, I tell you I barely recognized him – that's how much of a jump he's made in that time!

VERA: He's extremely curious –

MICHAEL: Bright –

VERA: Perceptive –

MICHAEL: He has a superb memory –

VERA: And yet he's such a good-looking kid, too!

MICHAEL: Just to give you an example. Do you know what he

asked me this morning? (*To* VERA) I forgot to tell you about that! All of a sudden, he comes to me and says, 'Daddy, can a frog drown?' What do you think about that? Isn't that awesome?

VERA: Did he really ask you that? If a frog can drown?

MICHAEL: Imagine that! He comes to me and says, 'Daddy, can a frog drown?'

VERA: Outstanding! I don't even know if I could have thought of that. Can a frog drown! Outstanding! Outstanding!

MICHAEL: You know, Ferdinand, sometimes I say to myself that to have a child and to bring it up is the only thing that has any meaning in life! Because it is such an awesome encounter with the mystery of life – such a lesson in life appreciation! Unless you actually go through it, you can never even understand it –

VERA: Absolutely, Ferdinand, it's an awesomely strange and beautiful experience: one day this tiny being shows up here – and you know he is yours – that without you, he wouldn't even be here – that you've made him and now he's here – and he's living his own life – and is growing before your eyes – and then he starts to walk – and say things – and reason – and ask questions – now isn't that a miracle?

VANEK: Certainly is –

MICHAEL: You know a child really changes you a lot – suddenly you begin to understand everything differently, more deeply – life – nature – people – and all of a sudden your own life – like it or not – acquires sort of a new dimension – a different rhythm, a different content, a different order – isn't that so, Vera?

VERA: Exactly! Just take the responsibility you suddenly have. It's up to you what kind of a person he will turn out to be – what he'll feel – think – how he'll live –

MICHAEL: But not only that: because it was you who tossed him into this world, who offered it to him for his use and who provides him with some orientation in it, you suddenly start feeling a much greater responsibility for this world that now contains your child – do you know what I mean?

VANEK: I guess so –

MICHAEL: I never believed this, but now I see how a child gives you a brand new point of view, a brand new set of values – and suddenly it begins to dawn on you that the most important thing now is what you do for that child, what sort of a home you create for him, what sort of a start you give him, what openings you provide – and in the light of this awesome responsibility you start seeing the utter insignificance of most of the things you had once thought world-shattering –

VERA: How did he put it? Can a frog drown? Do you see what that tiny head can give birth to? Isn't that fantastic?

VANEK: Mmn –

(*Pause.*)

MICHAEL: So what about you two?

VANEK: What about us two?

MICHAEL: Why don't you have a child yet anyway?

VANEK: I don't know –

VERA: Eva probably doesn't want one, does she?

VANEK: Oh no – she does –

VERA: I really don't understand that girl! Is she so afraid of all the worries that go along with having a child? Because if she really wanted a baby, you would have had one ages ago!

MICHAEL: You are the ones who will lose out by not pursuing this – because for the two of you, a child would definitely be the best possible solution! It would help you, Ferdinand, to see many things far more sensibly, realistically, wisely –

VERA: It would straighten out your relationship, because it would give you a common purpose in life –

MICHAEL: And what a good thing it would be for Eva!

VERA: You'd see how it would change her!

MICHAEL: How it would suddenly bring out the woman in her again!

VERA: How it would teach her to pay attention to the house –

MICHAEL: To cleanliness –

VERA: To routine –

MICHAEL: To you –

VERA: To herself –

MICHAEL: Seriously, Ferdinand, you ought to have a child, believe us!

VERA: You have no idea how happy we'd be for you!

MICHAEL: We really would, Ferdinand –

VANEK: I believe you –

(*Pause.*)

VERA: Of course, there are women who don't respond even to that – and then you really feel for the children –

MICHAEL: Of course, just to rely on the kid as some sort of panacea that will solve all your problems, that wouldn't be right either – a certain aptitude probably already has to be there before anything else –

VERA: Absolutely! For example, Michael here makes an ideal father: he drives himself hard at the office, till I feel really sorry for him sometimes, just so that he brings home some money – and then he still devotes almost all his free time to the family and to the home! Just take this remodelling he did. He came from the office and instead of stretching out and relaxing, he went right back to work – just so Pete can grow up in a nice environment from the very beginning, and learn to love nice things! And even while doing all that, he still found the time for Pete –

MICHAEL: Of course, Vera is awesome, too. Do you know what it is – to shop, take care of the kid, cook, clean up, do the laundry – while the apartment is a disaster area – despite all that to look just the way she looks right now? That really is no joke! I have to say I admire her more and more as time goes on –

VERA: A lot of that is because our marriage is working –

MICHAEL: Definitely! We get along just awesomely. I don't even remember us having any serious quarrels lately –

VERA: We are interested in one another, yet we don't limit or tie each other down –

MICHAEL: We are kind and attentive to one another without tiring each other with too much thoughtfulness –

VERA: And we always have things to say to each other, because we're fortunate enough to have exactly the same sense of humour –

MICHAEL: The same definition of happiness –

VERA: The same interests –

MICHAEL: The same taste –

VERA: The same views on family life –

MICHAEL: And what is extremely important: we also perfectly complement each other physically –

VERA: That's true, it is really extremely important! And Michael is awesome in that respect – he can be wild as well as tender – honestly selfish as well as awesomely attentive and giving – passionately spontaneous as well as inventively cunning –

MICHAEL: But Vera deserves all the credit for that, because she manages to excite and stimulate me again and again –

VERA: You'd be surprised, Ferdinand, how often we do it! And that's only possible because we always approach it as though it were our very first time, so that it becomes something new, something different for us every time. Something unique, unforgettable. In short, we really invest ourselves fully into it, and, consequently, for us it can never become just a matter of a stereotype or a boring routine –

MICHAEL: You see, Vera knows, too, that to be a good wife doesn't mean merely being a good homemaker and a good mother – she rightly feels that what it means more than anything else is to be a good lover! That's why she takes such wonderful care of herself. So that she keeps her sex appeal even while doing the heaviest chores – in fact, even more so then than at other times!

VERA: Do you remember the day before yesterday, Michael – when you got home early just as I was scrubbing the floor?

MICHAEL: It was beautiful, wasn't it?

VERA: Why do you think Michael isn't drawn to other women? Because he knows that he doesn't have some mop-swinging wifey at home, but a real woman who knows how to take as well as give –

MICHAEL: Of course, Vera is still just as attractive as always – I'd even say that now, after Pete, she has ripened even more –

she has an astonishingly fresh and youthful body now – well, judge for yourself!

(*Michael undoes* VERA*'s clothes, uncovering her breasts.*)

Not bad, right?

VANEK: Great –

MICHAEL: Do you know what I will do, for example?

VANEK: No –

MICHAEL: I'll kiss her, switching from her ear to her neck and back – which really turns her on and I like it, too – like this, look! (MICHAEL *starts to kiss* VERA, *alternating between her ear and her neck;* VERA *groans excitedly.*)

VERA: Don't, darling, no – please – wait – a little later, OK – come on –

(MICHAEL *stops kissing* VERA.)

MICHAEL: We'll talk a little more first, then we'll show you more – to give you an idea of the range of our technique –

VANEK: Won't I make you nervous by being here?

VERA: You silly boy! You're our best friend, right?

MICHAEL: And we'll be happy to show you how far you can take these things!

(*Pause.*)

VERA: So what about you two?

VANEK: How do you mean?

VERA: Do you still sleep with each other at all?

VANEK: Oh yes – now and then –

VERA: Not too often, right?

VANEK: That depends –

VERA: And how is it?

VANEK: I don't know – it's normal –

MICHAEL: I'm sure you don't put any effort into it – just go through the motions, so it's over and done with –

VANEK: We do our best –

VERA: I don't understand that girl at all! Why wouldn't she try a little harder at least in this –

MICHAEL: Is it really impossible for you to get her involved in this a little more?

VANEK: We really don't pay that much attention to it –

VANEK: See? That's where you go wrong, ignoring such an important thing! That's why you're in the shape you're in! Yet it would require so little effort – and maybe it would pull your relationship back up on its feet again!

MICHAEL: And what a good thing it would be for Eva – you'd see how it would change her!

VERA: How it would bring out the woman in her again!

MICHAEL: How it would teach her to pay attention to the house –

VERA: To you –

MICHAEL: To herself –

VERA: And what a change it would effect in you! Just imagine, suddenly there are no more reasons to go bar-hopping with your cronies –

MICHAEL: Chase waitresses –

VERA: Drink –

VANEK: I don't chase waitresses –

VERA: Ferdinand!

VANEK: I don't –

VERA: You don't like to talk about it, I know. But you know Michael and I have been talking about the two of you a lot lately, we've been thinking about you a lot – and we really care about how you two live!

MICHAEL: We're only trying to help, Ferdinand!

VERA: You're our best friend – we like you a lot – you have no idea how happy we'd be for you if your situation finally got resolved somehow!

VANEK: What situation?

VERA: Let's just drop it. Shouldn't I light the fire?

VANEK: Not for me –

MICHAEL: So I'll put on some music, all right?

VERA: Michael has just brought a ton of new records from Switzerland –

VANEK: Maybe later – OK?

(*Pause. Then suddenly the musical clock on the mantelpiece breaks into a period tune, startling* VANEK. *After a while, the clock falls silent again. Pause.*)

MICHAEL: But anyway – that's what I call art!

VANEK: What is?

MICHAEL: That Madonna –

VANEK: Mmn –

MICHAEL: Do you realize the dramatic tension that arises between her and that scimitar?

VANEK: Mmn –

(*Pause.*)

VERA: You probably don't use much woodpeak, do you?

VANEK: Not really –

VERA: If you'd like, Michael could bring you some from Switzerland –

VANEK: Oh yeah?

MICHAEL: You know that'd be no trouble at all for me.

(*Pause.*)

VERA: Have some more –

VANEK: No, thank you –

(*Pause.*)

MICHAEL: Why didn't you bring Eva with you?

VANEK: She didn't feel well –

MICHAEL: It's not any of my business, of course, but you should take her out now and then – give her a reason to put some nice clothes on, put on some make-up, do her hair –

VANEK: She does her hair –

MICHAEL: Ferdinand!

VANEK: She does –

MICHAEL: You don't like to talk about it, I know. But we're only trying to help –

VERA: We like you a lot –

MICHAEL: You're our best friend –

VANEK: I know –

(*Pause; the musical clock plays its tune.*)

MICHAEL: Did you get my card from Switzerland?

VANEK: That was from you?

MICHAEL: You didn't figure that out?

VANEK: Should have thought of it –

(*Pause.*)

VERA: (*To* MICHAEL) What did Pete ask you now? Can a frog drown?

MICHAEL: Right, imagine that –

VERA: Outstanding! Outstanding!

(*Pause.*)

MICHAEL: (*To* VANEK) Have some more –

VANEK: No, thank you –

(*Pause.*)

VERA: Do you know what we started to do again?

VANEK: What?

VERA: Going to the sauna!

VANEK: Really?

VERA: We've been going every week now, and you wouldn't believe how good it is for us. For the nerves, you know –

MICHAEL: Do you want to start coming with us?

VANEK: Not really –

VERA: Why not?

VANEK: I wouldn't have the time –

MICHAEL: Don't get offended, Ferdinand, but you're making a mistake! It would really get you into a better shape spiritually, psychically, as well as physically, and it would definitely be better for you and cost you less time, too, than the endless tongue-thrashing in bars with all those wise-guy cronies of yours –

VANEK: Whom do you mean by that?

MICHAEL: Well, all those various failures. Landovsky and so on –

VANEK: I wouldn't call them failures –

VERA: Ferdinand!

VANEK: Not at all –

VERA: You don't like to talk about it, I know. But we're only trying to help you –

MICHAEL: We like you a lot –

VERA: You're our best friend –

VANEK: I know –

(*Pause: the clock plays its tune.*)

MICHAEL: Do you know what Vera promised me?

VANEK: What's that?

**MICHAEL:** That she'll give me another child next year!

**VANEK:** That's nice –

**VERA:** I think Michael deserves no less –

(*Pause.*)

Do you know what Michael brought me from Switzerland?

**VANEK:** What's that?

**VERA:** An electric almond-peeler –

**MICHAEL:** You'll have to take a look at it, it's a beautiful thing –

**VERA:** As well as practical –

**MICHAEL:** Because Vera does a lot with almonds, so it saves her tons of time –

**VANEK:** I believe it –

(*Pause.*)

**VERA:** Have some more –

**VANEK:** No, thank you –

(*Pause.*)

**MICHAEL:** Listen, Ferdinand –

**VANEK:** Huh?

**MICHAEL:** Do you ever write anything any more?

**VANEK:** Not a whole lot –

**MICHAEL:** That's what we thought –

**VANEK:** Now that I have that job, I don't have the time for it, nor the concentration –

**MICHAEL:** But from what I hear, you weren't doing much writing anyway, even before you got this job –

**VANEK:** Not all that much –

**VERA:** Listen, didn't you maybe take that job because in your own mind it gave you an excuse for not writing?

**VANEK:** Not that –

**MICHAEL:** So what is your real reason for not writing? Is it just that it's not pouring out? Or are you going through some kind of a crisis?

**VANEK:** It's hard to say – the times, everything that is going on – you get this feeling of futility –

**MICHAEL:** Don't get offended, Ferdinand, but I think that the times are just another excuse for you, just like the job at the brewery, and that the real problem is inside of you and nowhere else! You're just all bent out of shape, you've given up on everything, you find it too tedious to strive for anything, to fight, to wrestle with problems –

VERA: Michael is right, Ferdinand. Somehow you should finally pull yourself together –

MICHAEL: Take care of problems at home – with Eva –

VERA: Start a family –

MICHAEL: Give your place some character –

VERA: Learn how to budget your time –

MICHAEL: Stop carousing –

VERA: Start going to the sauna again –

MICHAEL: Simply begin to live a decent, healthy, rational life –

VANEK: I don't feel that I'm doing anything irrational –

MICHAEL: Ferdinand!

VANEK: I don't –

MICHAEL: You don't like to talk about it, I know. But we're only trying to help you –

VERA: We like you a lot –

MICHAEL: You're our best friend –

VERA: You have no idea how happy we'd be for you if your situation finally got resolved somehow!

MICHAEL: Shouldn't I light the fire?

VANEK: Not for me –

VERA: So I'll put some music on, all right? Michael has just brought a ton of new records from Switzerland –

VANEK: Maybe later, OK?

(*Pause; the musical clock plays its tune.*)

MICHAEL: Listen, Ferdinand –

VANEK: Huh?

MICHAEL: Listen, honestly now. Are you serious with that brewery?

VANEK: What do you mean?

MICHAEL: You know, don't get offended now, but we just don't understand what the purpose of the whole thing is –

VERA: To just throw yourself away like that – to bury yourself in a brewery somewhere – only to ruin your health –

MICHAEL: All these gestures are completely senseless! What are you trying to prove? It's been a long time since that kind of thing impressed anybody –

VANEK: I'm sorry, but it was the only thing I could do in my situation –

MICHAEL: Ferdinand! Don't tell me that you couldn't do better than that – if only you really wanted to and tried a little harder – I'm convinced that with a little more effort and a little less ego on your part, you could've long been sitting in an editorial office somewhere–

VERA: You are, after all, basically an intelligent, hard-working person – you have talent – you have clearly proven that in the past with your writing – so why would you suddenly be afraid of confronting life?

MICHAEL: Life is rough and the world is divided. The world doesn't give a damn about us and nobody's coming to our rescue – we're in a nasty predicament, and it will get worse and worse – and you are not going to change any of it! So why beat your head against the wall and charge the bayonets?

VERA: What I can't understand is how could you have got mixed up with those Communists –

VANEK: What Communists?

VERA: Well, that Kohout and his crowd – you don't have anything in common with them! Don't be silly, forget about them and go your own way –

MICHAEL: We're not saying that breaking out of that charmed circle is going to be easy, but it's your only chance and nobody's going to do it for you! In these things, it's every man for himself, but you're definitely strong enough to withstand that isolation!

VERA: Just take a look at us – you could be just as happy as we are –

MICHAEL: You could have a home with character of your own –

VERA: Full of nice things and good family vibrations –

MICHAEL: A well-coiffed and elegant wife –

VERA: A bright kid –

MICHAEL: You could have a more appropriate job –

VERA: Make a few crowns –

MICHAEL: Later they'd even let you go to Switzerland –
VERA: Eat decent food –
MICHAEL: Dress better –
VERA: Go to the sauna –
MICHAEL: Now and then you could have some friends over –
VERA: Show them your place –
MICHAEL: Your kid –
VERA: Put on some music for them –
MICHAEL: Make groombles –
VERA: In short, live a little more like humans!

(VANEK *has quietly got up and begun shyly to back up to the door. When* VERA *and* MICHAEL *notice it, they stand up in surprise.*)

MICHAEL: Ferdinand –
VANEK: Mmn –
MICHAEL: What's the matter?
VANEK: Nothing's the matter –
VERA: You're leaving?
VANEK: I have to go now –
MICHAEL: Go where?
VANEK: Home –
VERA: Home? How come? Why?
VANEK: It's late – I get up early –
MICHAEL: But you can't do this –
VANEK: I really have to go –
VERA: I don't understand! Here we are in the middle of our unveiling –
MICHAEL: We wanted to give you a tour of the place –
VERA: Show you everything we have here –
MICHAEL: We thought you'd finish that bottle –
VERA: Eat the rest of the groombles –
MICHAEL: Take a look at Pete –
VERA: Michael wanted to tell you about Switzerland –
MICHAEL: Vera wanted to light the fire –
VERA: Michael wanted to play those new records for you –
MICHAEL: We thought you'd stay the night –
VERA: See how we make love –

MICHAEL: That we'd share a little of that family warmth you don't have at home –

VERA: Get into a different frame of mind –

MICHAEL: Pull you out of that mess you're living in –

VERA: Get your back up on your feet –

MICHAEL: Suggest some ways of how you can resolve your situation –

VERA: Show you what happiness is –

MICHAEL: And love –

VERA: Family harmony –

MICHAEL: A life that has some meaning –

VERA: You know that we're only trying to help you –

MICHAEL: That we like you a lot –

VERA: That you are our best friend –

MICHAEL: You cannot be this ungrateful!

VERA: We don't deserve this – not while we're trying to do so much for you!

MICHAEL: Who did you think Vera has spent the whole afternoon baking the groombles for?

VERA: Who do you think Michael has bought that whisky for?

MICHAEL: Who do you think we wanted to play those records for? Why do you think I wasted all that hard currency on them, and dragged them halfway across Europe?

VERA: Why do you think I dressed up like this, put the make-up and the perfume on, got my hair done?

MICHAEL: Why do you think we fixed this place up like this anyway? Who do you think we're doing all this for? For ourselves? (VANEK *is by the door now.*)

VANEK: I'm sorry, but I'll be off now –

VERA: (*Agitated*) Ferdinand! You can't just leave us here! You're not going to do that to us! You can't just pick up and go now; there's so much we still wanted to tell you! What are we going to do here without you? Don't you understand that? Stay, I beg you, will you stay here with us!

MICHAEL: You haven't even seen our electric almond-peeler yet!

VANEK: See you later! And thank you for the groombles –

(VANEK *is leaving, but before he closes the door behind him,*

VERA *breaks into hysterical sobs.* VANEK *stops and looks at her, not knowing what to do.*)

VERA: (*Crying*) You're selfish! A disgusting, unfeeling, inhuman egotist! An ungrateful, ignorant traitor! I hate you – I hate you so much – go away! Go away!

(VERA *runs to the bouquet that she got from* VANEK, *tears it out of the vase, and throws it at* VANEK.)

MICHAEL: (*To* VANEK) See what you're doing? Aren't you ashamed? (VANEK *is at loss about what to do for a moment, then picks up the bouquet, carries it hesitantly to the vase, puts it back in, slowly returns to his seat, and sits down with some embarrassment.* VERA *and* MICHAEL *watch tensely to see what he will do. As soon as they see that he has sat back down, they instantly return to their old selves, smiling as they sit down, too. A short pause.*)

VERA: Michael, won't we put some music on for Ferdinand?

MICHAEL: That's a good idea –

(MICHAEL *walks over to the record-player and the instant he turns it on, music starts pouring forth out of all the speakers: preferably some international hit, such as 'Sugar Baby Love' in the interpretation of Karel Gott.* The curtain falls; the music is booming on, the same tune over and over again, until the last spectator has left the theatre.*)

*See footnote on page 189.

# PROTEST

# CHARACTERS

**VANEK**
**STANEK**

*Stanek's study, Prague*

*Stanek's study. On the left, a massive writing desk, on it a typewriter, a telephone, reading glasses, and many books and papers; behind it, a large window with a view into the garden. On the right, two comfortable armchairs and between them a small table. The whole back wall is covered by bookcases, filled with books and with a built-in bar. In one of the niches there is a tape recorder. In the right back corner, a door; on the right wall, a large surrealist painting. When the curtain rises,* STANEK *and* VANEK *are on stage:* STANEK, *standing behind his desk, is emotionally looking at* VANEK, *who is standing at the door holding a briefcase and looking at* STANEK *with signs of embarrassment. A short, tense pause. Then* STANEK *suddenly walks excitedly over to* VANEK, *takes him by the shoulders with both arms, shakes him in a friendly way, calling out:*

STANEK: Vanek! Hello!

(VANEK *smiles timidly.* STANEK *lets go, trying to conceal his agitation.*)

Did you have trouble finding it?

VANEK: Not really –

STANEK: Forgot to mention the flowering magnolias. That's how you know it's my house. Superb, aren't they?

VANEK: Yes –

STANEK: I managed to double their blossoms in less than three years, compared to the previous owner. Have you magnolias at your cottage?

VANEK: No –

STANEK: You must have them! I'm going to find you two quality saplings and I'll come and plant them for you personally. (*Crosses to the bar and opens it.*) How about some brandy?

VANEK: I'd rather not –

STANEK: Just a token one. Eh?

(*He pours brandy into two glasses, hands one glass to* VANEK, *and raises the other for a toast.*) Well – here's to our reunion!

VANEK: Cheers –

(*Both drink;* VANEK *shudders slightly.*)

STANEK: I was afraid you weren't going to come.

VANEK: Why?

STANEK: Well, I mean, things got mixed up in an odd sort of way – What? Won't you sit down?

(VANEK *sits down in an armchair, placing his briefcase on the floor beside him.*)

VANEK: Thanks –

(STANEK *sinks into an armchair opposite* VANEK *with a sigh.*)

That's more like it! Peanuts?

VANEK: No, thanks –

STANEK: (*Helps himself. Munching*) You haven't changed much in all these years, you know?

VANEK: Neither have you –

STANEK: Me? Come on! Getting on for fifty, going grey, aches and pains setting in – Not as we used to be, eh? And the present times don't make one feel any better either, what? When did we see each other last, actually?

VANEK: I don't know –

STANEK: Wasn't it at your last opening night?

VANEK: Could be –

STANEK: Seems like another age! We had a bit of an argument –

VANEK: Did we?

STANEK: You took me to task for my illusions and my over-optimism. Good Lord! How often since then I've had to admit to myself you were right! Of course, in those days I still believed that in spite of everything some of the ideals of my youth could be salvaged and I took you for an incorrigible pessimist.

VANEK: But I'm not a pessimist –

STANEK: You see, everything's turned around!

(*Short pause.*)

Are you – alone?

VANEK: How do you mean, alone?

STANEK: Well, isn't there somebody – you know –

VANEK: Following me?

STANEK: Not that I care! After all, it was me who called you up, right?

VANEK: I haven't noticed anybody –

STANEK: By the way, suppose you want to shake them off one of these days, you know the best place to do it?

VANEK: No –

STANEK: A department store. You mingle with the crowd, then at a moment when they aren't looking you sneak into the washroom and wait there for about two hours. They become convinced you managed to slip out through a side entrance and they give up. You must try it out sometime!
(*Pause.*)

VANEK: Seems very peaceful here –

STANEK: That's why we moved here. It was simply impossible to go on writing near that railway station! We've been here three years, you know. Of course, my greatest joy is the garden. I'll show you around later – I'm afraid I'm going to boast a little –

VANEK: You do the gardening yourself?

STANEK: It's become my greatest private passion these days. Keep puttering about out there almost every day. Just now I've been rejuvenating the apricots. Developed my own method, you see, based on a mixture of natural and artificial fertilizers plus a special way of waxless grafting. You won't believe the results I get! I'll find some cuttings for you later on –
(STANEK *walks over to the desk, takes a package of foreign cigarettes out of a drawer, brings matches and an ashtray, and puts it all on the table in front of* VANEK.)
Ferdinand, do have a cigarette.

VANEK: Thanks –
(VANEK *takes a cigarette and lights it;* STANEK *sits in the other chair; both drink.*)

STANEK: Well now, Ferdinand, tell me – How are you?

VANEK: All right, thanks –

STANEK: Do they leave you alone – at least now and then?

VANEK: It depends –

(*Short pause.*)

STANEK: And how was it in there?

VANEK: Where?

STANEK: Can our sort bear it at all?

VANEK: You mean prison? What else can one do?

STANEK: As far as I recall, you used to be bothered by haemorrhoids. Must have been terrible, considering the hygiene in there.

VANEK: They gave me suppositories –

STANEK: You ought to have them operated on, you know. It so happens a friend of mine is our greatest haemorrhoid specialist. Works real miracles. I'll arrange it for you.

VANEK: Thanks –

(*Short pause.*)

STANEK: You know, sometimes it all seems like a beautiful dream – all the exciting opening nights, private views, lectures, meetings – the endless discussions about literature and art! All the energy, the hopes, plans, activities, ideas – the wine bars crowded with friends, the wild booze-ups, the madcap affrays in the small hours, the jolly girls dancing attendance on us! And the mountains of work we managed to get done, regardless! That's all over now. It'll never come back!

VANEK: Mmn –

(*Pause. Both drink.*)

STANEK: Did they beat you?

VANEK: No –

STANEK: Do they beat people up in there?

VANEK: Sometimes. But not the politicals –

STANEK: I thought about you a great deal!

VANEK: Thank you –

(*Short pause.*)

STANEK: I bet in those days it never even occurred to you –

VANEK: What?

STANEK: How it'll all end up! I bet not even you had guessed that!

VANEK: Mmn –

STANEK: It's disgusting, Ferdinand, disgusting! The nation is governed by scum! And the people? Can this really be the same nation which not very long ago behaved so magnificently? All that horrible cringing, bowing and scraping! The selfishness, corruption and fear wherever you turn! What have they made of us, old pal? Can this really be us?

VANEK: I don't believe things are as black as all that –

STANEK: Forgive me, Ferdinand, but you don't happen to live in a normal environment. All you know are people who manage to resist this rot. You just keep on supporting and encouraging each other. You've no idea the sort of environment I've got to put up with! You're lucky you no longer have anything to do with it. Makes you sick at your stomach!

(*Pause. Both drink.*)

VANEK: You mean television?

STANEK: In television, in the film studios – you name it.

VANEK: There was a piece by you on the TV the other day –

STANEK: You can't imagine what an ordeal that was! First they kept blocking it for over a year, then they started changing it around – changed my whole opening and the entire closing sequence! You wouldn't believe the trifles they find objectionable these days! Nothing but sterility and intrigues, intrigues and sterility! How often I tell myself – wrap it up, chum, forget it, go hide somewhere – grow apricots –

VANEK: I know what you mean –

STANEK: The thing is though, one can't help wondering whether one's got the right to this sort of escape. Supposing even the little one might be able to accomplish today can, in spite of everything, help someone in some way, at least give him a bit of encouragement, uplift him a little – Let me bring you a pair of slippers.

VANEK: Slippers? Why?

STANEK: You can't be comfortable in those boots.

VANEK: I'm all right –

STANEK: Are you sure?

VANEK: Yes. Really –

(*Both drink. Pause.*)

STANEK: How about drugs? Did they give you any?

VANEK: No –

STANEK: No dubious injections?

VANEK: Only some vitamin ones –

STANEK: I bet there's some funny stuff in the food!

VANEK: Just bromine against sex –

STANEK: But surely they tried to break you down somehow!

VANEK: Well –

STANEK: If you'd rather not talk about it, it's all right with me.

VANEK: Well, in a way, that's the whole point of pre-trial interrogations, isn't it? To take one down a peg or two –

STANEK: And to make one talk!

VANEK: Mmn –

STANEK: If they should haul me in for questioning – which sooner or later is bound to happen – you know what I'm going to do?

VANEK: What?

STANEK: Simply not answer any of their questions! Refuse to talk to them at all! That's by far the best way. Least one can be quite sure one didn't say anything one ought not to have said!

VANEK: Mmn –

STANEK: Anyway, you must have steel nerves to be able to bear it all and in addition to keep doing the things you do.

VANEK: Like what?

STANEK: Well, I mean all the protests, petitions, letters – the whole fight for human rights! I mean the things you and your friends keep on doing –

VANEK: I'm not doing so much –

STANEK: Now don't be too modest, Ferdinand! I follow everything that's going on! I know! If everybody did what you do, the situation would be quite different! And that's a fact. It's extremely important there should be at least a few people here who aren't afraid to speak the truth aloud, to defend others, to call a spade a spade! What I'm going to say might sound a bit solemn perhaps, but frankly, the way I see it, you and your friends have taken on an almost superhuman task: to preserve and to carry the remains, the remnant of moral conscience through the present quagmire! The thread you're spinning may be thin, but – who knows – perhaps the hope of a moral rebirth of the nation hangs on it.

VANEK: You exaggerate –

STANEK: Well, that's how I see it, anyway.

VANEK: Surely our hope lies in all the decent people –

STANEK: But how many are there still around? How many?

VANEK: Enough –

STANEK: Are there? Even so, it's you and your friends who are the most exposed to view.

VANEK: And isn't that precisely what makes it easier for us?

STANEK: I wouldn't say so. The more you're exposed, the more responsibility you have towards all those who know about you, trust you, rely on you and look up to you, because to some extent you keep upholding their honour, too! (*Gets up.*) I'll get you those slippers!

VANEK: Please don't bother –

STANEK: I insist. I feel uncomfortable just looking at your boots. (*Pause.* STANEK *returns with slippers.* VANEK *sighs.*) Here you are. Do take those ugly things off, I beg you. Let me – (*Tries to take off* VANEK*'s boots.*) Won't you let me – Hold still –

VANEK: (*Embarrassed*) No – please don't – no I'll do it – (*Struggles out of his boots, slips on slippers.*) There – Nice, aren't they? Thank you very much.

STANEK: Good gracious, Ferdinand, what for? (*Hovering over* VANEK) Some more brandy?

VANEK: No more for me, thanks –

STANEK: Oh, come on. Give me your glass!

VANEK: I'm sorry, I'm not feeling too well –

STANEK: Lost the habit inside, is that it?

VANEK: Could be – But the point is – last night, you see –

STANEK: Ah, that's what it is. Had a drop too many, eh?

VANEK: Mmn –

STANEK: I understand. (*Returns to his chair.*) By the way, you know the new wine bar. The Shaggy Dog?

VANEK: No –

STANEK: You don't? Listen, the wine there comes straight from the cask, it's not expensive and usually it isn't crowded. Really charming spot, you know, thanks to a handful of fairly good artists who were permitted – believe it or not – to do the interior decoration. I can warmly recommend it to you. Lively place. Where did you go, then?

VANEK: Well, we did a little pub-crawling, my friend Landovsky and I –

STANEK: Oh, I see! You were with Landovsky, were you? Well! In that case, I'm not at all surprised you came to a sticky end! He's a first-class actor, but once he starts drinking – that's it! Surely you can take one more brandy! Right?

(VANEK *sighs. Drinks are poured. They both drink.* VANEK *shudders. Short pause.*)

(*Back in his armchair*) Well, how are things otherwise? You do any writing?

VANEK: Trying to –

STANEK: A play?

VANEK: A one-act play –

STANEK: Another autobiographical one?

VANEK: More or less –

STANEK: My wife and I read the one about the brewery* the other day. We thought it was very amusing.

VANEK: I'm glad –

STANEK: Unfortunately we were given a rather bad copy.† Very hard to read.

VANEK: I'm sorry –

STANEK: It's a really brilliant little piece! I mean it! Only the ending seemed to me a bit muddy. The whole thing wants to be brought to a more straightforward conclusion, that's all. No problem. You can do it.

*Stanek is of course referring to *Audience*.

†Literary works circulating as *samizdat* texts in typescript are understandably often of poor quality. If one gets to read the, say, sixth carbon copy on onion skin, the readability of the script leaves much to be desired.

(*Pause. Both drink.* VANEK *shudders.*)

Well, how are things? How about Pavel?* Do you see him?

VANEK: Yes –

STANEK: Does he do any writing?

VANEK: Just now he's finishing a one-act, as well. It's supposed to be performed together with mine –

STANEK: Wait a minute. You don't mean to tell me you two have teamed up also as authors!

VANEK: More or less –

STANEK: Well, well! Frankly, Ferdinand, try as I may, I don't get it. I don't. I simply can't understand this alliance of yours. Is it quite genuine on your part? Is it? Good heavens! Pavel! I don't know! Just remember the way he started! We both belong to the same generation, Pavel and I, we've both – so to speak – spanned a similar arc of development, but I don't mind telling you that what he did in those days – Well! It was a bit too strong even for me! Still, I suppose it's your business. You know best what you're doing.

VANEK: That's right –

(*Pause. Both drink.*)

STANEK: Is your wife fond of gladioli?

VANEK: I don't know. I think so –

STANEK: You won't find many places with such a large selection as mine. I've got thirty-two shades, whereas at a common or garden nursery you'll be lucky to find six. Do you think your wife would like me to send her some bulbs?

VANEK: I'm sure she would –

STANEK: There's still time to plant them you know.

(*Pause.*)

Ferdinand –

VANEK: Yes?

STANEK: Weren't you surprised when I suddenly called you up?

VANEK: A bit –

STANEK: I thought so. After all, I happen to be among those who've still managed to keep their heads above water and I

*Stanek means Pavel Kohout.

quite understand that – because of this – you might want to keep a certain distance from me.

VANEK: No, not I –

STANEK: Perhaps not you yourself, but I realize that some of your friends believe that anyone who's still got some chance today has either abdicated morally, or is unforgivably fooling himself.

VANEK: I don't think so –

STANEK: I wouldn't blame you if you did, because I know only too well the grounds from which such prejudice could grow.

*(An embarrassed pause.)*

Ferdinand –

VANEK: Yes?

STANEK: I realize what a high price you have to pay for what you're doing. But please don't think it's all that easy for a man who's either so lucky, or so unfortunate as to be still tolerated by the official apparatus, and who – at the same time – wishes to live at peace with his conscience.

VANEK: I know what you mean –

STANEK: In some respects it may be even harder for him.

VANEK: I understand.

STANEK: Naturally, I didn't call you in order to justify myself! I don't really think there's any need. I called you because I like you and I'd be sorry to see you sharing the prejudice which I assume exists among your friends.

VANEK: As far as I know nobody has ever said a bad word about you –

STANEK: Not even Pavel?

VANEK: No –

*(Embarrassed pause.)*

STANEK: Ferdinand –

VANEK: Yes?

STANEK: Excuse me –

*(He gets up. Crosses to the tape recorder. Switches it on: soft, nondescript background music.* STANEK *returns to his chair.)*

Ferdinand, does the name Javurek mean anything to you?

VANEK: The pop singer? I know him very well –

STANEK: So I expect you know what happened to him.

VANEK: Of course. They locked him up for telling a story during one of his performances. The story about the cop who meets a penguin in the street –

STANEK: Of course. It was just an excuse. The fact is, they hate his guts because he sings the way he does. The whole thing is so cruel, so ludicrous, so base!

VANEK: And cowardly –

STANEK: Right! And cowardly! Look, I've been trying to do something for the boy. I mean, I know a few guys at the town council and at the prosecutor's office, but you know how it is. Promises, promises! They all say they're going to look into it, but the moment your back is turned they drop it like a hot potato, so they don't get their fingers burnt! Sickening, the way everybody looks out for number one!

VANEK: Still, I think it's nice of you to have tried to do something –

STANEK: My dear Ferdinand, I'm really not the sort of man your friends obviously take me for! Peanuts?

VANEK: No, thanks –

(*Short pause.*)

STANEK: About Javurek –

VANEK: Yes?

STANEK: Since I didn't manage to accomplish anything through private intervention, it occurred to me perhaps it ought to be handled in a somewhat different way. You know what I mean. Simply write something – a protest or a petition? In fact, this is the main thing I wanted to discuss with you. Naturally, you're far more experienced in these matters than I. If this document contains a few fairly well-known signatures – like yours, for example – it's bound to be published somewhere abroad which might create some political pressure. Right? I mean, these things don't seem to impress them all that much, actually – but honestly, I don't see any other way to help the boy. Not to mention Annie –

VANEK: Annie?

STANEK: My daughter.

VANEK: Oh? Is that your daughter?

STANEK: That's right.

VANEK: Well, what about her?

STANEK: I thought you knew.

VANEK: Knew what?

STANEK: She's expecting. By Javurek –

VANEK: Oh, I see. That's why –

STANEK: Wait a minute! If you mean the case interests me merely because of family matters –

VANEK: I didn't mean that –

STANEK: But you just said –

VANEK: I only wanted to say, that's how you know about the case at all; you were explaining to me how you got to know about it. Frankly, I wouldn't have expected you to be familiar with the present pop scene. I'm sorry if it sounded as though I meant –

STANEK: I'd get involved in this case even if it was someone else expecting his child! No matter who –

VANEK: I know –

(*Embarrassed pause.*)

STANEK: Well, what do you think about my idea of writing some sort of protest?

(VANEK *begins to look for something in his briefcase, finally finds a paper, and hands it to* STANEK.)

VANEK: I guess this is the sort of thing you had in mind –

STANEK: What?

VANEK: Here –

STANEK: (*Grabs the document*) What is it?

VANEK: Have a look –

(STANEK *takes the paper from* VANEK, *goes quickly to the writing desk, picks up his glasses, put them on, and begins to read attentively. Lengthy pause.* STANEK *shows signs of surprise. Where he finishes reading, he puts aside his glasses and begins to pace around in agitation.*)

STANEK: Now isn't it fantastic! That's a laugh, isn't it? Eh? Here I was cudgling my brains how to go about it, finally I take the plunge and consult you – and all this time you've had the whole thing wrapped up and ready! Isn't it marvellous? I knew I was doing the right thing when I turned to you! (*Returns to the table, sits down, puts on his glasses again, and rereads the text.*) There! Precisely what I had in mind! Brief, to the point, fair, and yet emphatic. Manifestly the work of a professional! I'd be sweating over it for a whole day and I'd never come up with anything remotely like this!

(VANEK *is embarrassed.*)

Listen, just a small point – here at the end – do you think 'wilfulness' is the right word to use? Couldn't one find a milder synonym, perhaps? Somehow seems a bit misplaced, you know. I mean, the whole text is composed in very measured, factual terms – and this word here suddenly sticks out, sounds much too emotional, wouldn't you agree? Otherwise it's absolutely perfect. Maybe the second paragraph is somewhat superfluous; in fact, it's just a rehash of the first one. Except for the reference here to Javurek's impact on non-conformist youth. This is excellent and must stay in! How about putting it at the end instead of your 'wilfulness'? Wouldn't that do the trick? But these are just my personal impressions. Good heavens! Why should you listen to what I have to say! On the whole the text is excellent, and no doubt it's going to hit the mark. Let me say again, Ferdinand, how much I admire you. Your knack for expressing the fundamental points of an issue, while avoiding all needless abuse, is indeed rare among our kind!

VANEK: Come on – you don't really mean that –

(STANEK *takes off his glasses, goes over to* VANEK, *puts the paper in front of him, sits again in the easy chair, and sips his drink. Short pause.*)

STANEK: Anyway, it's good to know there's somebody around whom one can always turn to and rely on in a case like this.

VANEK: But it's only natural, isn't it?

STANEK: It may seem so to you. But in the circles where I've to move such things aren't in the least natural! The natural response is much more likely to be the exact opposite. When a man gets into trouble everybody drops him as soon as possible, the lot of them. And out of fear for their own positions they try to convince all and sundry they've never had anything to do with him; on the contrary, they sized him up right away, they had his number! But why am I telling you all this, you know best the sort of thing that happens! Right? When you were in prison your long-time theatre pals held forth against you on television. It was revolting –

VANEK: I'm not angry with them –

STANEK: But I am! And what's more I told them so. In no uncertain terms! You know, a man in my position learns to put up with a lot of things, but – if you'll forgive me – there are limits! I appreciate it might be awkward for you to blame them, as you happen to be the injured party. But listen to me, you've got to distance yourself from the affair! Just think: Once we, too, begin to tolerate this sort of muck – we're *de facto* assuming co-responsibility for the entire moral morass and indirectly contributing to its deeper penetration. Am I right?

VANEK: Mmn –

(*Short pause.*)

STANEK: Have you sent it off yet?

VANEK: We're still collecting signatures –

STANEK: How many have you got so far?

VANEK: About fifty –

STANEK: Fifty? Not bad! (*Short pause.*) Well, never mind, I've just missed the boat, that's all.

VANEK: You haven't –

STANEK: But the thing's already in hand, isn't it?

VANEK: Yes, but it's still open – I mean –

STANEK: All right, but now it's sure to be sent off and published, right? By the way, I wouldn't give it to any of the agencies, if I were you. They'll only print a measly little news item which is bound to be overlooked. Better hand it over directly to one of the big European papers, so the whole text gets published, including all the signatures!

VANEK: I know –

(*Short pause.*)

STANEK: Do they already know about it?

VANEK: You mean the police?

STANEK: Yes.

VANEK: I don't think so. I suppose not –

STANEK: Look here, I don't want to give you any advice, but it seems to me you ought to wrap it up as soon as possible, else they'll get wind of what's going on and they'll find a way to stop it. Fifty signatures should be enough! Besides, what counts is not the number of signatures, but their significance.

VANEK: Each signature has its own significance!

STANEK: Absolutely, but as far as publicity abroad is concerned, it is essential that some well-known names are represented, right? Has Pavel signed?

VANEK: Yes –

STANEK: Good. His name – no matter what one may think of him personally – does mean something in the world today!

VANEK: No question –

(*Short pause.*)

STANEK: Listen, Ferdinand –

VANEK: Yes?

STANEK: There's one more thing I wanted to discuss with you. It's a bit delicate, though –

VANEK: Oh?

STANEK: Look here, I'm no millionaire, you know, but so far I've been able to manage –

VANEK: Good for you –

STANEK: Well, I was thinking – I mean – I'd like to – Look, a lot of your friends have lost their jobs. I was thinking – would you be prepared to accept from me a certain sum of money?

VANEK: That's very nice of you! Some of my friends indeed find themselves in a bit of a spot. But there are problems, you know. I mean, one in never quite sure how to go about it. Those who most need help are often the most reluctant to accept –

STANEK: You won't be able to work miracles with what I can afford, but I expect there are situations when every penny counts. (*Takes out his wallet, removes two banknotes, hesitates, adds a third, hands them to* VANEK.) Here – please – a small offering.

VANEK: Thank you very much. Let me thank you for all my friends –

STANEK: Gracious, we've got to help each other out, don't we? (*Pause.*) Incidentally, there's no need for you to mention this little contribution comes from me. I don't wish to erect a monument to myself. I'm sure you've gathered that much by now, eh?

VANEK: Yes. Again many thanks –

STANEK: Well now, how about having a look at the garden?

VANEK: Mr Stanek –

STANEK: Yes?

VANEK: We'd like to send it off tomorrow –

STANEK: What?

VANEK: The protest –

STANEK: Excellent! The sooner the better!

VANEK: So that today there's still –

STANEK: Today you should think about getting some sleep! That's the main thing! Don't forget you've a bit of a hangover after last night and tomorrow is going to be a hard day for you!

VANEK: I know. All I was going to say –

STANEK: Better go straight home and unplug the phone. Else Ladovsky rings you up again and heaven knows how you'll end up!

VANEK: Yes, I know. There's only a few signatures I've still got to collect – it won't take long. All I was going to say – I mean, don't you think it would be helpful – as a matter of fact, it would, of course, be sensational! After all, practically everybody's read your *Crash*!

STANEK: Oh, come on, Ferdinand! That was fifteen years ago!

VANEK: But it's never been forgotten!

STANEK: What do you mean – sensational?

VANEK: I'm sorry, I had the impression you'd actually like to –

STANEK: What?

VANEK: Participate –

STANEK: Participate? Wait a minute. Are you talking about (*points to the paper*) this? Is that what you're talking about?

VANEK: Yes –

STANEK: You mean I –

VANEK: I'm sorry, but I had the impression –

(STANEK *finishes his drink, crosses to the bar, pours himself a drink, walks over to the window, looks out for a while, whereupon he suddenly turns to* VANEK *with a smile.*)

STANEK: Now that's a laugh, isn't it?

VANEK: What's a laugh?

STANEK: Come on, can't you see how absurd it is? Eh! I ask you over hoping you might write something about Javurek's case – you produce a finished text and what's more, one furnished with fifty signatures! I'm bowled over like a little child, can't believe my eyes and ears, I worry about ways to stop them from ruining your project – and all this time it hasn't occurred to me to do the one simple, natural thing which I should have done in the first place! I mean, at once sign the document myself! Well, you must admit it's absurd, isn't it?

VANEK: Mmn –

STANEK: Now, listen Ferdinand, isn't this a really terrifying testimony to the situation into which we've been brought? Isn't it? Just think: even I, thought I know it's rubbish, even I've got used to the idea that the signing of protests is the business of local specialists, professionals in solidarity, dissidents! While the rest of us – when we want to do something for the sake of ordinary human decency – automatically turn to you, as though you were a sort of service establishment for moral matters. In other words, we're here simply to keep our mouths shut and to be rewarded by relative peace and quiet, whereas you're here to speak up for us and to be rewarded by blows on earth and glory in the heavens! Perverse, isn't it?

VANEK: Mmn–

STANEK: Of course it is! And they've managed to bring things to such a point that even a fairly intelligent and decent fellow –

which, with your permission, I still think I am – is more or less ready to take this situation for granted! As though it was quite normal, perfectly natural! Sickening isn't it? Sickening the depths we've reached! What do you say? Makes one puke, eh?

VANEK: Well –

STANEK: You think the nation can ever recover from all this?

VANEK: Hard to say –

STANEK: What can one do? What can one do? Well, seems clear, doesn't it? In theory, that is. Everybody should start with himself. What? However! Is this country inhabited only by Vaneks? It really doesn't seem that everybody can become a fighter for human rights.

VANEK: Not everybody, no –

STANEK: Where is it?

VANEK: What?

STANEK: The list of signatures, of course.

(*Embarrassed pause.*)

VANEK: Mr Stanek –

STANEK: Yes?

VANEK: Forgive me, but – I'm sorry, I've suddenly a funny feeling that perhaps –

STANEK: What funny feeling?

VANEK: I don't know – I feel very embarrassed – Well, it seems to me perhaps I wasn't being quite fair –

STANEK: In what way?

VANEK: Well, what I did – was a bit of a con trick – in a way –

STANEK: What are you talking about?

VANEK: I mean, first I let you talk, and only then I ask for your signature – I mean, after you're already sort of committed by what you've said before, you see –

STANEK: Are you suggesting that if I'd known you were collecting signatures for Javurek, I would never have started talking about him?

VANEK: No, that's not what I mean –

STANEK: Well, what do you mean?

VANEK: How shall I put it –

STANEK: Oh, come on! You mind I didn't organize the whole thing myself, is that it?

VANEK: No, that's not it –

STANEK: What is it then?

VANEK: Well, it seems to me it would've been a quite different matter if I'd come to you right away and asked for your signature. That way you would've had an option –

STANEK: And why didn't you come to me right away, actually? Was it because you'd simply written me off in advance?

VANEK: Well, I was thinking that in your position –

STANEK: Ah! There you are! You see? Now it's becoming clear what you really think of me, isn't it? You think that because now and then one of my pieces happens to be shown on television, I'm no longer capable of the simplest act of solidarity!

VANEK: You misunderstand me. What I meant was –

STANEK: Let me tell you something, Ferdinand. (*Drinks. Short pause.*) Look here, if I've – willy-nilly – got used to the perverse idea that common decency and morality are the exclusive domain of the dissidents – then you've – willy-nilly – got used to the idea as well! That's why it never crossed your mind that certain values might be more important to me than my present position. But suppose even I wanted to be finally a free man, suppose even I wished to renew my inner integrity and shake off the yoke of humiliation and shame? It never entered your head that I might've been actually waiting for this very moment for years, what? You simply placed me once and for all among those hopeless cases, among those whom it would be pointless to count on in any way. Right? And now that you found I'm not entirely indifferent to the fate of others – you made that slip about my signature! But you saw at once what happened, and so you began to apologize to me. Good God! Don't you realize how you humiliate me? What if all this time I'd been hoping for an opportunity to act, to do something that would again make a man of me, help me to be once more at peace with myself, help me to find again the free play of my imagination and my lost sense of humour, rid me of the need to escape my traumas by minding the apricots and the blooming magnolias! Suppose even I prefer to live in truth! What if I want to return from the world of custom-made literature and the proto-culture of television to the world of art which isn't geared to serve anyone at all?

VANEK: I'm sorry – forgive me! I didn't mean to hurt your feelings – Wait a minute, I'll – just a moment –

(VANEK *opens his briefcase, rummages in it for a while, finally extracts the sheets with the signatures and hands them to* STANEK. STANEK *gets up slowly and crosses with the papers to the desk, where he sits down, puts on his glasses, and carefully studies the sheets nodding his head here and there. After a lengthy while, he takes off his glasses, slowly rises, thoughtfully paces around, finally turning to* VANEK.)

STANEK: Let me think aloud. May I?

VANEK: By all means –

(*Halts, drinks, begins to pace again as he talks.*) I believe I've already covered the main points concerning the subjective side of the matter. If I sign the document, I'm going to regain – after years of being continually sick to my stomach – my self-esteem, my lost freedom, my honour, and perhaps even some regard among those close to me. I'll leave behind the insoluble dilemmas, forced on me by the conflict between my concern for my position and my conscience. I'll be able to face with equanimity Annie, myself, and even that young man when he comes back. It'll cost me my job, though my job brings me no satisfaction – on the contrary, it brings me shame – nevertheless, it does support me and my family a great deal better than if I were to become a night watchman. It's more than likely that my son won't be permitted to continue his studies. On the other hand, I'm sure he's going to have more respect for me that way, than if his permission to study was bought by my refusal to sign the protest for Javurek, whom he happens to worship. Well then. This is the subjective side of the matter. Now how about the objective side? What happens when – among the signatures of a few well-known dissidents and a handful of Javurek's teenage friends – there suddenly crops up – to everybody's surprise and against all expectation – my signature? The signature of a man who hasn't been heard from regarding civic affairs for years! Well? My co-signatories – as well as many of those who don't sign documents of this sort, but who none the less deep down side with those who do – are naturally going to welcome my signature with pleasure. The closed circle of habitual signers – whose signatures, by the way, are already beginning to lose their clout, because they cost practically nothing. I mean, the people in question have long since lost all ways and means by which they could actually pay for their signatures. Right? Well, this circle will be broken. A new name will appear, a name the value of which depends precisely on its previous absence. And of course, I may add, on the high price paid for its appearance! So much for the objective 'plus' of my prospective signature. Now what about the authorities? My signature is going to surprise, annoy, and upset them for the very reasons which will bring joy to the other signatories. I mean, because it'll make a breach in the barrier the authorities have been building around your lot for so long and with such effort. All right. Let's see about Javurek. Concerning his case, I very much doubt my participation would significantly influence its outcome. And if so, I'm afraid it's more than likely going to have a negative effect. The authorities will be anxious to prove they haven't been panicked. They'll want to show that a surprise of this sort can't make them lose their cool. Which brings us to the consideration of what they're going to do to me. Surely, my signature is bound to have a much more significant influence on what happens in my case. No doubt, they're going to punish me far more cruelly than you'd expect. The point being that my punishment will serve them as a warning signal to all those who might be tempted to follow my example in the future, choose freedom, and thus swell the ranks of the dissidents. You may be sure they'll want to show them what the score is! Right? The thing is –

well, let's face it – they're no longer worried all that much about dissident activities within the confines of the established ghetto. In some respects they even seem to prod them on here and there. But! What they're really afraid of is any semblance of a crack in the fence around the ghetto! So they'll want to exorcize the bogey of a prospective epidemic of dissent by an exemplary punishment of myself. They'll want to nip it in the bud, that's all. (*Drinks. Pause.*) The last question I've got to ask myself is this: what sort of reaction to my signature can one expect among those who, in one way or another, have followed what you might call 'the path of accommodation'. I mean people who are, or ought to be, our main concern, because – I'm sure you'll agree – our hope for the future depends above all on whether or not it will be possible to awake them from their slumbers and to enlist them to take an active part in civic affairs. Well, I'm afraid that my signature is going to be received with absolute resentment by this crucial section of the populace. You know why? Because, as a matter of fact, these people secretly hate the dissidents. They've become their bad conscience, their living reproach! That's how they see the dissidents. And at the same time, they envy them their honour and their inner freedom, values which they themselves were denied by fate. This is why they never miss an opportunity to smear the dissidents. And precisely this opportunity is going to be offered to them by my signature. They're going to spread nasty rumours about you and your friends. They're going to say that you who have nothing more to lose – you who have long since landed at the bottom of the heap and, what's more, managed to make yourselves quite at home in there – are now trying to drag down to your own level an unfortunate man, a man who's so far been able to stay above the salt line. You're dragging him down – irresponsible as you are – without the slightest compunction, just for your own whim, just because you wish to irritate the authorities, by creating a false impression that your ranks are being swelled! What do you care about losing him his job! Doesn't matter, does it? Or do you mean to suggest you'll find him a job down in the dump in which you yourselves exist? What? No – Ferdinand! I'm sorry. I'm afraid I'm much too familiar with the way these people think! After all, I've got to live among them, day in day out. I know precisely what they're going to say. They'll say I'm your victim, shamelessly abused, misguided, led astray by your cynical appeal to my humanity! They'll say that in your ruthlessness you didn't shrink even from making use of my personal relationship to Javurek! And you know what? They're going to say that all the humane ideals you're constantly proclaiming have been tarnished by your treatment of me. That's the sort of reasoning one can expect from them! And I'm sure I don't have to tell you that the authorities are bound to support this interpretation, and to fan the coals as hard as they can! There are others, of course, somewhat more intelligent perhaps. These people might say that the extraordinary appearance of my signature among yours is actually counterproductive, in that it concentrates everybody's attention on my signature and away from the main issue concerning Javurek. They'll say it put the whole protest in jeopardy, because one can't help asking oneself what was the purpose of the exercise: was it to help Javurek, or to parade a newborn dissident? I wouldn't be at all surprised if someone were to say that, as a matter of fact, Javurek was victimized by you and your friends. It might be suggested his personal tragedy only served you to further your ends – which are far removed from the fate of the unfortunate man. Furthermore, it'll be pointed out that by getting my signature you managed to dislodge me from the one area of operation – namely, backstage diplomacy, private intervention – where I've been so far able to manoeuvre and where I might have proved infinitely more helpful to Javurek in the end! I do hope you understand me, Ferdinand. I don't wish to exaggerate the importance of these opinions, nor am I prepared to become their slave. On the other hand, it seems to be in the interests of our case for me to take them into account. After all, it's a matter of a political decision and a good politician must consider all the issues which are likely to influence the end result of his action. Right? In these circumstances the question one must resolve is as follows: what do I prefer? Do I prefer the inner liberation which my signature is going to bring me, a liberation paid for – as it now turns out – by a basically negative objective impact – or do I choose the other alternative. I mean, the more beneficial effect which the protest would have without my signature, yet paid for by my bitter awareness that I've again – who knows, perhaps for the last time – missed a chance to shake off the bonds of shameful compromises in which I've been choking for years? In other words, if I'm to act indeed ethically – and I hope by now you've no doubt I want to do just that – which course should I take? Should I be guided by ruthless objective considerations, or by subjective inner feelings?

VANEK: Seems perfectly clear to me –

STANEK: And to me –

VANEK: So that you're going to –

STANEK: Unfortunately –

VANEK: Unfortunately?

STANEK: You thought I was –

VANEK: Forgive me, perhaps I didn't quite understand –

STANEK: I'm sorry if I've –

VANEK: Never mind –

STANEK: But I really believe –

VANEK: I know –

(*Both drink.* VANEK *shudders. Lengthy embarrassed pause.* STANEK *takes the sheets and hands them with a smile to* VANEK *who puts them, together with the text of the letter of protest, into his briefcase. He shows signs of embarrassment.* STANEK *crosses to the tape recorder, unplugs it, comes back and sits down.*)

STANEK: Are you angry?

VANEK: No –

STANEK: You don't agree, though –

VANEK: I respect your reasoning –

STANEK: But what do you think?

VANEK: What should I think?

STANEK: That's obvious, isn't it?

VANEK: Is it?

STANEK: You think that when I saw all the signatures, I did, after all, get the wind up!

VANEK: I don't –

STANEK: I can see you do!

VANEK: I assure you –

STANEK: Why don't you level with me?! Don't you realize that your benevolent hypocrisy is actually far more insulting than if you gave it to me straight?! Or do you mean I'm not even worthy of your comment?!

VANEK: But I told you, didn't I, I respect your reasoning –

STANEK: I'm not an idiot, Vanek!

VANEK: Of course not –

STANEK: I know precisely what's behind your 'respect'!

VANEK: What is?

STANEK: A feeling of moral superiority!

VANEK: You're wrong –

STANEK: Only, I'm not quite sure if you – you of all people – have any right to feel so superior!

VANEK: What do you mean?

STANEK: You know very well what I mean!

VANEK: I don't –

STANEK: Shall I tell you?

VANEK: Please do –

STANEK: Well! As far as I know, in prison you talked more than you should have!

(VANEK *jumps up, wildly staring at* STANEK, *who smiles triumphantly. Short tense pause. The phone rings.* VANEK, *broken, sinks back into his chair.* STANEK *crosses to the telephone and lifts the receiver.*)

Hello – yes – what? You mean – Wait a minute – I see – I see – Where are you? Yes, yes, of course – absolutely! – good – You bet! – Sure – I'll be here waiting for you! Bye bye.

(STANEK *puts the receiver down and absent-mindedly stares into space. Lengthy pause.* VANEK *gets up in embarrassment. Only now* STANEK *seems to realize that* VANEK *is still there. He turns to him abruptly.*

You can go and burn it downstairs in the furnace!

VANEK: What?

STANEK: He's just walked into the canteen! To see Annie.

VANEK: Who did?

STANEK: Javurek! Who else?

VANEK: (*Jumps up*) Javurek? You mean he was released? But that's wonderful! So your private intervention did work, after all! Just as well we didn't send off the protest a few days earlier! I'm sure they would've got their backs up and kept him inside!

(STANEK *searchingly stares at* VANEK *then suddenly smiles, decisively steps up to him, and with both hands takes him by the shoulders.*)

STANEK: My dear fellow, you mustn't fret! There's always the risk that you can do more harm than good by your activities! Right? Heavens, if you should worry about this sort of thing, you'd never be able to do anything at all! Come, let me get you those saplings –

# MISTAKE

# CHARACTERS

XIBOY
KING, a trustie
1ST PRISONER
2ND PRISONER
3RD PRISONER

*As the curtain rises, we see a door, left, with the* 1ST, 2ND *and* 3RD PRISONERS *crowding the doorway,* KING *in front. All four have shaven heads and a variety of tattoos on their arms and torsos –* KING *most of all. They are dressed in prison uniforms and are gazing intently at* XIBOY. *On the opposite side of the stage there is a tier of three iron bunks;* XIBOY *is sitting on the top one, like the others in prison garb and with shaven head but no tattoos.* XIBOY *is a newcomer and he looks with some apprehension at the group in the doorway. A long, tense silence . . .*

KING: (*To* XIBOY) I hear you lit a fag after slop-out . . .
(*Short pause.*)

1ST PRISONER: (*To* KING) 'e did – I saw 'im.

KING: (*To* 2ND PRISONER) That right?

2ND PRISONER: Sure, that's right.

KING: (*To* XIBOY) Don't you know when we fall out for breakfast?
(*Short pause.*)

1ST PRISONER: (*To* KING) Sure, he knows . . . Ten minutes after slop-out.

KING: (*To* 2ND PRISONER) Does 'e know?

2ND PRISONER: Sure he knows! They tell all the new boys, don't they . . .

KING: (*To* XIBOY) Now listen 'ere, friend. We have ten minutes between slop-out and breakfast. In that time we've all gotta get dressed, those as wants can wash or 'ave a piss, there's no objection to that, you understand, everyone's got a perfect right to do it, if they wanna, you can even start making your bed so we don't all start at once and get in each other's way. And we open the windows to get rid of all the farts first thing. That's the custom 'ere, that's the way it's done and always 'as been. Then we all grab our caps and food bowls and wait for the order to fall in. And when they yell 'fall in' we gotta look sharp and line up outside the cell. If we don't get out there quick enough, they send us back and we gotta wait our turn again. So we don't want anybody fart-arsing around holding things up looking for his things or tipping a fag-end or anything like that – and the rest of us get in the shit on 'is account. Understand? Because of one lousy slowcoach we ain't all gonna go back and 'ang around waiting. I 'ope that's clear. And if anyone thinks it ain't, we'll soon put 'im right!

1ST PRISONER: (*To* KING) It's clear, all right, and everyone does it just like you said.

2ND PRISONER: (*To* XIBOY) That's right – and if some cunt thinks 'e can mess us about, 'e'll do it just once and never again . . .

KING: (*To* XIBOY) So, as I said, there's a hell of a lot to do between slop-out and breakfast. No time for fart-arsing around. Much less for smoking. That's not the way we do things 'ere. Now, *after* breakfast, that's something else again, then you can light up if you've got any fags, that is. *Then* there's time and nobody gives a shit. But not before breakfast. That's how it's always been in this pad, and it's going to stay that way. Nobody's gonna tell me they can't wait a lousy twenty minutes for a smoke. That ain't asking too much, is it? (*To* 2ND PRISONER) Am I right?

2ND PRISONER: Sure you are.

1ST PRISONER: (*To* KING) We can wait.

KING: (*To* XIBOY) So, from now on remember – no smoking before breakfast . . .

1ST PRISONER: Specially as we're trying to air the fucking place . . .

KING: (*To* XIBOY) Yeah, that's right. And some people just can't stand the smell of smoke first thing in the morning. They don't like it, their lungs don't like it, they can't stand it. As is their right. Is that clear?

(XIBOY *says nothing, looks embarrassed and shrugs.*)

2ND PRISONER: (*Shouts at* XIBOY) Didn't you hear what 'e said?

(XIBOY *says nothing, looks embarrassed, shrugs.*)

Anyone we catch smoking after slop-out gets a fistful, see?

KING: (*To* XIBOY) What they do in other cells, that's their business. But nobody smokes in this one after slop-out. That goes for everybody, specially for new boys like you. That's all I wanted to say to you, friend. And not just for myself but for all of us. (*To* 2ND PRISONER) Right?

2ND PRISONER: Right.

1ST PRISONER: (*To* KING) That's what we all say – right . . .

KING: (*To* XIBOY) Everybody saw you smoking first thing, and everybody yakked about it. But I told 'em: 'e's a new boy, doesn't know the ropes yet. And so they stopped yakking. So you're OK for today. But next time just remember we don't hold with nobody trying to be clever and going it alone. Not on your life . . .

1ST PRISONER: (*To* KING) As long as I been 'ere, nobody ever had the nerve to light a fag before breakfast.

KING: (*To* XIBOY) So, as I said, you got away with it this time, but see it don't 'appen no more. Is that clear?

(XIBOY *looks embarrassed and shrugs*.)

2ND PRISONER: (*Yells at* XIBOY) What're you gawping at, you cunt? King asked you a question!

(*Silence*.)

KING: (*To* XIBOY) We're trying to be nice to you, see? So we'll skip it this once – but now you know and kindly keep your nose clean.

(*Longer silence*.)

Oh, and while we're on the subject . . . From tomorrow, you'll make your bed exactly like all the rest of us. If the others can do it, so can you. We don't want to lose a point every day just because some stupid bastard doesn't know how to make his bed properly, do we? We don't want the whole lot of us to get it in the neck on account of one miserable rookie what doesn't know how to make his bed. So you'd better hurry up and learn, cos if tomorrow your bed isn't just like everybody else's, we'll make you practice all evening.

2ND PRISONER: (*To* XIBOY) We'll make you do it ten times in a row, see if we don't.

KING: (*To* XIBOY) Blanket's gotta be two inches from the edge on both sides, the sheet neatly folded over, and so on and so forth . . . The boys'll show you how it's done.

1ST PRISONER: (*To* KING) I'll show 'im . . .

KING: (*To* XIBOY) Is that clear?

(*Silence.*)

Everybody in 'ere gets the 'ang of it sooner or later, so no reason why you shouldn't get the 'ang of it. Understand?

(*Silence.*)

2ND PRISONER: (*To* XIBOY) Bloody hell! Cat got your tongue, you bastard? Speak up when King asks you something!

1ST PRISONER: (*To* KING) What's the matter with 'im? Stupid idiot!

KING: (*To* XIBOY) Did you clean the washbasin?

(*Silence.*)

Your turn to scrub and clean this week, so you'd better look smart! And if you think you're just going to tickle the floor with the brush and that's it, you're bloody well mistaken. You get down and scrub the floor under the bunks, specially in the corners by the wall – the screws shine their torches down there. You dust everywhere, and the washbasin's gotta be washed, wiped dry and shined – and the same goes for the kaazie. Today it's a mess, so you can thank your lucky stars we haven't had the screws round 'ere. They'd 'ave shown you a thing or two. Tonight, before inspection, I'll come and look personal like. We're all in the same boat 'ere, nobody gets any privileges, 'specially not a rookie whose fag-end is still burning outside the prison gate!

2ND PRISONER: (*Yells at* XIBOY!) So why don't you come down off of there, you cunt, when King's talking to you!

(XIBOY *remains sitting on his bunk, smiling in embarrassment. Tense silence.* 2ND PRISONER *is about to lunge at* XIBOY *and drag him down but* KING *stops him.*)

KING: (*To* 2ND PRISONER) Wait a sec!

(*Silence.*)

(*To* XIBOY) Now look 'ere, me lad! If you've got it in yer 'ead that you're going to do as you bloody well please 'ere, or maybe play at being King, you've got another think coming! We know how to deal with the likes of you. Understand?

(*Silence.*)

IST PRISONER: (*To* KING) What a stubborn bastard!

2ND PRISONER: (*To* XIBOY) Come down off that bloody bunk, and be quick about it!

(*Silence* – XIBOY *doesn't move.*)

(*To* XIBOY) Well . . .?

(*Silence* – XIBOY *doesn't move.*)

KING: (*To* XIBOY) Now then, you, I don't take kindly to them as tries to make a monkey out of me. So don't get any ideas!

IST PRISONER: (*To* XIBOY) Down you come this minute and apologize to King!

(*Silence* – XIBOY *doesn't move, just sits there smiling in embarrassment.*)

2ND PRISONER: (*Yells at* XIBOY) You fucking mother-fucker!

(2ND PRISONER *leaps forward and catches* XIBOY *by one leg, pulling him down.* XIBOY *falls on the floor,* 2ND PRISONER *kicks him and returns to* KING*'s side.* XIBOY *rises slowly, looks at the others, puzzled. Silence.*)

3RD PRISONER: (*Softly*) 'ere, lads . . .

(*Silence – they all gaze at* XIBOY.)

KING: (*Without turning to* 3RD PRISONER) What?

(*Silence – they all gaze at* XIBOY.)

3RD PRISONER: (*Softly*) Know what? He's some kind of a bloody foreigner . . .

(*All three look questioningly at* KING. *Tense silence.*)

KING: (*After a pause, softly.*) Well, that's his bloody funeral . . .

(KING *starts out menacingly towards* XIBOY, *followed by* IST, 2ND *and* 3RD PRISONER. *They slowly edge closer to him.*)

Václav Havel was born in Czechoslovakia in 1936. Among his plays, those best known in the West are *The Garden Party*, *The Increased Difficulty of Concentration*, *The Memorandum*, *Largo Desolato*, *Temptation*, and three one-act plays: *Audience*, *Private View*, and *Protest*. He is a founding spokesman of Charter 77 and the author of many influential essays on the nature of totalitarianism and dissent, including 'An Open Letter to Dr Husák' and 'The Power of the Powerless'. In 1979 he was sentenced to four and a half years in prison for his involvement in the Czech human rights movement; out of this imprisonment came his book of letters to his wife, *Letters to Olga* (1988). In January 1983, for reasons of health, he was released from prison before his sentence was completed. In 1986 he was awarded the Erasmus Prize, the highest cultural award in the Netherlands. In November 1989 he helped to found the Civic Forum, the first legal opposition movement in Czechoslovakia in forty years; and in December 1989 he was elected President of Czechoslovakia.